Guillermo García Oropeza
Cristóbal García Sánchez

ONE HUNDRED *&* ONE
Beautiful SMALL TOWNS *in Mexico*

RIZZOLI
NEW YORK

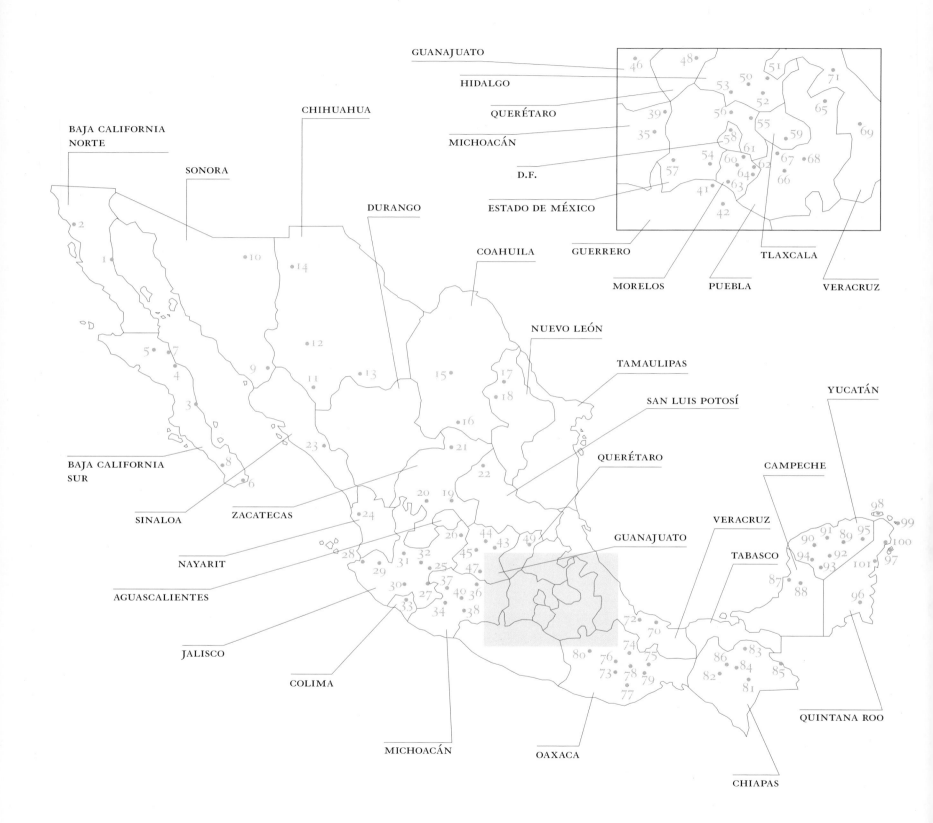

BAJA CALIFORNIA
NORTE

SONORA

CHIHUAHUA

GUANAJUATO

HIDALGO

QUERÉTARO

MICHOACÁN

D.F.

DURANGO

ESTADO DE MÉXICO

COAHUILA

GUERRERO

MORELOS

PUEBLA

TLAXCALA

VERACRUZ

NUEVO LEÓN

TAMAULIPAS

SAN LUIS POTOSÍ

YUCATÁN

QUERÉTARO

CAMPECHE

BAJA CALIFORNIA
SUR

VERACRUZ

SINALOA

ZACATECAS

GUANAJUATO

TABASCO

NAYARIT

AGUASCALIENTES

QUINTANA ROO

JALISCO

COLIMA

MICHOACÁN

OAXACA

CHIAPAS

REGIONAL CONTENTS

ALPHABETICAL CONTENTS

P R E F A C E

Mexico is a large country in both size as well as diversity. It is the thirteenth largest country in the world and is well known for its natural beauty and its more than sixty-eight hundred miles of coastline touching on four distinct bodies of water. Mexico also offers a splendid cultural and artistic legacy with its countless archaeological sites, its colonial towns, and the presence of fifty-nine different indigenous tribes, each with its own folklore and traditions. As of last year, no less than twenty-four of Mexico's natural and architectural treasures have been designated as UNESCO World Heritage Sites. In addition, Chichén Itzá was recently elected one of the "new" Seven Wonders of the World.

There are 2,750 miles between Mexico's eastern- and westernmost points and, in between, more than 12 percent of the species living on earth can be found. It ranks fourth in the world in terms of flora with more than twenty-six thousand different species, and most of the world's climate types can be experienced here. Its geography varies between tropical jungles and mountains that punctuate the landscape, and between mountain plateaus and vast deserts—all of which has created a vast biodiversity. Travelers to Mexico can visit what Jacques Cousteau called "the aquarium of the world" off the coasts of Baja California; bird-watch in the Sian Ka'an Biosphere Reserve, with its plethora of protected species; or enjoy the fascinating architecture at Tulum. There is also Batopilas, situated among the impressive, narrow passages of the Barrancas del Cobre; much to marvel at in Cuatro Ciénegas, where there are more than two hundred multicolored desert marshes; and much to enjoy in Comitán with its fifty-nine beautiful lakes.

Mexico's art is both ancient and magnificent. Its existence stretches back more than four thousand years to the enigmatic cave paintings of Baja California. Wonderful examples of pre-Columbian art can be found in the Mayan jewel of Palenque as well as in the elegant cultures of central Mexico such as Tula and Teotihuacan. Tajín near Papantla is like a fantasy while Monte Albán has an aura of serene grandeur. At the same time, treasures of colonial art can be enjoyed in opulent mining towns such as Guanajuato or in the innumerable beautiful monasteries that are found from the Sierra Gorda near Querétaro to the lower slopes of the Popocatépetl volcano. But there are also towns that shine with the genius of more popular art such as Tonanzintla and the colorful Tlacotalpan. Mexico's Romantic heritage is on display in the hundreds of haciendas that dot the Yucatán Peninsula as well as in the legacy of Gustave Eiffel found in Santa Rosalía.

Many Mexican towns are distinguished by their imaginative local crafts, including work inspired by the pre-Hispanic era such as Paquimé ceramics or the black earthenware vessels of Oaxaca. Other traditions find their inspiration in mestizo culture, such as the masks and wood-carved work of Pátzcuaro, the furnishings and ceramics of Tlaquepaque, or the silver jewelry of Taxco. Some pueblos are famous because of their beverages such as the wines from the valley of Guadalupe and Parras de la Fuente, which was the first vineyard in the Americas. Tequila has found its fame through its eponymous elixir of the gods while Coatepec is known as the land of aromatic coffee. Other pueblos are ideal places to rest and relax, such as the mountain hideaways of Valle de Bravo and Tapalpa, and spectacular ocean-side locations such as San José del Cabo, with its wildly contrasting landscapes, or Cozumel and Isla Mujeres located on the seductive Caribbean.

The 101 towns selected for this book represent an amazing and little-known Mexico, which is open to a range of travelers with varied interests. It promises 101 surprises and discoveries.

left:
A lovely sunset in San Miguel de Allende.

Loreto, a sleepy town, is surrounded by exotic wildlife and is bathed by the Sea of Cortés.

NORTHERN *Mexico*

SAN FELIPE
THREE LANDSCAPES IN ONE

LOCATED 125 MILES FROM THE AMERICAN BORDER, San Felipe is a simple fishing village on the shore of the Sea of Cortés and bordering the Baja California desert. Visitors from the United States and more distant locations like Australia, return repeatedly making lengthy stays in this picturesque locale. Its extensive beaches are an ideal place for enjoying rest and relaxation. San Felipe is a destination for travelers looking to enjoy nature. In contrast to the rest of the country, there are neither enigmatic archaeological sites nor richly designed colonial buildings. Its beauty is based on three pillars: its isolation, its tranquility, and its biodiversity.

Whether it is senior citizens, biologists, bird watchers, or fanatics of fishing, motocross, or surfing, all are seduced by the multiple attractions of San Felipe as well as the overall landscape of this exotic region. A visit to San Felipe is enhanced by exploring its three distinct geographical features. Once the aquatic pleasures and beach-related activities of the Sea of Cortés have been enjoyed to the fullest, it is worthwhile to visit the unique desert landscape. It is far from the ocean breezes and characterized by an intemperate and incessant heat. All-terrain vehicles, which allow visitors to travel farther into the sand dunes, are the best way to discover this incredible habitat.

Once the desert has revealed the extent of its diversity, visitors can travel into the mountains. Driving upward on a road through a forest, the profoundly narrow passages are imposing while the climate gradually becomes more agreeable, attaining a Mediterranean-like temperature. The first mountain range includes the Sierra de San Felipe and the Sierra de San Pedro Mártir, which is a nature reserve of 172,000 acres. This range stands out because of its white granite peaks, among them El Picacho del Diablo, the highest in Baja California at 10,170 feet. These mountains are home to the cougar, hawk, and ram as well as hundreds of species of birds. Among them are the beautiful golden eagle and the California condor, an enormous vulture splashed with white spots and black feathers with tones of red and yellow. This animal, which also has enormous longevity, has the longest wingspan of any North American bird. In the midst of this remote location the National Astronomical Observatory was built. There are many informal lookout points in the mountains where the visitor can contemplate the impressive surrounding landscape and enjoy spectacular vistas of the Sea of Cortés and the Pacific Ocean, as well as the desert.

The cardón, a huge cactus, is found throughout the Valley of the Giants in Baja California North.

facing page
Anchored boats along San Felipe's beautiful beach on the Sea of Cortés.

Ten miles south of San Felipe is the "Valley of the Giants." Here the cardón cactus (closely related to the saguaro, *Carnegiea Gigantea*) flourishes. It is the largest cactus species on the planet. These cacti can reach a height of sixty-five feet and weigh up to twelve tons. Thanks to its extended branches, which store huge amounts of water, the cardón can survive up to eight years during an extensive drought. This giant, which is found all over the region, produces a fruity juice similar to that of the prickly-pear cactus and from which the local indigenous groups make jellies, syrup, and alcoholic beverages. When the fruit matures in summer, birds, insects, and desert animals feast on its fruit and seeds—a spectacular scene. An adult cardón can live to be two hundred years old, though some can live for up to fifteen hundred years. One such giant was an impressive fifty-five-foot-tall, ten-ton cardón that Mexico donated as a gift to the Spanish government and displayed at the International Exposition in Seville in 1992.

The peaceful town of San Felipe is unique thanks to its exotic landscapes and extensive beaches that become sandy desert dunes leading to the mountains.
While some visit to rest and relax, others explore this exciting region in all-terrain vehicles. The Sea of Cortés is also ideal for kayaking, windsurfing, and sailing.
Fishing enthusiasts enjoy this area because it offers a nearly year-round bounty of corvina, white sea bass, and golden and triggerfish. Each year there are fishing competitions and regattas.
San Felipe is well known for its cuisine, which features seafood, especially shrimp.

VALLE DE GUADALUPE
LAND OF VINEYARDS

MEXICO IS KNOWN WORLDWIDE FOR ITS HIGH-QUALITY BEER AND TEQUILA. However, over the past several years, Mexican wines have evolved significantly and have won more than four hundred international prizes and recognitions in competitions in Europe and the United States. Mexico is in the New World–wine category, which includes countries such as Australia, Argentina, Chile, the United States, New Zealand, and South Africa. Today more than two hundred varieties of wine are produced in Mexico.

A vineyard in Mexico's wine-producing region, Valle de Guadalupe.

facing page
Barrels in a wine cellar at one of Mexico's vineyards.

Mexico's wine industry is centered in Valle de Guadalupe, located about eighteen miles northeast of the pleasant port of Ensenada in Baja California. This area falls within the internationally known wine-production zone—between the latitudes of 30 and 50 degrees. It has a Mediterranean climate with a rainy season in winter (the rest of the country has its rainy season during the summer). Also known as the Valle de Calafia, this region was discovered in 1795 by the Spaniard Ildefonso Bernal. Later, the Dominican friars established the mission of Our Lady of Guadalupe. Realizing the potential of the area's climatic conditions, they began to grow grapes, apricots, and olives. The Dominicans involved the local indigenous tribes in this agricultural work in addition to training them in cattle raising.

Wine development in Valle de Guadalupe proceeded rather slowly until the beginning of the twentieth century. At that time, President Porfirio Díaz sent more than three hundred Russian immigrants to the area to increase agricultural productivity. Later, the wineries employed French and Italian oenophiles as consultants, leading to a marked improvement in the quality of the wine produced. Thanks to these efforts, winegrowers in Valle de Guadalupe, as well as the neighboring Santo Tomas and San Vicente valleys, today export high-quality wines to more than forty countries. Some see resemblances between Valle de Guadalupe today and the early days of the Napa Valley in California.

Visitors to Mexico's wineries can take enjoyable tours of the facilities during which the owners and sommeliers personally describe the attributes of their products. The traditional harvest is celebrated in August, when the

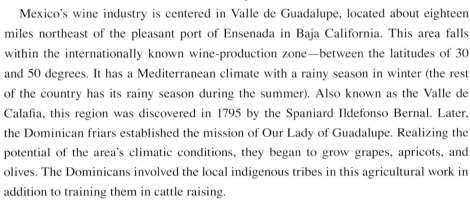

Valle de Guadalupe, situated in the Baja California desert, is lucky to have a warm climate with breezes from the Pacific Ocean, vital components for wine cultivation. In addition to delicious wines, the town is also known for its charming vineyard-surrounded hotels such as the Villa del Valle or the Adobe Guadalupe. These hotels feature delicious wines in a homelike setting, offer horseback-riding excursions, and have spa facilities. Good wine should be accompanied by good food and the area has two renowned restaurants: the iconic Rey Sol in Ensenada and La Laja in the heart of the Valle de Guadalupe.

wineries host fiestas, banquets, dances, auctions, concerts, and wine-tasting sessions. In Valle de Guadalupe, white wines such as Chenin Blanc, Colombard, Sauvignon Blanc, and Chardonnay are produced. Red wines include Cabernet Sauvignon, Merlot, Grenache, Carignan, Barbera, Nebbiolo, and Zinfandel.

Some of the most renowned wineries in Mexico—Monte Xanic, Santo Tomas, L. A. Cetto, Casa de Piedra, Chateau Camou, and Domecq—have won multiple awards. There are also outstanding smaller vineyards such as Barón Balche, Bibayoff, Valmar, Vinisterra, Aborigen, Tres Valles, Adobe Guadalupe, and Liceaga, among others. But there are lovely wines to be enjoyed and experiences to be had at lesser-known labels as well. Lupita Wilson's small organic vineyard is a unique, homey place, where the proprietress offers bottles of her own wine, rich pastries, and marmalade. Thanks to the generosity and knowledge of Valle de Guadalupe's celebrated oenophile, Hugo D'Acosta, humble growers have learned the secrets of the winegrowing art. Even in wineries with small reserves it is possible to enjoy notable wines.

LORETO
HISTORIC CAPITAL OF THE CALIFORNIAS

It was not until 1697, when the Jesuits arrived in the territory today known as Baja California, Baja California Sur, and California in the United States, that the area was successfully colonized. After founding Loreto and making it the capital of the Californias and the center of evangelization, the audacious Jesuits began to focus on colonizing the inhospitable lands of the north. These territories were inhabited by tribes such as the Mayos, Yaquis, Tarahumaras, Coras, and Pimas, among others. Another seventeen missions were built during the first century of the peninsula's evangelization.

By 1767 the Jesuits's efforts had borne surprising fruit. By the time King Charles III expelled them from the territory of New Spain, they had increased from the original fourteen pioneers to almost seven hundred members. There were more than one hundred thirty-three missions, twenty-five schools, and eleven seminaries, and the Jesuits were a powerful influence in twenty-five provinces. Jesuits preached the word of God in more than thirty indigenous languages and, contained within their libraries, possessed possibly the most important cultural inheritance of the era, an invaluable resource for today's ethnographers, cartographers, astronomers, botanists, and zoologists.

The missionaries not only performed their religious duties but worked as mechanics, teachers, doctors, cooks, and architects. In time, other colonizers, principally Italian, Belgian, and German Catholics, came to the peninsula to continue its colonization. They were invited, instead of the Criollo and Mestizo conquistadors, since the soldiers were restricted from entering the area because they were considered a bad influence on the newly converted natives.

Juan Maria de Salvatierra was the Jesuit who founded Loreto, and he chose this place because of its excellent location. Situated in the central part of the peninsula on the shores of the Sea of Cortés, where the mountains of the Sierra Giganta meet the desert, this palm-filled oasis is also near five beautiful islands: Coronado, Del Carmen, Danzante, Montserrat, and Santa Catalina. There are many creatures living along the coast, including humpback whales, sea lions, yellow-winged tuna, and sailfish. The lovely multicolored waters are a magnificent spot for divers and for aquatic sports.

A nighttime view of San Francisco Xavier Mission.

facing page
Our Lady of Loreto Church and its famous dome-topped bell tower.

Today Loreto's mission church continues to be the heart of the town. Next to the church is the Museum of the Missions, which houses a respectable collection of colonial-era tools, archaeological and religious objects, as well as the work of local artisans. Among its principal works are a life-size statue of Christ, a gilded cross, and large religious-themed oil paintings. To preserve the historical legacy of the missionary work here, a "Route of the Missions" has been created. This tour takes visitors to the principal religious sites of the peninsula. Loreto is an ideal place to begin this journey and walk the trails of the evangelists of the Californias, the foot soldiers of Saint Ignatius Loyola.

Saint Francis Xavier's manorlike mission is located about twenty-one miles from Loreto. Concealed in the middle of the Sierra Giganta mountains, this church is a classic example of the splendor of Jesuit architecture. Its facade has marble reliefs and in the interior, the principal retablo is baroque and has oil paintings of the Holy Trinity and Saint Ann. It also features an ornamented sculpture of Saint Francis Xavier and a beautiful statue of Saint Ignatius Loyola. The pueblo honors the work of the missionaries each year. In December, the faithful from around the region converge here to celebrate Saint Francis Xavier.

Exotic fauna live in the surrounding desert and provide striking visual contrasts beside capriciously formed desert plants including gigantic thistles and boojum trees that look like giant upturned turnips. The boojum's English name is derived from Lewis Carroll's poem *The Hunting of the Snark*.

MULEGÉ

A PARADISE OF CONTRASTS

MULEGÉ'S BEAUTY IS FOUND IN ITS DISSIMILAR ELEMENTS. It is a place where vegetation and desert mix, giving an extraordinary character to this splendid, diverse region of the Baja California peninsula. Pristine white beaches lead to the peaceful turquoise waters of the Sea of Cortés. It is spectacular natural scenery that can only be compared to the Caribbean. But the bays of Mulegé are not only surrounded by palms but by many cactus plants. There are golden dunes of sand surrounded by imposing ridges of reddish rock.

Mulegé is an oasis fed by a river. Its remote location has isolated it from the rest of the country and it is a perfect refuge from which to explore nature. Many scientists come to this region to study its vast marine ecosystem or to explore the millennium-old caves and their ancient paintings. It also provides an unparalleled view of the stars. From the time of its discovery by the Jesuit Juan Maria de Salvaterra in 1702, Mulegé's visitors have marveled at its varied natural ecosystem.

It was first used as a port and then was part of the Santa Rosalía Mission, which was the third Jesuit area from which Baja California was colonized. Even though construction of this mission was not finished until 1766, from the beginning it served as a center of evangelization and a place to study the region's biodiversity. The church was constructed of stone and its base is in the form of an L. Its rustic interior is graced with a sculpture of the protectress of town, Our Lady of Santa Rosalía, which dates from the eighteenth century.

During the 1847 war between Mexico and the United States, Mulegé was the scene of an intense battle. The Mexican troops defeated the Americans earning the town the moniker, "heroic."

Over the passage of time, the unusual military fort here was transformed into an unusual prison. It is said that the Jesuits who were charged with the social rehabilitation of the prisoners not only did not put bars on the windows but allowed the prisoners to leave for work in the morning and return in the evening. Today, the municipal museum occupies this ancient prison.

Protected by Conception Bay, Mulegé is renowned for its spectacular beaches and landscapes. Among these are Santispac, El Requeson, El Burro, Coyote, Punta Prieta, and Punta Arena. The smooth sand dunes of El Gallito have become popular for motorcycling. For more adventurous spirits, it is worthwhile to climb to the top of nearby ridges to enjoy the magnificent coastal views.

A view of Mulegé with its mountainous backdrop.

facing page
A tranquil scene at Santispac Beach thanks to the beautiful waters of the Sea of Cortés.

Diving and snorkeling are ideal activities in the crystal clear waters of the Sea of Cortés, as are sailing and kayaking. For those who like to explore, the seventy-five-hundred-year-old cave paintings found in San Borjita and at the Hacienda La Trinidad are a must. These ancient caverns are painted with human figures, desert animals, and fish, as well as images of utensils and rudimentary tools.

Mulegé is an enclave for Canadian and American visitors. It is normal to see all-terrain vehicles as well as motor homes on the local highways. The majority of homes are built on the banks of the river delta. Though there is no dominant architectural style, houses are simple and have Mediterranean-inspired decor. From their palm-covered terraces residents have wonderful views of the valley.

SAN IGNACIO
C A V E   P A I N T I N G S

FEW JOURNEYS ARE AS REWARDING AS EXPLORING THE MARVELOUS CAVE PAINTINGS of the Sierra de San Francisco of Baja California. These splendid murals, which can be found throughout more than three hundred sites in the area, appear like a heavenly gallery open to the world. It is estimated that the prehistoric paintings here are more than four thousand years old. Spread out over an extensive 4,633-square-mile area, these cave paintings were declared a World Heritage site by UNESCO in 1993. There are many wonderful surprises in store during one's visit.

Travelers to the caves start in the beautiful town of San Ignacio, founded by the intrepid Jesuit father Francisco Maria Piccolo in 1728. Surrounded by the reddened earth of the Sierra de San Francisco, San Ignacio is a pleasant oasis in the middle of the desert. Thanks to an underground river that supplies water, this picturesque pueblo of fishermen sits beside a lake bordered by tulles and dried reed grass and is shaded by date palms and leafy trees from India. The region is also famous as one of the principal sanctuaries for migrating gray whales.

In 1993 UNESCO declared the whale sanctuary part of the cultural patrimony of humanity. This eco-region not only has the largest concentration of gray whales on the planet, but throughout its over six million acres protects a natural habitat that is home to more than four hundred species of plants, an estimated quarter of the plants native to Baja California.

If Henry IV of France was correct in his admission that "Paris was worth a Mass," it can also be said that viewing these cave paintings in their natural setting is worth the challenging journey. Getting to these prehistoric paintings requires climbing winding mountain trails, spending the night in the mountains, and riding a burro or horse. Only after this trek can visitors view these great treasures. A short tour takes three to four days; a more extensive trip takes six to ten days. But the rewards are well worth the effort. Incredible panoramic views of the Sea of Cortés, the Pacific Ocean, the diverse desert landscape, and colorful plains can be enjoyed from this mountaintop.

It is believed that the Cochimí tribe inhabited the area with the cave paintings. Depictions in these paintings include an incredible variety of human figures as well as land and sea animals. These ancient paintings help us realize that it is not in life but in art that transcendence is experienced. Red and black are the predominant colors featured, though orange, blue, and white are also used. After seeing these marvelous paintings in person, the adventurous traveler can echo the words of Pablo Picasso: "Some painters transform the sun into a yellow spot, others transform a yellow spot into the sun."

Cave paintings at Cueva del Ratón.

facing page
A panorama of San Ignacio.

The principal cave painting sites are found in El Vizcaino's biosphere reserve. Foremost is La Pintada, which is known for its size and diversity of images. It is 327 feet long and 16 feet high. Also significant are La Flecha, Los Músicos, La Soledad, and La Boca de San Julio. Of singular importance are the remote, rarely visited caves of San Gregorio and San Gregorito. La Serpiente, El Mono Alto, La Super Nova, and Los Corralitos are caves found on the Rancho de Santa Marta. The most accessible of the caves in the Sierra de San Francisco is the Cueva del Ratón with its walls covered in images of humans and animals.

San Ignacio exudes quiet and tranquility with narrow streets radiating from the main plaza. After the Jesuits were expelled from Mexico, the town's mission was given to the Dominicans. The main door of the church is a Moorish arch crowned with a medallion that has an eight-pointed star and a fleur-de-lis, symbols also used in the Dominican churches of Oaxaca. Its facade, built on a base consisting of blocks of volcanic rock, is organized on two planes with simple cornices and pilasters. To honor the church's benefactors, the design includes symbols of the Spanish empire: two castles and two crowned lions. A surprisingly beautiful main retablo, made of gilded wood, can be found inside. There are seven oil paintings dedicated to Our Lady of Pilar, the apostles Peter and John, and saints Vincent and Dominic.

SAN JOSÉ DEL CABO
A PARADISE BETWEEN TWO SEAS

MOTIVATED BY THE DESIRE TO FIND AN ABUNDANT SUPPLY OF PEARLS, the Spanish conquistadores arrived in the lower part of Baja California in 1534 at a place known as Los Cabos. But they were greeted with hostility by the nomadic tribes living in this area rich in natural beauty and eventually were repelled. The Spaniards retreated; however, they maintained the myth that they had encountered a place of unbelievable riches, similar to the legendary El Dorado. Hearing of these legends, pirates and privateers made Los Cabos both a refuge and a place from which to ambush passing ships.

In 1730 the San José del Cabo mission was founded and during the following years the southern peninsula developed slowly. In 1888, as part of a plan to spur the economic development of the region, President Porfirio Díaz ordered the division of Baja California into two territories. This did not bring the desired results. The beautiful region had to wait until the 1950s when an ex-president of Mexico turned businessman, Abelardo L. Rodríguez, built a beautiful and exclusive hotel there. It became the favored summer vacation spot for the American president Dwight Eisenhower. Next, the sophisticated Hotel Palmilla opened with its fabulous golf course. With this, the southern half of the peninsula became a sophisticated tourist destination.

The region known as Los Cabos includes the picturesque town of San José del Cabo, the modern port of Cabo San Lucas, and the marine park Cabo Pulmo. San José del Cabo maintains its lovely ambience largely because of its colonial atmosphere with a tropical touch. Its charming streets are lined with old homes that have been converted into boutiques and restaurants. The unusual Palacio Municipal, with nine arches across its facade, contains murals that tell the story of the peninsula's past. On the edge of town are many private residences as well as deluxe hotels.

The Cabo Pulmo aquatic park is a protected area. It has a spectacular coral reef with marine animals such as dolphins, manta rays, turtles, whales, and numerous fish. Visitors can view these inhabitants through the crystal-clear water. As surprising as its natural beauty has been the orderly growth of the region. In just fifty years the Cabo area has consolidated its position as the principal tourist destination of the peninsula. Even though the explorers did not discover their El Dorado, today's visitors are still able to enjoy other treasures.

A live display of plants at the Cactus Museum.

facing page
Pristine Love Beach, the site of iconic arch formations and incredible blue water.

Baja California's natural beauty is astonishing. It is estimated that over thirty-two hundred species of marine life live in the Sea of Cortés (prestigious marine researcher Jacques Cousteau considered the region the aquarium of the world). Its banks of coral reefs, and the incredible diversity of marine life there, make it a great place to go snorkeling and diving. Especially enjoyable sights are the cascading sand, the colonies of sea lions, and the Banco la Gorda, all obligatory for the more intrepid marine enthusiast. For those who love fishing, Los Cabos is known as the world's marlin-fishing capital and offers an unparalleled fishing experience year-round.

Los Cabos is a coastal paradise where the waters of the Pacific Ocean meet the Sea of Cortés. Its golden beaches are great places to enjoy private moments. The arch formed by the erosion of the sea is both the symbol of Cabo San Lucas and the guardian of the beautiful Playa del Amor. El Medano is Los Cabos's primary beach and where the splendid landscape of the region can be enjoyed. There is a brand-new golf course with an endless carpet of grass set amidst the golden dunes. An array of formidable desert plants such as thistles and cacti adorn the course. In San José there is a museum dedicated to teaching about the hundreds of animal species that inhabit the desert.

20

The simple mission church of San José dominates the main plaza of the town. As is typical in Mexico's small towns, vendors sell balloons, cotton clothing, artwork, and ice cream. While San José del Cabo is peaceful and picturesque, neighboring Cabo San Lucas is intense and sophisticated and known for its high level of service. It has a modern marina and many restaurants, and it offers a wide range of entertainment. Beautiful views of both the Pacific Ocean and the Sea of Cortés can be enjoyed at the tip of the peninsula—the place to be to view breathtaking sunrises and sunsets.

above
Lovely San José Church.

left
A romantic panoramic view
of Cabo San Lucas at sunset.

below
One of many picturesque
streets in San José del Cabo.

SANTA ROSALÍA
GUSTAVE EIFFEL'S LEGACY

AFTER THE END OF MEXICO'S FIGHT FOR INDEPENDENCE IN 1821, the country fell under French influence. Throughout the nineteenth century, Mexico adopted many of France's social customs, as well as its cuisine and way of life. At the same time, French religious teaching orders such as the Marists and Ladies of the Sacred Heart flourished. In architecture, cities chose to employ the French styles then in vogue in Paris. All this intensified economic relations between the two countries and led to the establishment of French companies throughout Mexico. This is what happened with the French mining company El Boleo, which discovered rich copper deposits in Baja California. President Porfirio Díaz gave the company permission to begin extracting minerals in 1885 in order to create jobs and a viable town; today the town is known as Santa Rosalía.

Yaqui Indians from Sonora were imported as mine workers while the French supervised mining operations. For the town's urban design, the mining company directors adopted a plan that was typical of other French mining towns. Celebrated French engineers had perfected a system of prefabricated buildings, and they wanted to increase their business by sending products abroad to places such as Mexico. Santa Rosalía is unique among Mexican towns because it includes both wood houses and prefabricated steel buildings.

During the 1889 Paris World Exposition, a young Frenchman named Gustave Eiffel displayed a beautiful church building constructed of galvanized steel. Eiffel, who would later build his famous tower in Paris, incorporated the latest advances in prefabricated building. After the exposition, the building was dismantled and shipped to Brussels where it was reassembled and then exhibited until 1895. Its next stop was supposed to be Africa, but the French director of Santa Rosalía's mine acquired it and sent it there instead. It became the icon of the town.

Santa Rosalía is built on two small plateaus separated by a river that flows into the Sea of Cortés. The northern part of town is the area where the French built; the southern is Mexican. Its heart, where the majority of the town's businesses are located, lies along the banks of the river. One such business is El Boleo, a famous French bakery. Steam locomotives, commemorating a distant era, are displayed as monuments in various plazas. A charming place, Santa Rosalía has narrow streets and buildings that are adorned with abundant, colorful plants and flowers. Even after the mines closed it continued to be the French jewel of the peninsula—and still is to this day.

The office of El Boleo mining company.

facing page
Beautiful stained-glass windows at Santa Barbára Church in Santa Rosalía.

In addition to the beautiful Santa Barbara Church, San Ignacio's other prefabricated buildings include the present-day Municipal Archive and Museum, also attributed to Eiffel. It has a distinctive French facade complemented with a balustrade and wood decorations. This building was the mining company headquarters, but today it houses a considerable collection of mining tools and utensils. There are other historical French-designed buildings such as the city hall and post office.

Santa Barbara is a lovely church attributed to Gustave Eiffel. It is ninety-six feet long and fifty-one feet wide. Its framework is made of forged iron and the walls are made of steel with woven wire insulation. Its altar is lit by beautiful stained-glass windows in the French neo-Gothic style. The windows, framed by colorful floral and geometric designs, represent Christian biblical scenes such as the adoration of the Magi and the holy women gathered at the cross. The design of the altar and the interior clearly reflect the influence of the French Gothic while outside the church has a bell tower topped by a red roof.

TODOS SANTOS
BOHEMIAN OASIS IN BAJA

LOCATED FIFTY MILES SOUTH OF LA PAZ AND FORTY-FIVE MILES NORTH OF LOS CABOS, Todos Santos is an oasis in the Baja California desert. It is a place with exceptionally rich natural beauty—attractive beaches and an abundance of tropical biodiversity. A large variety of birds are found there, as well as gray whales, dolphins, and a range of marine species. Todos Santos is one of the jewels of the Baja peninsula.

From its founding, the Jesuits understood the potential of this location, and in 1733 they established the mission of Santa Rosa de las Palmas; it later became known as Todos Santos. Given its plentiful water and proximity to the United States, the town rapidly became a prosperous center for growing and refining sugarcane. By the middle of the nineteenth century there were eight sugar mills, and it was during this time that the region reached its cultural and economic apogee. Todos Santos was the point of reference for social refinement in Baja California—because of its ability to attract artists and its seductive lifestyle, which was further enhanced by numerous theaters and galleries.

The architecture of Todos Santos was eclectic with colonial-style buildings and Mediterranean-inspired adobe houses. In 1950 a lengthy drought left Todos Santos in ruins. Miraculously, thirty years after the catastrophe, the water of the oasis returned and with it agriculture flourished once again. But this time organic vegetables, not sugarcane, were planted.

A view of the town from above.

facing page
Mediterranean-style homes can be found in Todos Santos's desertlike environment.

Thanks to the efforts of prolific artist Charles Stewart, who opened a studio there, the village's cultural atmosphere was also revived. He persuaded a community of international professional artists to relocate to the town. Following these artists, some dozen galleries opened. Today, Todos Santos has more than twenty artisan shops selling a range of Mexican ceramics, textiles, and carved wood. It was recently chosen to be included in a group of *pueblos mágicos* chosen by the Mexican government. These small towns are selected for their overwhelming cultural and historic value. Once one visits, it is easy to understand why people like to linger there. The most

Todos Santos's beaches are exceptional. To the north, Las Pocitas and La Pastora offer both great waves on which to practice surfing as well as golden sands to enjoy. To the south is Playa Punto Lobos, which is primarily used by fishermen. Continuing on to Los Cabos, Las Palmas is an ideal place to swim in the peninsula's turquoise waters. At San Pedrito one can see surfers enjoying the challenging waves. For nature lovers, Los Cerritos's expansive beach is a wonderful place to collect shells, swim, snorkel, or simply watch the gray whales that swim near the shore.

famous attraction in Todos Santos is neither a church nor an archaeological site but a hotel—the Hotel California, where the Eagles composed their iconic song of the same name. Every year, thousands of American tourists travel to Baja to visit the hotel. Perhaps the Eagles's immortal lyrics state the attraction of this place best: "You can check out anytime you like, but you can never leave."

Todos Santos offers wonderful culinary experiences. At Miguel's, patrons can enjoy excellent *chiles rellenos*. For more refined pallets, Juerg Wiessendanger and his young German chef Andre offer a delicate fusion of Mexican and Swiss cuisine, accompanied by an exclusive selection of more than two hundred Mexican wines. The majority of the town's restaurants offer organic produce from local farms, as well as fresh-baked breads. Todos Santos's worldly atmosphere, artistic community, and outstanding cuisine lead many people to compare it to Carmel, California.

ÁLAMOS

A COLONIAL CITY RESTORED

CALLED THE "GARDEN OF THE GODS" BY ITS ORIGINAL INHABITANTS, the Mayo and Yaqui Indians, the magnificent area where Álamos is located is rich in silver deposits. After the Spanish discovered silver in the Promontorios, Aduana, Cabras, and Quintera mines, the local population grew rapidly. During its colonial heyday at the end of the eighteenth century, it was known as the "City of Silver." This visible prosperity turned Álamos into the most important city in northwestern Mexico and created a regional pride in the balanced development of its economy, architecture, and culture.

Agriculture, business, and cattle raising were all, in turns, important to the economy. Cereal and oranges were exported to the United States while a money exchange was built to mint silver for China, England, India, and the United States. Many majestic buildings, plazas, and churches were constructed. All of this development came to an end at the beginning of the twentieth century: the silver mines had been exhausted, there was a drought, and social upheaval led to the revolution. A beautiful city became a ghost town. Today, though its former economic glory has not been completely re-established, Álamos has resurrected its splendid colonial ambience.

Álamos had two famous citizens. One was the actress María Felix, known as La Doña, who was an icon of the Golden Era of Mexican cinema. During her career she made forty-seven films in various countries including Mexico, Italy, Argentina, and Spain. Felix, known for her incredible beauty and short temper, married two other Mexican celebrities, the renowned actor and singer Jorge Negrete and the prodigious composer Agustin Lara. Lara dedicated the famous song "María Bonita" to her; today it is a nickname used to sweetly refer to the Sonoran actress. La Doña's family home contains mementos of her life.

The other great figure was the multifaceted Alfonso Ortiz Tirado, a surgeon, scientist, and tenor, who was well known throughout Latin America as an orthopedic specialist. He was the primary physician of Agustin Lara, as well as the painters Diego Rivera and Frida Kahlo, the latter of which he operated on several times. At the same time, Dr. Ortiz Tirado had a career as a tenor, singing in many countries in the Americas and in Europe. His successful musical career enabled him to be a philanthropist, and he built the celebrated Children's Hospital in Mexico City.

The memorial plaque on the hospital reads: "I built this temple with my song to alleviate suffering." Álamos honors the "Tenor of the Americas" each year at the end of January, hosting the prestigious Dr. Alfonso Ortiz Tirado cultural festival.

View of the church from the gazebo in the plaza.

facing page
Overlooking Álamos's plaza, church, and buildings.

Immaculate Conception Church served as the seat of the first bishop. It was built in a baroque style and has three naves. The delightful Plaza de las Armas, planted with palms, has a unique kiosk in the center reflecting a Romantic design, with musical allusions inside. Nearby are important buildings. Crossing over to the "Street of the Kiss" takes you to Alameda Park, planted with ancient laurels from India as well as poplars (*alamos*) that give the town its name. At the city market it's possible to buy the famous "jumping beans."

Álamos, a beautiful town, has 188 historic buildings. The Municipal Palace, which does not look particularly colonial, is decorated with steel columns and has a brick facade with a row of windows topped by a tower. Nearby is the former money exchange as well as a cultural center that previously was used as a jail. A typical Álamos house has an interior patio with a garden. A number of the grander homes have been restored and converted into lovely hotels and office buildings. The magnificent La Hacienda de los Santos is a hotel that fits in beautifully with the nearby colonial mansions as well as the local mill. It has many Spanish-influenced decorative touches as well as beautiful gardens and pools.

MAGDALENA DE KINO
INHERITANCE OF MISSIONS

IN THE IMPLACABLE DESERT REGION OF SONORA AND ARIZONA, the distinctions between two states—between two countries—are almost nonexistent. Here there is simply one form of life, one cultural inheritance, one common form of survival. Facing the enormous heat of summer and the overwhelming cold of winter, the people who live in this extraordinary environment have also grown together; ranching and mining development are their primary work. They also share the same ethnic roots, food, art, and, above all, the spiritual influence of the heroic Father Kino.

Eusebio Kino was born in 1645 in a small town in the mountains of the Italian Tyrol near the city of Trent. He studied science, letters, and theology at the Jesuit college in Innsbruck, Austria. Later he studied mathematics at Germany's University of Ingolstadt; he arrived in New Spain in 1681. Over the next thirty years he dedicated himself to exploring this desert region on horseback and evangelizing the natives. He founded more than twenty missions. Among those that stand out in Arizona are San José de Tumacácori (a U.S. National Historic Park) and San Xavier del Bac near Tucson, both of which have notable architectural designs with interiors rich in frescoes and statues. Particularly noteworthy in Sonora, Mexico, are La Purísima Concepción de Nuestra Señora de Caborca, San Pedro y San Pablo de Tubutama, known for excellent plaster reliefs, and San Diego del Pitiquito, with its remarkable hidden frescoes.

Father Kino was an excellent cartographer and his 1705 map of the region was used for more than a century. Thanks to his exhaustive explorations (he made more than forty-two expeditions to Arizona alone) and travels on the Colorado and Gila rivers, he was the first to prove that Baja California was a peninsula and not an island, as had originally been thought. He made notable astronomical observations for which he was named a "royal cosmographer," and he published the book *Explaining Comets*. In addition to his evangelical work, he spoke multiple dialects and taught thousands to read and write. He taught campesinos about agriculture and ranching, and he helped to improve the working conditions for miners. At the end of his life he wrote about his experiences in a famous book, *Celestial Favors*.

He spent his final years in the town of Magdalena de Kino, where he died in 1711. He had a major influence on the region. This is why a statue of him can be seen in the National Statuary Hall in the U.S. Capitol, a collection that honors prominent citizens from each state. Father Kino represents the state of Arizona. Each year, thousands of pilgrims come to Magdalena de Kino to visit his mausoleum and to express their profound veneration.

Eusebio Kino Square's clock tower.

facing page
The lovely Santa Maria Magdalena Church.

A memorable nature experience can be enjoyed in this wonderful area. Its greatest beauty lies outside the walls of Magdalena de Kino, where one can explore the extraordinary fauna and flora of the region. More than three hundred species of animals and three thousand flowers exist in this desert ecosystem. Expeditions are offered to wildlife refuges in both the U.S. and Mexico, and fabulous flowers and animals such as antelope can be seen on the trip. La Proveedora petroglyphs, near Caborca, is also worth a visit. These petroglyphs are shaped out of the rocky hillside and depict animals, human activities, and geometric designs estimated to be about one thousand years old.

Nuestra Señora de María Magdalena Church stands out in the lovely Plaza Monumental where Father Kino's mausoleum is located. Notable buildings with porticos as well as stores and restaurants surround it. Several blocks to the west is the Municipal Palace featuring an eclectic architectural mix of Greek, Roman, Arabic, Spanish, and colonial influences. It has walkways with arches as well as an important stairway. The town of Magdalena de Kino is famous for its fruit preserves and its saddlery. It is the ideal place to begin a tour of the region's missions and enjoy repasts of traditional beef dishes, wheat cakes, and *bacanora*, a liquor made from wild cactus.

BATOPILAS
SILVER JEWEL OF THE COPPER CANYON

A TRANSPLANTED AMERICAN NAMED ALEXANDER SHEPHERD RE-ESTABLISHED MINING IN THIS TOWN, and brought it the latest technologies of the time. But Shepherd's story started in Washington, D.C. On the corner of Pennsylvania Avenue and Fourteenth Street in that city a bronze sculpture rests upon a granite base. A solitary name is inscribed upon it: Shepherd. For most of the city's residents, this name means nothing. Nevertheless, much of the splendor of Washington as it is today is due to the efforts of Alexander Shepherd.

At the end of the Civil War, the American capital was in as much need of reconstruction as the South, but powerful groups preferred to move the capital. Yet, Shepherd, a brilliant man who had made his fortune in the construction and plumbing industries and was a close friend of President Grant, undertook all necessary actions as governor of the District of Columbia to retain the capital in Washington. He also strengthened those foundations that would secure its permanence.

As part of his great reconstruction project, in only eighteen months Shepherd assigned contracts for more than $30 million worth of work, equivalent to one-fourth of the value of all real estate property in the city at that time. Enraged taxpayers and officials suggested Shepherd had not only put public finances at risk, but had also enriched himself. Despite these suppositions of illegal activity, no proof of embezzlement ever surfaced. Instead it was found that he did not possess a considerable fortune at all; on the contrary, he had acquired substantial debts. Pressured by this situation, Shepherd left for a self-imposed exile in Mexico.

Shepherd had heard of a mining town in Chihuahua located in an enclave within the Batopilas Canyon, part of Copper Canyon; it was said that the bottom of the river was covered with silver, not sand. He explored the area, becoming convinced of the existence of riches buried in the mountains. Shepherd had never run a mine. However, he raised three million dollars and, backed by Mexican president Porfirio Diaz, in a very short time he re-established silver-mining operations; he also became the region's feudal lord. He persuaded local businessmen to build the Chihuahua railway, paving the way for Batopilas to become only the second town in Mexico to have electricity.

It is said that he amassed a fortune of more than twenty million dollars during the eight years he ran the mine. He then returned to Washington, D.C., and received a hero's welcome from those who had forced him to leave. Some time later, he returned to Mexico where he died in 1902. The silver veins are now exhausted, but the Batopilas region's natural wealth and beauty lives on.

Ramón Figueroa, world-renowned Raramuri violin maker.

facing page
Solitary Satevó Church rests at the bottom of the Batopilas Canyon.

Tarahumaras (or Raramuris, as they call themselves) are indigenous people of Copper Canyon, specifically Batopilas. Perhaps the most homogenous people in the Americas, they have preserved their traditional way of life. A respect for nature and humans is paramount in the Tarahumaras' value system. The Tarahumaras produce a rich variety of crafts, some of an exceptional quality. Such is the case of the renowned Rarámuris Patrocinio Lopez and Ramon Figueroa, who produce fine, exquisite violins, earning them numerous invitations to display their creations and music in various countries in America and Europe, including Cremona, Italy, the birthplace of the famous Stradivarius violins.

The Jesuits Christianized the people of the region during the seventeenth century, and they built missions that are scattered throughout the mountain range. Satevó Church sits on a riverbank and is framed by the canyon. Travelers on foot can follow the river's course—one of the most fascinating routes within Copper Canyon. The three-day trek from Batopilas to Urique passes through the ravines and cliffs of its famous canyons.

The Tarahumaras are remarkable runners, as has been true of indigenous peoples throughout Mexico over the centuries, who needed to be superb athletes to survive; for example, when powerful Aztec emperor Moctezuma I reigned, he ate fresh fish for lunch. In the early morning, fishermen caught the fish for his lunch in the Gulf of Mexico. Messengers transporting the day's catch then had to run 250 miles inland and climb six thousand feet in order to reach Mexico-Tenochtitlán by Moctezuma's noontime lunch.

A twenty-six-mile marathon is easy for the Tarahumaras compared to their own races, during which these world-class runners cover distances of more than sixty-two miles. When Tarahumaras run, they don't wear fancy high-tech sneakers; in fact, most of them run shoeless. Their unique abilities have been researched by top running organizations throughout the world, as well as by NASA and the U.S. Army.

The road leading to Batopilas winds its way through the mountains, which are arranged in tiers of varied greens and blues. Hikers descend six thousand feet over forty miles of terrain. Halfway through the journey they pass the small mining town of La Bufa. As they near the bottom of the canyon, the landscape becomes a mix of both tropical and desert vegetation, and slowly the best-kept secret of the mystic Copper Canyons—Batopilas—is discovered.

above
Alexander Shepherd's hacienda.

below
A donkey strolls undisturbed along the quiet streets of Batopilas.

right
An impressive view of the canyon frames the Bufa mine.

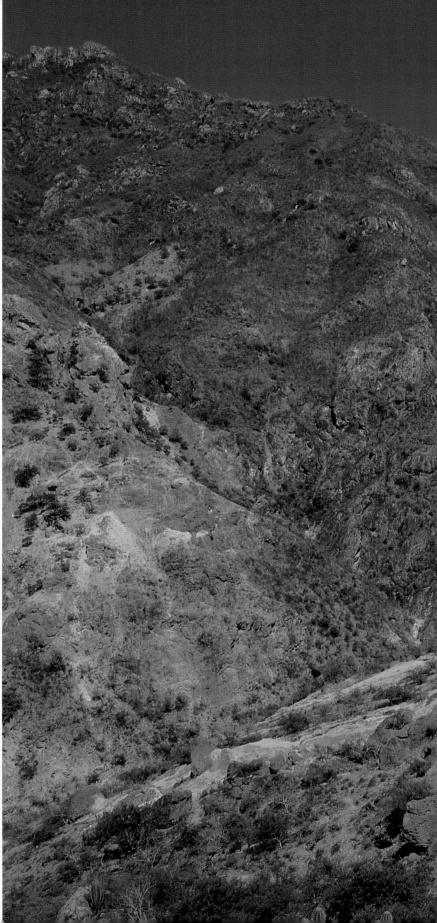

CREEL

GATEWAY TO THE COPPER CANYON

As is commonly said, "the Copper Canyon is what the Grand Canyon would like to be when it grows up." This spectacular series of canyons in Chihuahua is four times longer and one and a half times deeper than the Grand Canyon. Many of its canyons surpass the Grand Canyon in scale. After centuries of erosion, constant lava flows, and the accumulation of tons of ash, the plateaus broke up into canyons up to one and a quarter miles deep and several miles wide. In total, these canyons include more than thirty-seven thousand miles of mountains, with cliffs and precipices covering half its surface.

The Copper Canyon is among Mexico's most spectacular sights, and Creel is the perfect starting point to see it, reached either by highway or by the famous "Chepe," the train linking the 584 miles from Chihuahua to Los Mochis. One can see splendid views of the canyon throughout the rail journey, which crosses 410 bridges and goes through 99 tunnels.

The train traverses the entire Septentrión Canyon and some areas of the Urique Canyon. Stop for an excursion at Temorís, the gateway to the Chínipas Canyon, and at Bahuichivo, the starting point to the Cerocahui Mission. From there, one can descend to the lowest point of the canyon, enjoying spectacular views; the picturesque mining town of Urique is there. Those travelers who seek to enjoy unbeatable luxury and comfort can travel by train on the renowned *Orient Express*, which departs from the United States and visits different sites in Chihuahua and Sonora.

In Creel, several trips can be arranged to points throughout the region. Visit Guachochi, at the entrance to Sinforosa Canyon, with its six-thousand-foot cliffs. From there one can reach Norogochi, site of some of the best Holy Week festivities, along with those celebrated in the towns of Arareko, Cusárare, and Basíhuare. Visiting the Caborachí Mission is quite interesting, as many Tarahumara paintings are preserved there. Discovering the canyons requires several intense days of traveling and Creel is the natural point from which to enter these monumental, magical, and marvelous canyons.

From Creel travelers can go to Divisadero, which offers an incomparable panorama of the Urique Canyon, the deepest in the sierra. In Basaseachi, travelers enter the Candameña Canyon, considered by many to be the most beautiful and accessible. It is also known as the canyon of waterfalls. Two of Mexico's highest waterfalls—Basaseachi, at over eight hundred feet, and Piedra Volada, at nearly fifteen hundred feet—are there. Nearby is the imposing Peña del Gigante boulder, a rock monolith with a wall twenty-nine hundred feet high.

A fine portrait of the Virgin Mary housed at the Loyola Museum.

facing page
Hidden in the mountains is the beautiful town of Creel.

A dozen miles from Creel is Cusárare, a typical Tarahumara village with two beautiful treasures: a lovely one-hundred-foot-tall waterfall and the Loyola Museum, home to an outstanding collection of forty-five religious paintings from the sixteenth and seventeenth centuries. Owing to the tireless efforts of Father Luis Verplancken and to the support of the local indigenous people, the current museum was built next to the simple mission. The highlight of its collection are twelve paintings by Miguel Correa depicting the life of the Virgin Mary.

A few minutes from Creel is San Ignacio Arareko, a Tarahumara community on the shores of a peaceful lake and surrounded by pine forests. Some of the most colorful Holy Week festivities are celebrated here. Around Arareko there is a series of interesting rock formations, two of which are known as "the mushroom" and "the frogs"; these are beautiful places to practice mountain biking or simply to explore. South of Creel is the striking Rukíraso waterfall. To the west is Bisabírachi Valley, with its natural scenery and abundant rock formations. Back in Creel, the Arts and Crafts Institute displays artifacts of Tarahumara culture; regional crafts are also sold.

HIDALGO DEL PARRAL
PANCHO VILLA'S HOME

MEXICO HAS TWO GREAT REVOLUTIONARY HEROES. One is Emiliano Zapata, the *caudillo* (military leader) of the south, who was a tireless fighter for social equality through his ideals of land and liberty; the other is General Francisco "Pancho" Villa, who organized the powerful northern division with his intrepid soldiers, known as Los Dorados. This army played an essential role in organizing the revolution during its multiple phases, which, all told, lasted more than ten years. Though neither Zapata nor Villa would become president, they both agreed that it would be best to have a civilian guide the country.

Alvarado Palace.

facing page
Hidalgo Theater.

Pancho Villa was, without a doubt, the most famous Mexican revolutionary, he was known throughout the world. He was at the center of worldwide media attention and traveled surrounded by journalists. Hollywood moguls financed uniforms and arms in exchange for the rights to film his battles. Among other well-known journalists, Villa attracted the attention of John Reed who, after graduating from Harvard, decided to cover military conflicts around the world. Reed accompanied Villa during his battles in hopes of capturing the essence of Villa's personality, as well as that of Venustiano Carranza. Reed synthesized his experiences of the country's revolution in the book *Insurgent Mexico.* Subsequently, Reed covered World War I, and traveled to Russia to meet Lenin. He witnessed the October Revolution, which he covered in his book *Ten Days That Shook the World,* published in 1919. His life was memorably portrayed in the film *Reds,* starring Warren Beatty.

The mining town of Hidalgo del Parral played an important role in the life of Pancho Villa. While he was governor of Chihuahua State, Villa established a money-exchange house in the town as a way to supply the revolutionary troops with funds. Here coins with enough silver could be exchanged at a one-to-one rate with American dollars. Later, it was the citizens of Hidalgo del Parral who, with a small group of soldiers, repelled American troops chasing Villa after his 1916 invasion of Columbus, New Mexico. Over eleven months, more than ten thousand American soldiers commanded by John J. Pershing failed to trap the revolutionary, eventually ending the effort. Interestingly, this was the last important mounted military operation and the beginning of the use of mechanized military vehicles. Pershing would go on to lead American troops during World War I. In 1923, after Villa retired as a revolutionary to dedicate himself to his ranch and philanthropy, the icon of Mexico's fight for independence, known as the "Centaur of the North," was assassinated in Hidalgo del Parral.

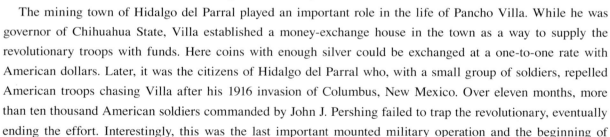

A symbol of Hidalgo del Parral is the Palacio de Alvarado. This elegant building was the property of Virginia Griensen and Pedro Alvarado. He was the wealthy owner of the Palmilla mine and was famous for offering to pay off the national debt, a gesture that President Porfirio Díaz refused because it was the debt of the nation, not just one patriot. Don Pedro Álvarez was a well-respected and loved person as well as being a father figure to and personal friend of Pancho Villa. There is also a Villa museum in Hidalgo del Parral where revolutionary-era objects are displayed. Each July the famous Cabalgatas Villistas takes place during which three thousand horsemen re-enact the adventures of the "Centaur of the North."

Hidalgo del Parral is a town with a majestic feel. Among its historic buildings are the Hidalgo Theater, the work of the French architect Amérigo Rouvier, with a seating capacity of nearly twelve hundred people. It was inaugurated during the Porfiriato, with a performance of Verdi's *Il Trovatore*. Casa Elisa Griensen combines the Austrian and the Mozarabic in its architecture. Casa Stallforth is a palatial French residence with a beautiful facade, which is surpassed only by the beauty of the interior, with its delicate paneled roofs and finished woodwork. Virgen de la Soledad Church contains a beautiful retablo and the Centro de Documentación preserves its genuine colonial feel. At the popular Mina la Prieta attraction, it's possible for visitors to go down into the mine and learn about the mining process, which was the principal economic activity of the town from the time of its founding in 1631.

NUEVAS CASAS

ANCIENT REMAINS AND ART OF THE DESERT

A ceramic piece by Juan Quezada, a master craftsperson of Mata Ortíz.

facing page
An archaeological site at Paquimé.

CHIHUAHUA IS MEXICO'S LARGEST STATE, EQUAL IN SIZE TO A MEDIUM-SIZE EUROPEAN COUNTRY. While a significant portion of the state is desert, it has rugged mountains as well as forests and fields. Chihuahua is the center of an immense region that stretches as far into Mexico as it does into the United States—a cultural region that some have named Oasisamerica. For many years, Mexico's northwest was little studied by anthropologists and archaeologists. But in the mid-twentieth century, Dr. Charles di Peso developed a chronology for the region that divided its history into three archaeological eras. The first was a lengthy ancient period that began more than five thousand years before Christ and ended in around 1000 B.C. It was a period of hunters and nomad gatherers who eventually evolved into an agrarian society that developed an architecture based on clay dwellings.

It was from these origins that the town of Paquimé arose. It became the center of an advanced civilization that created magnificent ceramics, designed shell and turquoise jewelry, extracted copper from mines, developed water hydraulics, and built paved roads across the mountains. It was connected—both culturally and commercially—with indigenous communities of the Pacific as well as the great civilizations of central and southern Mexico. But around the year 1475, a few years before the European discovery of America, Paquimé started to decline, and was abandoned and then forgotten until it was rediscovered by archaeologists.

Today, Paquimé is the most important site of Mexico's ancient north. It is near the town of Nuevas Casas and Mata Ortíz, a town famous for its ceramic art. Paquimé impressed the Spanish explorers, as revealed in the chronicles of Spaniard Baltasar de Obregon, who wrote, "this great city has buildings that appear to have been constructed by the ancient Romans. There are many large houses, both strong and tall. They have five or six stories with towers and fortified walls. The houses have large and magnificent patios covered with large and beautiful tile flooring that appears to be like jasper . . ."

Paquimé was added to the patrimony of humanity by UNESCO, although the site needs further exploration and restoration. Its buildings are not made of adobe but of clay cast in wooden forms, similar to the way cement is made today. The houses were sunk into the ground and had private patios. There were also open, public spaces with raised mounds, some in the shape of serpents, which apparently served a ritual purpose.

Juan Quezada's ceramic work has its roots in an ancient tradition, but it is infused with a powerful personal vision. He has become the premier artisan in Mexico and his world-renowned work commands extremely high prices. The ceramic pottery of Mata Ortíz employs geometric, anthropomorphic, and fantastic motifs, a wonderful combination of contemporary images blended with primitive designs used by the original tribes of the region. It is as if from somewhere deep within a collective memory, a new inspiration has emerged and been transformed into something living and modern, all because of the work of a humble potter.

Mata Ortíz is near Paquimé, and it is the center of a cultural phenomenon: the renaissance of the traditional ceramic art of the region. In 1976 an American art historian and anthropologist, Spencer Heath MacCallum, discovered ceramic work in an antiques shop in Deming, New Mexico. The store's owner did not know where the pieces were from but supposed they originated in Mexico. MacCallum began his search for the source of the work and did not stop until he arrived in Mata Ortíz, where he found their maker. The potter's name was Juan Quezada. MacCallum encouraged Quezada to create more ambitious pieces, which he took with him, promising to return. This was the beginning of a wonderful relationship between an artisan of Mata Ortíz and an American academic.

A place known as Las Cuarenta Casas is located within the Paquimé archaeological site. It features steep clay cave dwellings. The name *Cuarenta* (the Spanish word for forty) is symbolic only; it does not refer to the exact number forty but to "many" homes. Little is known about the history of these unique dwellings other than what archaeologists can glean from its remains. It seems that the golden age of Las Cuarenta Casas was during the heyday of Paquimé, around the year A.D. 1200; at that time it was used as a transit point between Paquimé, the Pacific coast, and the Gulf of California. Among objects traded commercially at Paquimé were seashells, a large number of which have been discovered among its ruins. Las Cuarenta Casas was also used as a fortress to protect the region, for its commercial routes, and as a site of religious celebrations. It was abandoned in about A.D. 1340.

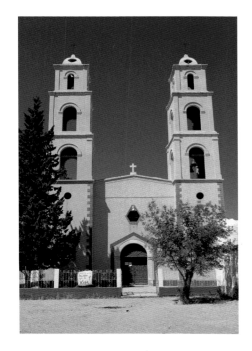

above
San Antonio de Padua
Convent's yellow facade.

left
Cuarenta Casas's
archaeological site.

below
Inside the ruins at
Cuarenta Casas.

CUATRO CIÉNEGAS
ANCIENT REEFS AND THE ORIGIN OF LIFE

IN THE MIDDLE OF A DESERT WHERE TEMPERATURES CAN REACH 130 DEGREES FAHRENHEIT, over five hundred aquifers can be found in one area. It is an amazing and unique phenomenon, and, as a result, Cuatro Ciénegas is used by scientists as a living laboratory. The ancient interconnected water system that supports this ecosystem has not changed in more than thirty-five thousand years and has had no significant geological alterations in millions more. For these reasons it is an extraordinarily rich source for research—equal to that of the Galapagos Islands.

Cuatro Ciénegas has many watery reefs, also known as cellulite stone carpets, that are gathered together in colonies of sedimentary multilayered rocks. They look similar to corals. These reefs are important because they are the most ancient evidence of life on earth, examples of an evolutionary line that has maintained its integrity throughout time. These were the first reefs that formed, making this a place where it is possible to study the development of the earth from its inception. Some scientists are also using Cuatro Ciénegas to study the history of the solar system. But, most importantly, reef systems were the first organisms to recycle carbon and thus are the original source of oxygen. For over two billion years these reefs have been expanding in the oceans of the world, not only creating a significant amount of oxygen but saturating the oceans with this oxygen. This eventually led to the formation of the ozone layer above the earth.

Cuatro Ciénegas's nature reserve covers nearly two hundred thousand acres. This humid desert has a rich biodiversity that is unique among the world's desert ecosystems. It is home to more than one thousand species of flora and fauna, of which seventy-seven species are endangered. Of primary importance is the Bisagra turtle, which evolved with claws instead of feet or fins. It also has a flexible shell that it can open or close depending on its defensive needs. For some scientists, the greatest treasure of Cuatro Ciénegas is that it has maintained its food chain intact for more than 550 million years. Its microorganisms have retained their affinity with primitive marine species, having adapted to living in unique environments such as one in which there is a total absence of phosphorous in the water and a high degree of solar radiation.

Surrounding Cuatro Ciénegas are dunes that are nearly 98-percent gypsum. They were formed more than 150 million years ago during the Mesozoic Era and its sediments are the same as the Sea of Tethys, the precursor of the Mediterranean Sea. For this reason, NASA considers Cuatro Ciénegas to be one of the few "model" ecosystems in the world that allows scientists to understand earth's primitive evolution and to design studies to explore the possibility of life on other planets such as Mars.

A charming street in Cuatro Ciénegas.

facing page
Crystal-clear blue waters of Poza Azul.

Amidst Cuatro Ciénegas's impressive ecosystem are more than two hundred individual spring-fed pools of water, the majority of them crystal clear and pure. Their size can vary from about three feet to more than one hundred wide, and they can reach depths of fifty-nine feet. Some of these are thermal springs and visitors can bathe in a number of them, including Los Mezquites, La Playita, and La Becerra. One of the most beautiful is the blue pool. Its high percentage of organic life imparts brilliant colors.

Venustiano Carranza, the revolutionary leader and president of Mexico, was born in the picturesque pueblo Cuatro Ciénegas de Carranza. His old house has been converted into the Carranza Museum and is home to a special collection of objects, images, and archives of Mexican life during revolutionary times, including a valuable facsimile copy of the constitution of 1917. Cuatro Ciénegas is also well known for its wine, especially that of the Ferrino Winery, one of the pioneering vineyards of the Americas.

PARRAS

FIRST VINEYARD OF THE AMERICAS

GRAPE CULTIVATION BECAME WIDESPREAD IN MEXICO SOON AFTER VINES WERE BROUGHT THERE IN 1524. By King Charles V's royal decree, each ship that set out for the Americas was required to carry grapevines and olive plants. Conquistador Hernán Cortés, who was the first captain-general and governor of New Spain, ordered that all landholders seed one thousand vine shoots for every one hundred natives in their service. This would have the effect of both diminishing the importation of wine from Europe and meeting the demand for wine by the colonizers of New Spain.

Because the development of farmland was essential, expeditions of colonists included at least one missionary trained in agriculture and languages. In 1574, one such expedition left Zacatecas for Coahuila in search of gold. In the middle of a brutal desert, the conquistadores encountered a palm-filled oasis rich in springwater and uncultivated plants; today this place is called Parras de la Fuente. They had stumbled upon a microclimate ideal for vineyards.

The colonizers' first efforts to grow vines at this site were unsuccessful. But it was not long before Fray Agustin Espinoza arrived. He studied Irritila, which was the predominant language of the natives of the region, and founded the Santa Maria de las Parras mission as well as a hospital. Under his direction, vineyards flourished in this fertile land and produced the first high-quality wine in the Americas.

Wine production rapidly increased, not only in Parras de la Fuente but throughout the country. The fertile lands of the new continent responded to agricultural development, while the friaries and monasteries became important research and training centers for farmers. But when the wine industry in Mexico reached a high point, and threatened the interests of producers in Spain, the king intervened and issued a decree prohibiting the production of wine in the colonies. He ordered the destruction of thousands of plants and limited cultivation only to ecclesiastical use. After taking this hit, the residents of Parras de la Fuente resumed their agricultural activities and also developed the textile industry that continues to this day.

Parras de la Fuente is also known for producing sweets with figs and pine nuts. Each August the community celebrates its grape harvest with a festival. Traditional dancing, parties, and wine tastings are featured. Residents celebrate the harvest as well as the fact that their town is home to the first vineyards in the Americas.

Santo Madero Church perched at the top of a hill.

facing page
An evening view of Santa Maria de las Parras Church.

Santo Madero Church, built on the edge of the Sombreretillo ridge, has simple architectural details and functions as a sort of popular gathering place. From it there is a great view of the town and its valley rich in springwater. For those visitors interested in further exploration of the area, the Lima and Fuques canyons are worthwhile. Less adventurous travelers may prefer staying in town, walking the quiet streets and discovering its beautiful hidden spaces. Wandering peacefully through the town's plazas and seeing its historic buildings is a lovely way to spend a visit—in addition to enjoying the delicious northern Mexican cuisine accompanied by a generous glass of local wine.

Parras de la Fuente is a beautiful colonial town. The lovely San Ignacio Church as well as the Municipal Palace—built of pink marble—are both found in the Plaza Zaragoza. The palace is two stories with balconies edged in the neo-classical style. A nearby park is the site of the Santuario de Guadalupe, which was built in the seventeenth century. It has a three-part baroque retablo with a spiral column design constructed in honor of the Jesuits' founder. On one side of the building is the former San Ignacio College, which has been converted into the Matheo Museum. The Museum of Culture, representative of Coahuila architecture, exhibits personal items of Parras's most famous citizen, Francisco Madero, who was a leader of the revolutionary movement in Mexico. It was Madero who set the stage for the eventual democratization of Mexico.

During vacations or days off, Parras de la Fuente residents gather beneath the beautiful clock in front of the parish church of Santa María. In the streets, milk prepared according to ancient traditions is still delivered by carts in the early morning. Wine, whether or not for home or for sale, continues to be made according to the teachings of Don Lorenzo García. He was one of the founders of Parras and worked hard to grow vines, while diverting springwater from almost nine miles to the north. While living here he wrote to King Philip II of Spain asking for "mercy"—a gift of land that he received on August 18, 1597. The land was given with the express purpose of planting vines to produce wine and brandy. This was the formal birth of Hacienda San Lorenzo, today Casa Madero, considered the first winery in the Americas. Its Riesling and Cabernet Sauvignon wines are considered world-class.

above
The town's Clock Square at night.

below
Barrels at the Casa Madero Winery.

right
Milk is still delivered in the traditional way, a throwback to an earlier age.

BUSTAMANTE
AN EDEN WHERE BREAD IS KING

UNLIKE DUSTY DESERT TOWNS, BUSTAMANTE, LOCATED IN THE NORTHEASTERN STATE OF NUEVO LEÓN, is green, leafy, and full of rich traditions. Its first inhabitants were the Tlaxcalteca people, who, after being defeated by the Spaniards, were converted into allies. They helped to conquer the Mexica empire and then later explored northern Mexico in search of minerals. The town was founded as San Miguel de Aguayo de la Nueva Tlaxcala, at the spring of San Lorenzo. Over time it was renamed Bustamante, but the Tlaxcalteca have not been forgotten and the annual fair is called Our Lady of Tlaxcala.

While the Spanish brought Christianity, they allowed for a mix of faiths. An artistic example of this is the figure of Christ made from corn paste applied to a bamboo frame and known as El Señor de Tlaxcala, which is found in the parish church of San Miguel. The church's architecture is a fusion, characteristic of both the conquest as well as the mud construction of the indigenous people. The main plaza is oriented to the four cardinal points but is dominated by a sculpture of Saint Michael the Archangel. Religious festivities combine the fervor of Christian pilgrims with the mysticism of native *matachine* dancers.

The Good Friday "Procession of Silence," commemorating the Virgin Mary's journey to Jesus' tomb, is one of oldest traditions still observed in Bustamante, brought to Bustamante by the first Spanish missionaries. Many people in Bustamante and other communities in Mexico still participate in this event, a sign of the fervent and unswerving faith of the country. These traditions have not changed over time, still carried out as they originally were in Spain.

The Spanish brought valuable knowledge about efficient agricultural techniques. Nuts and oranges are still an important part of Bustamante's agricultural output. Because of its abundant humidity and a unique non-desertlike microclimate, Bustamante is the garden of Nuevo León; its simple adobe homes are adorned with groves of orange and walnut trees. Homemade sweets are made from locally grown fruit and the town is justly famous for its sweetened breads such as *semitas, polkas,* and *coyotas. Mezcal* has also been produced as a folk industry since the seventeenth century. Bustamante is proud of its ecotourist attractions.

Tourists can camp in Bustamante Canyon, swim in warm springs, or explore approximately two miles of rock formations in its famous caves. It's a wonderful place from which to experience the eastern Sierra Madre mountains. Its proximity to the United States augments this town's unique international flavor, where one can hear both Mexican *corridos* and American country music on the local radio station. Bustamante is a place to experience cultural traditions, the simple pleasures of life, and a moment of tranquility underneath the shade of a large walnut tree.

Bustamante's incredible caves.

facing page
Lázaro Caso bakes bread in a traditional oven in Bustamante.

The imposing caverns of Bustamante are located in the Sierra de Gomas. The entrance is in the lower part of the Cono canyon. Even though the exact depth of the caverns is not known, speleologists estimate that it is one of the largest cavities known in the world. Their actual distance is almost 2 miles and some of its chambers are more than 300 feet wide and are more than 60 feet high. Even though the access is rather rustic, undertaking this expedition is quite worthwhile

Bustamante is known for its cuisine. Typical of the region is *cabrito al pastor*, a baked dish featuring young goat that is celebrated throughout the state. Homemade sweets of milk and nuts are the best of the region. Breadmaking is considered a craft of artisans; these bakers turn out empanadas, *cemitas, molletes,* and coyotas made with locally grown wheat and nuts. Some use traditional adobe ovens and colonial-era recipes to give their breads a delicious traditional taste reminiscent of the breads made by Don Lázaro Caso.

VILLA DE GARCÍA
DESERT CAVERNS

NUEVO LEÓN IS THE SECOND MOST PROSPEROUS AND INDUSTRIALIZED STATE IN MEXICO. If the country did not have such an intense concentration of resources in immense Mexico City, it would certainly be in first place. This position is even more surprising when one considers that Nuevo León lacks extensive coastline, petroleum reserves, and biodiversity. Its climate is almost exclusively arid. However, it does have an exceptional source of wealth: its people. Known as *Neoloneses,* they are incessant workers—practical, and, above all, unwilling to conform to the status quo.

The first Spanish explorers came to this region in search of precious minerals. They did not find any silver, but they did establish ranches. Because of this, towns began to flourish throughout this area. They featured simple adobe construction and a particular northern architectural style. With the passage of time, industries began to grow, as did commercial relations with its American neighbors. With the building of the railway and modern production techniques, Nuevo León has focused its productive energy on diverse areas such as cement, beverages, glass, steel, and technology.

But to really know the state, it is best to venture beyond the industrial smoke stacks and skyscrapers of Monterrey and to visit the nearby valleys and mountains. This is the way to discover what these small neighboring towns have to offer. To the south is Santiago, with its Cola de Caballo waterfalls. Nearby is Linares and its fertile orchards. It is also known nationally for *Glorias,* rich sweets made of nuts and milk chocolate. A little farther south, in the middle of rugged mountains, is Iturbide. Here, the faithful but proactive inhabitants of Nuevo León proudly live out the local motto, "God gives you the means, but then it's up to you to make it." Northeast of the capital is Boca de Potrillos, with its hundreds of enigmatic petroglyphs, as well as the dramatic canyons of Portrero Chico. There are more than six hundred places to rock climb or mountain bike. Finally, to east lies the peaceful town of Villa de García and its millenia-old caverns.

Villa de García has the simplicity of a well-planned colonial town, where the focal point of social life is the central plaza. The plaza's kiosk is surrounded by benches and places to rest and people watch. There are also balloon and ice-cream vendors, shoeshine men, and musicians. Nearby, doves scatter at the sound of the bells of the local church announcing some festivity. Dominating this esplanade is City Hall, and nearby are colorful homes and bountiful orchards.

An overhead cable car in Villa de García provides wonderful views.

facing page
Dramatic formations in García Caves.

García's ancient caverns were formed more than fifty million years ago. These caves cover an interesting, nearly one and a quarter mile route of haphazardly placed stalagmites and stalactites. There are sixteen rooms, among them El Mirador de la Mano, La Octava Maravilla, El Salón del Aire, and El Sal de la Luz. Some of the caverns are nearly 1,000 feet long and 344 feet high. The temperature inside is 64 degrees F, which remains constant year-round.

The famous caverns of García are located on Fraile Mountain at a height of thirty-six hundred feet. They are only five miles from the town of Villa de García and twenty-four miles from Monterrey. The only way to get to the entrance of the caverns is by funicular. Inside the caverns are marine fossils, which may indicate that this desert region surrounded by imposing mountains was submerged in water thousands of years ago. Nearby there are also pieces of shells and snails. The caverns were discovered in 1843 and have become the principal natural attraction of the region.

GUADALUPE
HOME OF COLONIAL-ERA MASTERPIECES

SITUATED WHERE THE NORTHERN PART OF THE COUNTRY BEGINS, Zacatecas is one of the most beautiful cities in Mexico. It became an important mining town with a rich supply of silver. Near this colonial town is the Guadalupe monastery, founded by the Franciscans and today converted into an excellent museum of colonial art. This Museum has 27 permanent exhibition galleries that are divided into two areas. The first is the history of the convent from its beginnings until a recent visit by the Holy Father. The other part is a museum whose great stairway is dedicated to Saint Michael the Archangel and whose galleries are devoted to a particular theme such as the Baroque or the masters of colonial painting.

Guadalupe was founded because the Franciscans wanted to establish a series of apostolic colleges across the Spanish empire's immense territory. The goal was to build colleges to spread the faith. These colleges were grand institutions.

By the end of the eighteenth century there were between four hundred people in residence here, including priests, friars, novices, and students. This was partly because the missionary territory they had to cover was enormous—not only northern Mexico but across the Río Grande into Texas. In this vast area were many native tribes that were both primitive and savage—none were on an equal footing with the indigenous civilizations of central Mexico with their grand ceremonial centers and advanced culture. Certainly, the Franciscans had one of the more difficult tasks in the evangelization of Mexico.

The great hero in this effort was the founder of Guadalupe, Friar Antonio de Margil de Jesús. Friar Antonio was born in Valencia, Spain, in 1657; he died in Mexico City in 1726. When he was twenty-six years old he was sent to establish a college in Querétaro. Once it was established, he was sent on a journey to investigate possible locations for other colleges, first in the south of Mexico and then in Central America. Subsequently, he received the order to found a college in Guadalupe, in northern Mexico.

But Friar Antonio was not allowed to rest there; he was sent back to Zacatecas in the mountains of northwestern Mexico, and then on to Texas. He always traveled on foot, carrying with him the minimum supplies necessary; the total number of miles traveled measures in the thousands between places as far away as Florida all the way to Panama, none of which kept him from writing religious works and corresponding regularly. He died at the great friary the Franciscans built in Mexico City. Friar Antonio was one of the great missionaries at a time when the Franciscans were given the task of evangelizing the savage north of Mexico, a territory that appeared to stretch into infinity.

Annunciation of the Virgin Mary by Cristobal de Villalpando.

facing page
Guadalupe's splendid monastery.

Guadalupe's collection of colonial paintings is perhaps the best in Mexico. Among the church's greatest treasures is a series of fourteen oils of the Virgin Mary by Miguel Cabrera, an eighteenth-century painter. In the philosophy gallery there are four paintings by Cristobal de Villalpando, another great colonial painter who created vast compositions in a baroque style. The "gallery of the ladies" has portraits of elegant women dressed up to symbolize the saints.

The church of Guadalupe is one of the finest examples of baroque architecture in northern Mexico. Its facade is figured in quarried red stone carved with an image of the patroness of the church, the Virgin of Guadalupe. It is a massive, solid facade as is its single bell tower with circular columns. At the end of the nineteenth century, the friars added a clock tower. Entered through a carved door, the cloister of San Francisco surrounds the principal patio, which contains genuine artistic treasures such as the life of San Francisco in twenty-four panels and the marvelous "royal staircase," which has a wonderful San Cristobal on its landing. Also well worth visiting are the nursing cloister with its beautiful chapel, the cloister of the Passion, that of the bishops, and the "Naples chapel."

J E R É Z

BIRTHPLACE OF A POET

MEXICO'S MOST IMPORTANT POET, RAMÓN LÓPEZ VELARDE, WAS BORN IN JERÉZ, a town in the northwestern Mexican state of Zacatecas. In his great poem *La Suave Patria,* he was able to paint a portrait of the entire country in a seamless mural of words. Perhaps he was able to write this poem precisely because Velarde was a native of Jerez. Though it is not a prosperous mining town, it is filled with beautiful buildings and it is closely tied to the land and landscape. It is a quiet, harmonious place, like a poem.

The region around Jerez is very dry and ranching is the most important activity in a region where the work of local artisans has a finer, lighter character than the local culture of ranching would indicate. These works include leather works or wide sombreros with their decorative embroidery which are rarely seen except on feast days. This is in contrast to the real clothing such as sarapes that are used as protection from the cold. Jerez is a typical western town and in its Mexican style is austere, but not without elegance.

Jerez is also a part of the vast western geographical region extending southward from Canada, where primitive bands of indigenous peoples flourished but where signs of civilization only gradually appeared. The natives of this region were called Zacatecas. Though they did not compare with the great Mayan and Toltec civilizations, they knew about astronomy and the movement of time. They also developed a vast knowledge of herbal medicine that still survives in Mexico.

They were governed by the wisdom and knowledge of ancient wise men and an example of a classic primitive tribe of ancient North America that lived in an vast and difficult place. Their religion was very simple with only three gods. A child god was the lord of the rains. Another, the god of science, was consulted for various problems. The third, the god of battles, is always depicted carrying a bow and arrow.

The sun also served as a form of god created during the first morning even before the creation of time, triumphantly appearing amid the darkness and chaos of a world inundated with water. This sun god came down to earth, and he constructed a ladder on a mountain, as well as four cosmic posts that helped support the sky. He then traveled in the four cardinal directions, tracing a parallelogram cross, called a *tskuri*, that gave form to the world. At this moment the cycle of time was created and life was organized into contrasts: light/darkness, day/night, desert/sea, dry/rain, heaven/the underworld. Near Jeréz, the Zacatecas constructed a parallelogram-type cross to commemorate this world organization. Only the southern section of the cross, some primitive pyramids, and the remains of a palace still exist.

Night view of the Humboldt archway.

facing page
A magnificent example of the eclectic architecture of the town:
the *Ex-escuela de la Torre* and the *Santuario de Nuestra Señora de la Soledad.*

Though a simple place, Jeréz had cultural ambitions; a theater was built, a sign of interest in a world outside its own. Daily life in Jeréz was bound to celebrations of the church year, and the political struggles and threats of revolution at the beginning of the nineteenth century made its citizens nervous. But Jeréz did not lose its sense of harmony, qualities that were described so beautifully by its favorite son, Velarde.

56

Founded in 1570, Jeréz was built as a defensive military fort and because of its location was called Jeréz de la Frontera (Jeréz of the Frontier). Its primary purpose was to protect the silver shipments being transported south from the nearby city of Zacatecas; the area was rife with rebellious natives. Colonial architecture mixes with the romantic eclecticism of the nineteenth century in Jerez. The best example of this is the Santuario de la Soledad, whose virgin is the patroness of the town. In Mexico it is traditional to refer to the Virgin Mary as *La Generala,* or "the General." Curiously, in Jerez she is called *La Tres Veces Generala,* or the "three-times general."

SOMBRERETE
MINES OF THE EMPIRE

SOMBRERETE IS A MINING TOWN LOCATED IN THE WESTERN MOUNTAINS OF MEXICO. Its atraction after the conquest was based on its rich mineral deposits. A pioneer named Juan de Tolosa arrived in 1555, bringing with him a group of Spaniards, a few Franciscan friars, and some indigenous allies. They stopped on an uneven strip of land with a spring nearby and named it Sombrerete. The name derived from the Spanish word for hat—*sombrero*.

San Francisco Church and Convent.

facing page
Sombrerete's impressive bell tower and dome-topped buildings.

It got this name because the shape of a nearby mountain reminded them of the three-cornered hat popular at the time.

Supplies of gold, silver, iron, and mercury were discovered, and the town soon prospered. Its importance increased in the eighteenth century when it was named a "royal depository," making it a center for buying and selling precious metals. It also served as a tax-collection center for the faraway king of Spain.

Some of its mineral veins were among the richest in Mexico—competing with those of Taxco, Guanajuato, and Zacatecas. A local aristocracy was born, some members of which the king was inclined to grant titles of nobility. At the same time, this generosity created a fugitive class of millionaires who fled to Spain with fortunes and titles, but famous Spanish galleons continued to deliver the fabulous riches of Mexico and Peru to Spain.

Two families of Sombrerete managed to gain titles of nobility, one nothing less than that of Marquis, and the other -the Campa y Cos family- the title Conde de San Mateo de Valparaiso. Of course, a part of these fortunes was invested in building palatial homes locally and in Mexico City. Today, the building in the capital that houses the headquarters of the central Bank of Mexico was once the town home of the aforementioned Conde de San Mateo de Valparaiso, a building constructed with all the splendor of the late Baroque. By the beginning of the nineteenth-century, Sombrerete had thirty-four mine related haciendas.

During colonial times, the silver Mexican peso was recognized as a strong currency as far away as China, a country with which Mexico had a very active commercial relationship. The presence of mining riches attracted farmers and cattlemen who in turn built their own haciendas; these existed until the revolution.

Franciscans have been in Sombrerete since its founding, so it is not surprising that they built one of their most important churches in the town. Named in honor of Saint Matthew the Evangelist, the monastery itself is enormous, with two full floors and many outbuildings. Though construction began in the sixteenth century it was not completed for two centuries. Consequently, while late baroque in style, it incorporates many colonial features. There is also a Third Order chapel that reflects the influence of the Italian Renaissance, known in Spain as the plateresque, or plated, style; the facade reflects all of the luxury of the late baroque.

In the mid-twentieth century these lands were returned to local farmers. This policy did not affect agrarian production and today Sombrerete is one of Mexico's most important agricultural regions.

A monument commemorates the mine owners of Sombrerete, those that not only produced fabulous riches but became important people. An example was Don Fernando de la Campa y Cos, the Conde de Valparaiso, who, apart from building his own palaces, generously donated the money to build the most opulent church in Sombrerete. Though it was built in the eighteenth century, it was designed in a late Mexican-baroque style adorned with a wealth of swirling columns and sculptures. A few miles from town is one of Mexico's most spectacular geological formations, the Sierra de los Organos ("ridge of organ pipes"). Here seven gigantic columns appear together like the pipes of an organ.

REAL DE CATORCE
THE PAST MADE PRESENT

DURING THE LENGTHY COLONIAL ERA, HUNDREDS OF MINING TOWNS WERE FOUNDED. Few reached the economic heights of Real de Catorce. It was one of the three most important mining towns in New Spain, along with Zacatecas and Guanajuato. At its zenith, Real de Catorce had a population of more than forty thousand, which consolidated its position as the economic center of northern San Luis Potosí State.

A view of the old mining town, Real de Catorce.

facing page
The entrance gates of Guadalupe Cemetery.

Real de Catorce is surrounded by the eastern Sierra Madre mountain range, a desertlike region that once was famous as a hideout for bandits. Historians speculate that this was a reason the town received far less in investment compared to the worth of the minerals taken away. The bandits continually seized shipments of minerals and merchandise and in one attack killed fourteen Spanish soldiers (thus the fourteen in its name). By the twentieth century the region became inhospitable because of the social chaos caused by Mexico's revolution, the decreasing international price of silver, and the exhaustion of the principal mineral veins. These combined factors turned Real de Catorce into a virtual ghost town.

But prior to the arrival of the Spanish, the region had been used by the Huicholes as a ceremonial site. These indigenous people remain one of the purest ethnic tribes in Mexico, with much of their heritage remaining intact. Every year the Huicholes begin a three-hundred-mile-long pilgrimage over the mountains of Jalisco and Nayarit to Wirikuta. This is their name for the sacred zone formed by the Quemado Ridge located near Real de Catorce. Here, at what they consider to be the center of the world, they bring offerings and celebrate the mystic ritual of the hunt for the "Blue Deer."

For this celebration the pilgrims purify themselves by fasting, confessing their sins, and abstaining from sex. The ritual occurs under the direction of a spiritual guide who, according to Huichol beliefs, has the ability to establish contact with the sacred Blue Deer. This figure is central to their complex religious beliefs and is made to appear in the real world through their use of peyote, a high-grade hallucinogenic substance that comes from cacti. The spiritual guide administers the peyote to the purified pilgrims who then have access to this mystical experience. These peyote-induced visions enable the Huichol leaders to determine the ideal circumstances for hunting and planting. They also are able to recommend remedies for illnesses.

Real de Catorce's unique ambience has seduced writers, painters, and international movie directors, as well as hippies, pilgrims, and extreme-sport enthusiasts. For decades, its mysterious corners have enchanted visitors, as has the beauty of its landscape and its picturesque ancient streets and buildings. Huicholes sell their lovely crafts in the park. They make exquisite textiles and art created with embedded colored glass beads designed in complex geometric shapes and floral patterns. The region's simple gastronomy includes the traditional *cabuches* and delicious *gorditas* made with onion and cheese, with palm flowers, nopales, and *chile cascabel* and *huevo rojo*.

When one enters into Real de Catorce, a town whose past is still present, a beautiful light will persist during the walk among the town's beautiful buildings. The combination of the town's melancholy, nostalgic architecture and feel and its natural surroundings makes it unique.

Getting to Real de Catorce requires driving up steep, craggy, dusty roads through a landscape featuring an immense variety of exotic desert plants including nopales crowned by colorful prickly pears, flowering maguey cactus plants, and the biznaga cactus with its white flowers. An imposing ridge interrupts the road at the peak of the mountain. To get to Real de Catorce from there, drivers must go through the narrow, minelike one-and-a-half-mile-long Ogarrio Tunnel under the ridge. At the end of the tunnel the brilliant light adorning Real de Catorce says this singular prelude has come to an end. But when one reaches the outskirts of town and the Panteón de Guadalupe, the saffron-colored rays of the sun will finally disappear over the horizon.

Real de Catorce's charm lies in the extraordinary atmosphere that evokes the past and the town's colonial heyday. Its melancholy stone-paved streets invite visitors to explore this memorial to mining, where vestiges of the once-sumptuous lives of the inhabitants still exist. Defying the passage of time, ancient buildings such as the bull ring, the *palenque,* and the money-exchange house still stand. At the center of town is the Immaculate Conception Church, which has a beautiful interior and a crowded side altar honoring Saint Francis of Assisi. Bordering the church is the parish museum exhibiting a collection of documents and antique objects. Real de Catorce's natural scenery complements the ambience of the town. To the east it is guarded by copper-colored rocky ridges; to the west the town overlooks an immense desert valley that functions as a sort of "backyard" garden.

above
Two all-terrain taxis on a street
in Real de Catorce.

left
A panorama of Real de Catorce
as night approaches.

below
A typical street representative of
the rustic ambience of the town.

COSALÁ
THE TREASURE OF THE SIERRA MADRE

SINALOA STATE HAS A THREE-TIERED ECONOMY AND GEOGRAPHY: the thistle-abundant coast, a fertile tomato-growing plain, and the mineral-rich mountains. Apart from its riches, little is known about the beautiful mountains of the Sierra Madre Occidental. During the conquest, generous deposits of silver were discovered; as a result, several marvelous mining towns were founded. This rich region was immortalized in the film the *Treasure of the Sierra Madre* directed by John Huston, which had a notable performance by Humphrey Bogart.

Surrounded on one side by tropical mountains, Cosalá is like a secret destination hidden within the state of Sinaloa. It has maintained its ancient way of life; few modern influences have permeated. At its apogee as a mining town, Cosalá was home to more than fifty mines and eight mineral-treatment plants. By 1810 and the beginning of the independence movement, it was the most prosperous mining town in western Mexico. It attracted the newly insurgent army looking for financing, even though it failed in its efforts because of the effectiveness of the royal army, which tenaciously guarded its treasure. By the mid-twentieth century, however, the mineral veins had run out and a strike, combined with low productivity, led to mine closings. Today, the town still maintains its charm.

Looking down a quiet street in Cosala.

facing page
Cosala's main square and kiosk with the San Francisco Church beyond it.

Cosalá's peaceful atmosphere is reminiscent of two other small mining towns at the base of the imposing Espinazo del Diablo. This craggy region in the south of the Sierra Madre is known for its impressive gorges and spectacular vistas. First is Concordia, with its serene architecture of white houses with tile roofs. Equally notable is the visual feast of its Churrigueresque-style church with hierarchical sculptures of Saint Sebastian, Saint Barbara, and the Virgin of Guadalupe. The artisans of this town are known for their pottery and hand-carved woods. Heading along the highway a few miles toward Durango is rustic Copala, with its narrow and sinuous stone-paved streets bordered by red trees and tall palms.

Among the three towns of Cosalá, Concordia, and Copala, Cosalá has the best-preserved colonial identity, perhaps because of its relative distance from the major cities of Sinaloa. Visitors can enjoy an express trip back in time to the colonial era and the town design reflects this. King Phillip II decreed that the alignment for urban development of new settlements was to be based on the central plaza, which would be the focal point for the entire town. The parish church, convents, and later the Municipal Palace as well as the houses of the more powerful families were situated according to this.

Cosalá's uniform architecture distinguishes the town. Houses have reed grass and tile roofs mounted by cornices. Their adobe walls are painted in multicolored tones. The hilly stone-paved streets twist and turn randomly. During the year, Cosalá celebrates many fiestas—most importantly that of the Virgin of Guadalupe. Thousands of candles are lit and placed on benches, porticoes, and windows to illuminate the arrival of the Virgin Mary. The pilgrimage ends with a fireworks display. Cosalá's artisans are well known for their beautifully crafted saddles and other horse-related equipment.

In the center of the Plaza de Armas is a kiosk of forged copper and wood surrounded by beautiful gardens. At the center of this esplanade are San Francisco Church and its friary, which for a time during the revolution was home to Pancho Villa's soldiers.

The present Municipal Palace was once the sumptuous residence of Don Francisco Iriarte, the town's leading citizen who not only occupied the post of vice-governor, but was also the editor of the first newspaper of northwestern Mexico. The newspaper's offices were located in an adjoining office, La Chinche, which today is the Casa de Cultura. Nearby is a small lane, Pérez Meza, which is a charming colonial aside. After San Francisco, the other important church in this town is the parish of Saint Ursula, built by the Jesuits; its monastery was located near the Leyva Plaza and faces the antique sundial.

MEXCALTITÁN
A MYTHIC PLACE

ONE OF THE MOST ENDURING MYSTERIES OF ANCIENT MEXICO IS THE ORIGIN OF THE AZTECS. This civilization, also known as the Mexica, became the great phenomenon of the pre-Hispanic world: a nomadic and savage tribe that arrived late in history and in just a few years took possession of central Mexico. Later, the Aztec empire spread to Central America. It was at this time that they built a capital, México-Tenochtitlan. This extraordinary city, built in the middle of a lake, became the richest and most powerful place in Mexico.

The Aztecs did not exist for long, though. They arrived in A.D. 1345 in a valley with a lake that had been populated since earliest times. But their city and its empire were conquered by the Spanish and the city itself destroyed in 1521. If we compare this fleeting presence to other civilizations like that of Teotihuacán, Oaxaca, or the Mayans, which lasted thousands of years, the Aztecs were like a comet barely lasting two centuries. A brutal yet civilized culture capable of creating powerful art and a beautiful literature, the Aztecs were hated and feared by their neighbors who, when the opportunity arose, eagerly allied with the Spanish to defeat and obliterate them.

The origin of the Aztecs has been a controversial academic question since the colonial era began. But some men of action among the original conquistadores undertook the great adventure of seeking this origin in a mythic place called Aztlán. They organized large expeditions led by the terrible Nuño de Guzmán, the conqueror of western Mexico. He supposedly arrived at Aztlán but passed through because he did not find the fabulous riches he thought existed at the birthplace of the Aztecs. Other conquistadores such as Vázquez Coronado organized expeditions to look for the "Seven Caves" or the "Seven Cities of Gold." Finding these places, along with El Dorado and the Fountain of Youth in the Amazon, became obsessions for some men who were motivated by ambition and greed.

Historians place Aztlán in various parts of Mexico such as Lake Chapala or in the Californias. Erudite scholars such as Humboldt placed Aztlán in Oregon, while the prolific historian Padre Tello placed it in Asia. Seler considered it to be simply a mythic place and referred to it as being like the Land of the Dead or Mictlán, somewhere that is always in the north. For specific reasons, including the fact that it is a round island resembling a full moon and similar to the Aztec capital itself, serious historians such as Jiménez Moreno believe that Aztlán is in fact Mexcaltitán in Nayarit State.

An arcaded building on the plaza.

facing page
A view of the island from the air.

Mexcaltitán is a unique town, named a "pueblo mágico" by the Mexican government. One of the few car-free places in existence, both people and goods are transported in canoes. Agriculture is impossible, since the surrounding soil has a high saline content; as a result, fish are a primary source of food. The island's cuisine is greatly appreciated in western Mexico. Fish preparations have a certain pre-Hispanic influence. Both the parish church and the island's principal fiesta are dedicated to saints Peter and Paul. There is an annual canoe competition between two teams of fishermen, each representing one of the apostles.

Mexcaltitán, a word that means "in the house of the moon," is reminiscent of the Aztec capital constructed in the "navel of the moon." Mexcaltitán is in the middle of a lagoon of the same name on the northern coast of Nayarit State. It is circular and has a diameter of a third of a mile. Lifestyles of the locals on the island have an astonishing similarity to ancient life in México-Tenochtitlan, the Aztec capital. In the rainy season, two grand waterways cross in the center of the city while another waterway circles the island; it is called the "Venetian Circle." Just like México-Tenochtitlan, during the rainy season the streets become canals and the people are deluged except for houses built high enough to avoid flooding; people travel via canoes. The area has numerous herons; in fact, the traditional name of the cradle of the Aztecs was Aztlán, the "place of the herons."

Central Mexico's mighty volcano, Popocatéptl.

CHAPALA
A PEACEFUL ESCAPE

MEASURING FIFTY-THREE MILES FROM EAST TO WEST AND OVER FIFTEEN MILES AT ITS WIDEST POINT, Lake Chapala is Mexico's largest lake. The name Chapala is of Indian origin and means "the great lake." Because the town of Chapala, the most well-known place on the lake, is at an altitude of five thousand feet above sea level, it has a temperate climate that is generally very consistent. Locals claim it has the best weather in the world. While this can be debated, it is cool in the summer and only slightly cooler in the winter. It has become a favorite summer destination for the residents of Guadalajara.

For most of its history, Chapala was a quiet lakeside village where farmers and fishermen led a peaceful existence. But an unusual event changed everything. From the end of 1876 until 1910, with only a short four-year break, Mexico was governed by the dictator General Porfirio Díaz; he has the distinction of being the longest-serving dictator in Latin American history. A powerful man who was able to bring peace, he also brought economic development to Mexico but at a high social cost—one that would lead both to the revolution of 1910 and his eventual exile in Paris.

In 1904, at the height of his power, Díaz decided to accept the invitation of a political crony to visit his summer house in the village of Chapala; he continued these visits over the next five years. Díaz's presence was the "miracle" that led the affluent citizens of nearby Guadalajara to discover that Chapala was a perfect place for summer retreats. Despite being difficult to reach—nearly thirty miles on horseback—they began building summer homes there; designs were akin to houses in the Italian lake district or Victorian homes.

Notable figures such as the Englishman Septimus Crow and the German Karl Eismann moved into splendid villas featuring shady gardens with immense trees, a period known as Chapala's belle époque. Even though the Mexican Revolution would prevent Porfirio Díaz from returning to Chapala, the twentieth century began relatively calmly. The lake continued to draw notables such as the British writer D. H. Lawrence, who was inspired by his visit to write *The Plumed Serpent*.

Chapala owes much of its charm to people such as Christian Schjetman. He thought that the town would benefit from a boating culture aside from that of the fishermen. In 1910 he opened an elegant yacht club, while at the same time starting a navigation company with two small steam ships, the *Vikingo* and the *Tapatia*. But to succeed, there needed to be a railway from Guadalajara as well as a station, the design of which was commissioned from the architect Guillermo de Alba. Unfortunately, an unexpected rise in the lake's waters ruined his boats, the railway, and the railway station, which was abandoned as some sort of romantic folly. It was recently restored and today is a cultural center.

Prolonged droughts wreaked havoc on the area and it fell into decline. Eventually, a change in the water-management system restored the lake to its original splendor. Today, taking the trip from Guadalajara to Chapala on a modern highway enables visitors to enjoy lovely lake vistas and a reinvigorating setting.

Chapala's old railway station.

facing page
Ajijic sprawls out along the riverbank.

One of the lakeside towns is Ajijic, and like Chapala it was "discovered." But in this town, the discoverers were Americans who began arriving after World War II and into the fifties and sixties. Hippies were especially attracted to its beauty and inexpensiveness. Among its many notable visitors was playwright Tennessee Williams, who mentions his stay at Ajijic in his journals. In recent decades Ajijic has become a haven for other transplanted people—this time senior citizens from the United States and Canada. Thanks to their ample financial resources, they have discovered the marvelous climate and the splendid gardens. Every type of semitropical flower grows in abundance there, and the bougainvillea vines growing on the walls create a colorful display. Ajijic continues to attract artists and tourists who prefer a slower-paced life.

LAGOS DE MORENO
A PLACE FAR FROM THE VICEROY

IN CONTRAST TO THE GREAT PRE-HISPANIC CULTURES of central and southern Mexico and the Gulf of Mexico, the lands of the west and north were populated by more primitive tribes who fiercely resisted the Spanish. These tribes were called Chichimecas; the Spanish would fight them for centuries without totally subduing them. Many of these tribes sought refuge in less accessible regions.

Once the Spanish conquered a territory, they immediately began settling it both with fellow Europeans as well as indigenous people from other parts of the country with whom they had alliances. Lagos de Morenos was one of those places. Its original name was Santa María de los Lagos, but Moreno was added later in honor of a hero of the independence movement. It was founded in 1563 when the "very magnificent gentleman" Hernando Martel chose a site amid vacant fields on which to build a church and plaza. The king of Spain would have a home here on the off-chance that he would come to this lonely place. Thus began the history of Lagos, which was filled with the stories of Spaniards who came to these parts while still being threatened with attack by the native population.

Prosperity came to this region, mostly because it became a crossroads connecting the central part of the country with lands to the west. It also served as an important transit hub for silver being transported from the rich mines of Zacatecas to the capital. Large cattle ranches and dairy farms also flourished, and Lagos became an important milk supplier. It still is to this day.

In 1600 there were twenty thousand cattle in the area, a success that was built on thanks to the prosperity of the nearby mining towns. Lagos transformed from a virtually unknown, nonexistent place to an agreeable colonial outpost. This was especially true in the eighteenth century, when its principal buildings were constructed. Among these were the magnificent parish church, today the heart of Lagos, along with monasteries and the grand houses of its wealthier citizens.

Peace didn't exist in Santa Maria de los Lagos for long, though. At the time of the War of Independence, when the Spanish threatened to burn the town to the ground, the population here entered the fray of Mexico's tumultuous history, which included civil wars between liberals and conservatives, foreign invasions, frivolous and authoritarian dictators, and, finally, one of the great revolutions of the twentieth century that, from 1910, rocked Mexico. Lagos has survived into the twenty-first century and today is a civilized and pleasant place.

Two men sit on a bench and talk on the Plaza de Armas.

facing page
The bridge at the entrance to Lagos de Moreno.

The parish church's imposing stature dominates the community, but there are many other interesting religious buildings. Among them is the church of the "Light"; surprisingly, its cupola was inspired by Sacre Coeur in Montmartre, Paris. However, the majority of the churches took inspiration from less exotic locales, combining the colonial with the Romantic of the nineteenth century. The most attractive is the Capuchin convent with a facade that has original seemingly Arab-inspired drawings. Lagos also has an enchanting theater dating from the end of the nineteenth century, named after children's writer Rosas Moreno.

One of Lagos's mayors provided the country with an amusing anecdote, at the town's expense, as well as a bridge over a river. It was on this bridge, built in 1860, that the mayor inscribed the following words: "This bridge begins in Lagos and goes higher." The parish church was completed in 1796, but it was not until the nineteenth century that Lagos completed its colonial-era building, one that includes the impressive cathedral-size parish church with its two tall bell towers that stands in front of a large park. According to the historian Miguel Toussaint, it was the "final great building" of the vice-regal period. Lagos's parish church was built in the late-baroque style. The church has a moderate, formal richness even though the interior had the more traditional rich retablos, which were destroyed in the nineteenth century.

El Calvario Church sits atop a hill and has a large esplanade with a panoramic view. Constructed next door was a church that had a facade meant to look like St. Peter's in Rome. It has an octagonal cupola and its interior has an interesting work in carved wood. The patron of Lagos, Nuestro Padre Jesus del Calvario, is venerated here. Lagos has many interesting homes including that of a rich miner from Guanajuato, the Conde de Rul. Another is that of the Marquis of Guadalupe, famous in Mexico for his interest in *charreria*. In this sport contestants ride on horseback and work cattle, a sort of rodeo but within the Spanish aristocratic tradition. Lagos is also the birthplace of Mariano Azuela, one of Mexico's greatest writers and the author of *The Underdogs*, the classic novel of the Mexican Revolution.

above
An eagle ornaments the facade of Mexico's municipal president's palace.

left
El Calvario Church and its impressive steps at night.

below
One of Lagos de Moreno's typical streets, which leads toward the main parish church.

MAZAMITLA
AN ARCHITECT'S INSPIRATION

MAZAMITLA IS A MOUNTAIN TOWN IN JALISCO STATE that recently was declared a *pueblo mágico* by the federal government. It is located near Lake Chapala and is surrounded by beautiful forests. Its cool, dry climate is constant year-round. Many people in the nearby city of Guadalajara have built weekend houses there. It is a type of ecological tourism.

Many people don't think that Mazamitla has existed for a long time, but there is evidence that tribes arrived there in 1165. They spoke Náhuatl, the great language of central Mexico spoken by the Aztecs and the one in which the majority of pre-Hispanic literature was written. But Mazamitla did not become part of the empires of central Mexico. Instead, it became part of the empire of another warring tribe, the Tarascos of nearby Michoacán State. The architectural style of Mazamitla today is the same as that found in Michoacán's small mountain towns.

Hernán Cortés arrived in Mexico in 1521 and with the fall of the Aztecs' capital Mexico-Tenochtitlán, the civilization was defeated and destroyed. Suddenly an adventurer who was a dropout from law school and a not-so-successful rancher in Cuba became the owner of a large part of Mexico, including Mazamitla. This particular territory was conquered by Cristóbal de Olid, one of Cortés's captains, who wanted to get to the Pacific and, if possible, the Far East.

Cortés lost possession of Mazamitla, and the king and the viceroy decided that the local inhabitants would own the land and water. Mazamitla's tranquil colonial life began—a peace that would continue after independence. It was a simple, sleepy Mexican town. Its only famous moment over the centuries was when Father Hidalgo, the revolutionary leader of the independence movement, passed through Mazamitla with his army. They stopped to celebrate Mass on an improvised altar—the trunk of an oak tree—that is today considered an important historical relic.

Mazamitla has lovely stone streets and houses with thick adobe walls and roofs of wood and red tile. The large roofs serve as protection against the frequent rains. The heart of these homes is the central patio; the heart of town is the central plaza with its white church. As is appropriate for a mountain town, many of Mazamitla's other buildings have columns with capitals and wood roofs; larger homes have balconies. The climate is cool by Mexican standards, which makes it an inviting place to relax while enjoying a hot drink, eating regional cakes and sweets, and wearing locally crafted wool clothing.

A view of the distinctive-looking San Cristobal Church.

facing page
Looking down at the valley where Mazamitla nestles into the surrounding landscape.

Nearby is a somewhat celebrated town, San José de Gracia, with a similar look and architecture to Mazamitla, including houses with large patios. It was founded one hundred years ago for the very large Gonzáles family. One family member, Luis González, revolutionized Mexican history with a book based on his doctoral thesis *Pueblo en Vilo*. An important, widely translated work that eventually found its way onto library bookshelves, it was the first work of "micro history," investigating what actually happened in a town, in a neighborhood, and in a family. González wrote it on benches around San José de Gracia.

Until recently, the only people who visited Mazamitla, and braved the long trip on terrible roads, were those who had homes there. The Barragán family lived in Guadalajara in the early twentieth century and sent their children to Mazamitla for summer vacations. One of their children, Luis, later studied civil engineering and began building homes in Guadalajara and Mexico City. But Luis had a genius that led him to create a unique architectural style that combined traditional Mexican influences with contemporary touches. His style included closed walls, intimate patios, and a great simplicity; it was luxurious in addition to revealing a love for gardens and water. Luis Barragán went on to win architecture's prestigious Pritzker Prize, the profession's version of a Nobel Prize. Barragán always felt that he owed a debt of inspiration to Mazamitla.

PUERTO VALLARTA
A COSMOPOLITAN PARADISE

SOME YEARS AGO A FRIEND CLAIMED TO HAVE ENCOUNTERED PARADISE. During his youth he had tried many vocations, including that of a sailor, and during one trip he had arrived at the perfect place. It was a small fishing town on the Pacific coast of Mexico that was paved with cobblestone streets; seemed to dangle from green, junglelike hills; had a wide, slow river running through it; featured small, intimate beaches; and was dotted with lovely red-tile roofed white houses. He decided to retire there as soon as possible. The place had a name: Las Piedras (The Stones). Of course, I looked this place up but had no luck. I suspected it was only an invention, a sailor's yarn. Many years afterward I discovered that, in fact, this was the original name of Puerto Vallarta, renamed to honor a nineteenth-century Mexican politician and diplomat, Ignacio Luis Vallarta.

This town has an unusual history. Until the 1960s, Puerto Vallarta was known only to locals and adventurous tourists. Then someone in Hollywood decided to film *The Night of the Iguana* there. It was based on a play by Tennessee Williams and starred Ava Gardner and Richard Burton (Elizabeth Taylor accompanied Burton, which became tabloid fodder). Forgettable as the movie was, it put Puerto Vallarta on the map. Yet another Hollywood icon, John Huston, also discovered this town and decided to retire there. Today a sculpture in a little square in town honors him.

A harbor in the bustling city.

facing page
Town buildings abut the water's edge.

Tourism soon increased exponentially; Las Piedras was no longer the remote spot remembered by my friend. "Vallarta" became as famous among international travelers as Acapulco or Cancún. Its transformation spurred development all along Mexico's Pacific coast. With all of the expansion, however, Puerto Vallarta manages to retain the ambience of a small village. Its geography—steep hills, the wide Cuale River that runs through town, and the ocean itself—has imposed natural limits and helped to contain its growth. The city's scale remains comfortably human and manageable.

Puerto Vallarta's streets radiate outward from the Malecón (the boardwalk) and rise high into the hills. Walking around the town itself becomes a minor sport, one with unexpected rewards: art galleries, stores with colorful fashions, and some of the most refined restaurants in the country, such as the Café des Artistes. But for all its sophistication, Puerto Vallarta is also a genuine Mexican town with its marketplace and its homes with their open, flower-filled patios. Nearby, the river and hills with houses ensure this transformed paradise will always remain tempting.

Heading north from Puerto Vallarta is a surprisingly developed tourist area that has in very little time grown rapidly. It includes hotels, apartment buildings, nine golf courses and houses that seem to be hanging from the hillsides. More adventurous travelers might prefer visiting the nearby islands where it is possible to live a little more primitively. The most spectacular growth has occurred, however, farther to the north in Punta Mita as well as at Marina Vallarta which is part of a system of marinas along the Pacific coast which support coastal navigation. With slips for 400 boats, the marina is distinguished both by its lighthouse which is its symbol as well as by having all the accoutrements of grand tourism but found in a small area.

Puerto Vallarta's center and symbol is a very traditional Mexican church made unique because it is literally crowned with a huge metallic *corona* (crown) that reminds locals of that of the famous beer. This fits with the festive and casual spirit of the town. As is typical, the parish church has its plaza and is very close to the Malecón, the boardwalk and the gathering place for both visitors and locals. On the outskirts of Puerto Vallarta are a few exclusive golf courses. It is possible to participate in other sports as well. There are excellent places for diving, strong winds ideal for kite- and windsurfing and sailing, in addition to challenging waves for surfers. During the winter, whales that have migrated south arrive to mate and can be seen on the horizon.

SAN SEBASTIÁN DEL OESTE
THE CONQUEROR AND THE TOWN

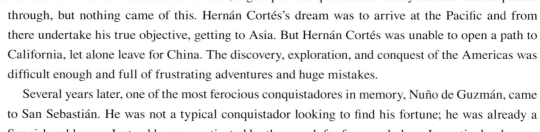

SAN SEBASTIÁN DEL OESTE IS LOCATED ON THE EDGE OF THE SIERRA MADRE, close to the Pacific Ocean. Because it is near the ocean this countryside of mountains and cloud-covered forests has a beautiful landscape both peaceful and suggestive, like a Chinese watercolor. In pre-Hispanic times the region was populated by minor tribes who left no traces of art or architecture. In 1524, a group of conquistadores led by Hernán Cortés passed through, but nothing came of this. Hernán Cortés's dream was to arrive at the Pacific and from there undertake his true objective, getting to Asia. But Hernán Cortés was unable to open a path to California, let alone leave for China. The discovery, exploration, and conquest of the Americas was difficult enough and full of frustrating adventures and huge mistakes.

Several years later, one of the most ferocious conquistadores in memory, Nuño de Guzmán, came to San Sebastián. He was not a typical conquistador looking to find his fortune; he was already a Spanish nobleman. Instead he was motivated by the search for fame and glory. In particular, he was obsessed with surpassing Cortés and founding his own kingdom that would be more powerful than New Spain. To achieve this he used every malicious cruelty he could, including burning hundreds of indigenous towns and persecuting the inhabitants while searching for mines that would finance his irrational project. After conquering western Mexico, he turned his attention to the north—an immense area that seemed to have no end. Finally, Don Nuño's excessive ruthlessness brought him down—even the Spanish were scandalized. He was sent back to Spain in chains.

But when Don Nuño came to San Sebastián in 1530, he was at the high point of his infamy and for that reason the natives did not resist, allowing him to explore the region in peace. But Nuño found nothing of interest. Disappointed, he continued with his voracious conquest. The irony is that

Peaceful San Sebastián del Oeste's picturesque red-tile roofs.

facing page
A cozy terrace in San Sebastián overlooking the mountains.

while Nuño was dying in Spain, enormous silver deposits were discovered in San Sebastián. These would have been more than sufficient to finance all of his dreams of building a royal Spanish kingdom that would surpass and humiliate Hernán Cortés's New Spain. San Sebastián in fact became "royal"—*Real* de San Sebastián. All of the great mining towns were given this royal name because, at least in theory, they belonged to the King of Spain. This discovery began a bonanza that transformed San Sebastián into one of the largest towns in the region.

San Sebastián del Oeste is an ideal place for hiking, especially early in the morning when you can admire the mountain plants and trees. It is also possible to enjoy the local tropical flora when traveling by car to Puerto Vallarta on the coast.

As happens in many places that once knew great prosperity and then later lost everything, San Sebastián was almost completely abandoned. Those who stayed decided to preserve the beauty and character of the town. Slowly but surely, San Sebastián's fame grew and more visitors arrived. They were enchanted with the tranquility, simplicity, and integrity of this ancient mining town. High-quality hotels that complemented the local feel of the town were constructed. For tourists from Puerto Vallarta, it is an opportunity to visit a nearby mountain enclave that contrasts nicely with the tropical heat of the port town. San Sebastián can become a special tourist destination without losing its charming colonial atmosphere.

During the colonial period, the silver mines were a huge boon for San Sebastián. The town was built according to the Spanish model: at its center a church was built in honor of Saint Sebastian, a martyr and important figure in Catholic art. The church did not survive and was rebuilt in the nineteenth century when the town and the mines were at their heights of productivity. But in 1888 a strike by the miners led to the closing of the principal mine; thus began San Sebastián's decline. In 1921 the last mine was closed and the town became a shadow of its former self, dwindling to a mere five hundred inhabitants. Until the end of the twentieth century, the town existed in almost total isolation because there were no decent roads. This isolation only came to an end when an eccentric veteran pilot of World War II flew his old "Flying Tiger" airplane into San Sebastián from Puerto Vallarta. This was the start of San Sebastián's rise as a tourist destination.

TAPALPA
WHITE WALLS AND RED TILES
HIDDEN IN THE MOUNTAINS

ABOUT ONE HUNDRED MILES FROM GUADALAJARA, Tapalpa ("land of colors") occupies a small valley surrounded by mountains in the western state of Jalisco. Surrounded by pine forests, the town manages to avoid the heat produced by nearby salt lakes and offers fresh, cool weather year-round. Up until a few years ago, Tapalpa was quite an adventurous place to even reach, accessible only by a narrow, winding road; its few visitors found themselves walking on cobblestoned, crooked streets leading to the large central square with Saint Anthony's Church at its center. Houses here typically were built with thick adobe walls and wooden beams, and were covered with red tiled roofs, the traditional mountain style of folkloric architecture. Nowadays, many people have built second homes here in the abundant wooded areas and enjoy walking through the surrounding mountains for relaxation. Tapalpa also offers charming small hotels and restaurants serving international cuisine, but this attractive tourist town hasn't lost its rural, solid simplicity.

Built on a hillside, Tapalpa rolls gently across the hills. In order to construct its focal point, Saint Anthony's Church, a large space had to be leveled. This created a plaza complete with an archway and stone fountains built with the region's brown stone. Erected by the Franciscan friars in 1650, this church has a large white dome and a commanding tower. Life around the church is vibrant and colorful, and there is a nearby crafts market every Sunday. Woolen and carved wooden crafts are sold alongside huaraches, Mexico's traditional leather sandals. Children's toys, furniture, and candies are also sold. The people of Tapalpa have a sweet tooth and enjoy fruit-punch wines, sherbet ice cream in a variety of flavors, and *rompope,* a sort of local eggnog flavored with vanilla.

The geography of the region around Tapalpa is very beautiful. Just beyond the town limits is the "Sierra del Tigre". Spread out before the town is a large dry lake that is in total contrast to the local landscape. Following the highways south from the town there is a point where beneath the midday heat there rises majestically in the distance twin volcanos known as that of "Ice" and of "Fire". The surrounding mountains of Tapalpa have become a playground for those who take part in sports such as rock climbing and mountaineering, as well as hang- and paragliding for which Tapalpa has attained international fame. The World Cup in this sport takes place here as well as in Italy.

Distinctive white and red houses line a street in Tapalpa.

facing page
Tapalpa viewed from the tower of its church.

In Las Piedrotas (Big Stones), hikers can find a sculptural and rather mysterious group of enormous rocks in the middle of a rolling landscape, or they can go to the Salto del Nogal, a waterfall more than three hundred feet high. Tapalpa's traditional cuisine is a blend of the indigenous and the colonial. Its main dish is *borrego al pastor,* a goat-calf barbecue often accompanied by enchiladas as well as the very typical *tamales de acelga* made with Swiss chard and traditional corn dough.

About one hundred miles from Guadalajara, Tapalpa occupies a small valley surrounded by the high Sierras. By Mexican standards its weather is cold; for international travelers it's perfect: temperatures average sixty-degrees Fahrenheit. Tapalpa's streets are cobblestone, bordered by narrow sidewalks that travelers can explore on foot. Although tourism has increased in recent years and one can find nice hotels and restaurants, the character of the town remains untouched and maintains its old ways and customs. Rancheros still ride their horses in the streets, and houses are built in traditional styles with lush plant-filled patios.

The landscape of the Tapalpa region is spectacular, and traveling south one reaches San Gabriel, hometown of Juan Rulfo, Mexico's most famous novelist who wrote tragic and magical stories of this mountain land. Another pleasant town in the vicinity—still untouched by tourism—is Atemajac de Brizuela. Tapalpa's simple pleasures help visitors escape everyday tensions and stress. Indifferent to the passage of time, one walks through the town's streets and discovers that the past is still very much alive. Some people go to the village fountains for water or go shopping with the neighbors, and it seems that everyone is selling something handmade. Others simply stroll through town for the sheer pleasure of sightseeing and letting time pass by.

above
A nighttime scene of Tapalpa's covered corridors.

right
A view overlooking Tapalpa's red-tile roofed buildings, as well as the surrounding hills.

right
The main square of town at night.

84

TEQUILA
ELIXIR OF THE GODS

TEQUILA IS THE ICONIC BEVERAGE OF MEXICO. Extracted from a blue-green cactus—the *Agave tequilana weber*—it is grown in the western region of the country. Either clear or amber-colored, tequila is used in many mixed drinks (the margarita being the most famous), but in the past it was drunk straight—in the afternoon, served in a *caballito* (a small four-inch-tall glass), and accompanied by just a few grains of salt on the back of the hand combined with a few drops of lemon juice. Tequila was also served as an aperitif.

Tequila is produced in the northern part of the state of Jalisco. The town was recently named a World Heritage site by UNESCO. Bluish-green hirsute plants cover the rolling hills around the village of Tequila and the slopes of a nearby volcano. Some of the oldest distilleries are actually found in the charming rural village itself. The history of tequila dates back to pre-Columbian times when this beverage was consumed by priests and the elderly. But after the conquest, the Spaniards developed a taste for tequila and the famous Spanish botanist Jeronimo Hernandez even described its medicinal effects. But tequila was not to remain a medicine only and a formal distillery was opened in 1758.

The first distillery owner was Jose Antonio Cuervo, proprietor of the large estate of Villoslada. In 1795 tequila received a decree of royal patronage. Next, its production benefited from distillery techniques brought by the Spaniards. Tequila helped the economy of the region in the last years of the colonial era and, thanks to its revenues, the beautiful palace of the provincial governor was built. When Mexico gained independence in 1821, it became the most popular drink in the country and thus new entrepreneurs started producing it. One was Cenobio Sauza who, in 1873, exported tequila for the first time to the United States: a total of three barrels and five bottles. Nowadays some 117 million liters are exported yearly worldwide.

There are three types of tequila: *blanco,* or silver, which is the youngest; *reposado,* aged, golden tequila; and *añejo,* extra aged, with its characteristic deep golden color. Though tequilalike products are made in many regions, only the one made in Jalisco is worthy of its now-famous name. Tequila is made using colonial-era techniques. The process begins with the removal of the agave cactus plant's pineapple-shaped "heart." The hearts are cooked in an oven for between twenty-four to thirty-six hours; they are then milled. These ground hearts are then put in a barrel and distilled until the tequila obtains its crystal clear purity. In order to produce reposado or añejo, tequila is aged in huge oak barrels.

The territory surrounding the village of Tequila certainly is beautiful and original. So much so that a famous local architect who was very devout was inspired to propose that the Almighty had felt uneasy after creation and thus on the seventh day, He interrupted His rest and entertained himself by designing and creating the *Agave tequilana weber,* the blue agave cactus plant whose heart becomes the basis of tequila. Though this is an apocryphal story, it shows the local people's appreciation for what has now become an international drink. Today this hard liquor enjoys commercial success, and it is represented by over 715 brands. It is packaged in many bottle shapes and sizes, some of them as capricious as bottles of French perfume.

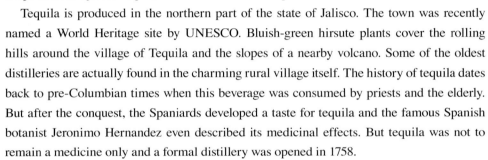

Archangel Gabriel protects Tequila.

facing page
Agave plantations around Tequila.

Tequila is still a rural village, though its main product has an international presence. It is not a place of great architectural value, but it certainly has character and atmosphere. It can be reached by road but also by railroad on a special "Tequila Train" (during the journey tequila is served). The village of Tequila is the capital of the tequila-producing region and has been designated a "denomination of origin"—like those granted to the places in France that produce cognac or champagne.

TLAQUEPAQUE
A POTTER'S VILLAGE

An exquisite colorful vessel by Jesus Guerrero-Santos, a noted contemporary ceramicist.

TODAY'S SAN PEDRO TLAQUEPAQUE HAS BEEN SUBSUMED INTO THE URBAN CONTINUUM OF GUADALAJARA, Mexico's second city. But at one time it was a quiet village, and though it was fairly near Guadalajara it was still considered far away. As a result, it was particularly attractive to Guadalajara's affluent residents, who felt it was much safer to be there in the event of an earthquake. It became fashionable for the rich to build second homes there; soon Tlaquepaque, an unassuming potters' village, became fashionable. Beautiful houses were built on the town's more attractive streets, such as the wide Calle Independencia; today, Independencia's surviving grand mansions house restaurants and chic art galleries. But Tlaquepaque has kept its small-town atmosphere.

Tlaquepaque was first founded by natives. In this community of indigenous peoples, pottery was an important craft—and still is to this day. All through colonial times and then after independence, the artisans of Tlaquepaque practiced their craft with gusto. After the conquest, both Spanish and native tastes and techniques were blended together. The characteristic red ceramics were decorated in a simple but joyful style. Colorful ceramics combining both naive and sophisticated touches are the result; they are definitely Mexican in feel. Tlaquepaque's ceramics range from very humble pottery to works of art. Some of its traditional craftsmen, such as Panduro, whose miniatures depicted Mexico's way of life in the early twentieth century, even rose to national fame. Later, artistic innovators brought new styles and techniques. Artists such as Jorge Wilmot produced a charming fusion of the native with an oriental delicacy and a modern simplicity.

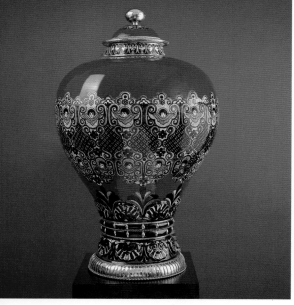

left
A view of El Refugio.

Tlaquepaque still has the feel of a small town. El Refugio (a former hospital), highlights a panorama of domes and traditional architecture. But this potters' village is also a playground for the region. Many people come to Tlaquepaque to eat, drink, and listen to music. The palenque is the town's arena for cockfighting but it also attracts famous musical artists from all over Mexico who come here to perform. The palenque is also famous for its galleros, the men who raise and train fighting cocks. Among Tlaquepaque's crafts, we also find the production of the typical Mexican equipales. These wide, comfortable chairs and sofas are an essential part of Mexican furniture and decoration. The equipal, in fact, was one of the few types of furniture used in pre-Columbian times.

Tlaquepaque is a veritable showplace of Mexican crafts of all kinds: in addition to pottery, textiles, metal, and woodwork are sold in the shops in the center of town. But ceramics reign supreme and the town's famous Museo de la Ceramica houses a beautiful collection of this work. Many visitors go to Tlaquepaque not in search of beautiful crafts, but to visit the enormous *parian* found in the center of town. This covered area is one of the largest cantinas in the world. Places to eat and drink monopolize a whole block, and the mariachi music never stops. The Parian's special dish is *birria*, a kind of local barbecue that is consumed with very cold beer.

Pottery is Tlaquepaque's real specialty though it has also become a showplace for many other Mexican crafts. The ceramics produced in Tlaquepaque range from very humble pottery in a more popular style to the work of craftsmen like Jesus Guerrero-Santos, who has created a fusion of the baroque, the popular, and the contemporary. Using new high-temperature techniques, his elegant vases combine baroque complexity with a popular simplicity. The use of metals gives his creations a luxurious feel. In Tlaquepaque, many of the old traditions are preserved, such as the taste for miniatures, some of which are quite risqué, or portraits of popular characters or of historical figures.

C O M A L A
A VITAL, SPIRITED TOWN

MEXICO'S MOST FAMOUS NOVEL, BY JUAN RULFO, tells the story of a young man who is looking for his father, "a certain Pedro Páramo," who had abandoned him and his mother and who could presumably be found in Comala. In the novel, Comala was a sinister and dark town full of ghosts and dusty winds, a sort of earthly purgatory most suitable for the perfect villain, a cynical politician and womanizer. In reality, though, Comala is one of the happiest towns in Mexico, a place full of life and vigor.

The portrait *La Niña en Primera Comunión* by Alejandro Rangel Hidalgo.

facing page
A quiet cobblestone street with Comala's impressive volcanic neighbor rising in the background.

It is a tropical place where gigantic trees grow. It has imposing neighbors, the Volcán and Nevado de Colima (Colima Volcano and Snow-covered Mountain)—and from Comala you can appreciate this spectacular geological presence amid the lush greenness of the tropical west coast of Mexico. But the town is not impressed at all by its towering neighbors and has become a good example of provincial Mexican insouciance and joie de vivre. Its center and core is, of course, the plaza with the typical kiosk and church. But here the *portales*, arcades that are found all over Mexico, have evolved into a long, huge cantina where people go to drink cold beer and listen to mariachi music. Favorite songs include the famous *sones* of western Mexico such as "La Negra" or "El Niño Perdido." Comala, the place of the dead in Rulfo's novel, is a colorful and noisy place of the living.

In the joyful Comala, the visitor is able to enjoy a very unusual type of pleasure, places that only serve appetizers. The appetizer, or "botana" is one of the most typical of Mexican culinary pleasures and is made up of small portions that can vary from pork pate to nuts. They can include a wide variety of ingredients that include reduced portions of shrimp or tamales or tacos, all specialities of Mexican cuisine but always served in miniature. These appetizers are always served with beer or drinks while listening to mariachi music.

Many artists have been attracted by the town's casual, upbeat atmosphere, including the mythical Alberto Isaac, an important movie director, a political cartoonist, a humorous painter, a ceramist, and a national swimming champion. Isaac lived amidst a large, unkempt, junglelike garden with a pool and a house built in a traditional style.

Comala's ambience is dedicated to the *dolce far niente*. Cobblestone streets are everywhere, and the pace of life is slow. Men in typical campesino attire ride horses in the streets while cars and pickups patiently wait for them. Comala's weather has much to do with this lifestyle; tropical but not too hot, the temperature encourages people to take it easy.

On the outskirts of Comala is Nogueras, a magnificent colonial hacienda that once produced lemon oil. At the time of the revolution, the plantation owners lost the land and the big house fell into ruins. One of the family heirs, Alejandro Rangel Hidalgo, was an impeccable draftsman and painter. With sponsoring by UNESCO, he created Christmas cards that became an international success. And against all business logic, Hidalgo left Mexico City where he had triumphed and returned to Nogueras to rescue his family home from decline. Today Nogueras has been nicely restored and houses a charming museum of pre-Columbian art.

Alejandro Rangel Hidalgo, an artist whose work was often supported by the New York Graphic Society, was that exception in modern artists: an utterly precise and punctilious draftsman and colorist. No wonder his influences were the Flemish masters and Greek icon makers. Hidalgo did careful research before drawing even one line. Quite surprisingly, Hidalgo's work became very popular. His techniques were also applied to the furniture he designed and built in Comala, products that were very successful—so much so that they were used to furnish Los Pinos, the Mexican presidential residence.

ANGANGUEO
KINGDOM OF THE BUTTERFLIES

THIS TYPICAL OLD MINING TOWN IS LOCATED IN CENTRAL MEXICO. Mine operations started in 1792 and continued well into the twentieth century; the mines once belonged to the Spaniards, British, French, and Americans. The gold, silver, and copper mined here brought the town significant commercial and cultural prosperity. In 1887 Angangueo even became one of the first towns in the region to have railway service. It is an orderly and cheerful place, where all the houses display pots of red flowers and where local festivals are enthusiastically celebrated (especially important is the Day of the Cross, on May 3, featuring an impressive fireworks display).

Monarch butterflies rest after their long journey south.

facing page
The old mining town awaits its "royal" visitors.

Yet Angangueo's popularity today does not stem from its wealth of metal or its peaceful atmosphere, but rather because it is the primary sanctuary for monarch butterflies. Each year the monarchs escape the cold climates of Canada and the northern United States, taking refuge in the forests around Angangueo. The migration of the monarch butterflies is a fascinating phenomenon, and it has inspired experts from the three countries to study and protect them. Various organizations work together to try to maintain the ecological balance of the region so it remains hospitable. With their distinctively patterned yellow and black wings, the monarchs are undoubtedly one of the most beautiful butterflies found in nature.

The scientific name of monarch butterflies is *Danaus plexippus;* the name originates from Greek mythology. Danaus and Aegyptus were the twin sons of King Belus. Danaus had fifty daughters, the Danaides; his brother Aegyptus had fifty sons. Aegyptus commanded that his sons marry the Danaides, who refused. Instead, their father led their escape to Greece. Aegyptus and his sons followed them there, and Danaus consented to the wedding. However, he gave each of his daughters a knife, so that, on their wedding night, they would kill their husbands. Only one, Lynceus, escaped death and, years later, he took his revenge by killing Danaus.

The term *danaus* means sleeper and *plexippus* means transformation. Carolus Linnaeus originally baptized this butterfly as *Papillo plexippus,* yet someone improved upon the name, including the legend of the Danaides in order to somehow explain the migratory nature of this butterfly. The name "monarch" was bestowed in honor of William III of the House of Orange and the king of England. In North America it is also known as the King Billy, wanderer, and milkweed butterfly. In Mexico it is known only as "monarch."

On average, adult butterflies live from four to five weeks. Nevertheless, to be able to undertake their long journey to Mexico, a true biological miracle takes place: a "Methuselah generation," with an average lifespan of seven to eight months, is born. This phenomenon would be akin to having a generation of humans that could live more than five hundred years. Without this long-lived generation, the extraordinary migration that allows the butterflies to hibernate and regenerate could not occur. The monarch butterfly also inhabits other places on earth, in Asia and South America, but, apparently, without undertaking migrations such as those in North America. It is believed that some monarch butterflies have flown across the Atlantic, arriving in Spain, Ireland, and the United Kingdom.

Each year in November, Angangueo welcomes the monarch butterflies and the thousands of tourists who flock to witness this extraordinary event. After the butterflies fly back to the north, Angangueo resumes being an old mining town. Americans Bill and Joyce Parker stayed on in Angangueo after visiting. Bill Parker was a photography enthusiast who spent years assembling a collection of images on life in this mining town; it is now housed in the Parker Museum.

CUITZEO
A LAKE AND A MONASTERY

LOCATED IN THE STATE OF MICHOACÁN, Cuitzeo was one of the largest lakes in Mexico though over time it has diminished in size. The first settlers there were Otomí Indians; they were followed by a tribe that spoke Náhuatl, the language of central Mexico. Later, when the Tarascos dominated Michoacán, they took possession of Cuitzeo and turned it into an important place where they widened the river by almost twenty-seven feet and constructed a ceremonial center with a temple that no longer exists.

Augustinians were sent to evangelize Cuitzeo during the colonial era. They also changed the plan of the town, basing it on a Roman model with straight streets; they left the ceremonial area in the center. Beginning in 1550, the Augustinians began building churches and monasteries across Michoacán dedicated to Saint Mary Magdalene, to whom the Augustinians were clearly devoted. Eventually they would construct five monasteries honoring her in the state. Why were they so devoted to Mary Magdalene? Possibly it's because both Magdalene and Augustine, the founder of the order, were sinners who eventually repented.

Large open spaces still characterize the church and monastery, though they were even bigger in the past. Over time the small chapels built at the corners of the church have disappeared as has the great cross in the church atrium. The church's facade is in the plateresque style, the first European style to arrive in Mexico. Though its overall plan is rather modest, the facade was imagined by an architect who wanted the design to appeal to the native Tarascans; for example, in place of the shield of the King of Spain, with its castles and lions, the sculptors of Cuitzeo placed the Augustinian shield with a heart pierced by three arrows, something that related to traditions of the ancient religions. The shield is mounted atop an eagle, but in this case it is less like an imperial Austrian eagle than one native to Mexico.

Other shields on the facade have images of pelicans or a large vessel, a reference to the word *cuitzeo*, which means "large earthenware jar." Other parts of the facade are decorated with Augustinian symbols accompanied by plants and flowers of the region, and decorative angels appear more native than European.

The town of Cuitzeo has very white architecture, which contrasts with the green of the lake's waters. Today the lake is traversed via a modern causeway, but during the nineteenth century a narrow roadway was built for the muleteers to deliver their merchandise on horseback. Numerous species of birds make their homes around the lake, and their movement creates a sense of tranquility. In comparison to other more boisterous towns, Cuitzeo has maintained a quiet, provincial calm.

A Judgment Day fresco in the church.

facing page
Entrance to the former convent of Santa Maria Magdalena.

On the side of the church is a door with six arches that serves as the entrance to a porter's lodge; one wall has a large fresco of the Last Judgment. At the center of the fresco is the figure of a powerful Christ appearing as a severe judge with open arms. To one side of him are two groups of male saints; on the other is a group of female saints. Placed above this are clouds on which float a small angelic army; above, a mature God the Father governs all. The somewhat damaged lower portion of the fresco displays a confused humanity. Fantastic gargoyles in the figures of dragons and sirens decorate the monastery, which is definitely worth a visit.

Cuitzeo's church and monastery took a long time to build. The monastery is enormous and the church itself had beautiful retablos, which were destroyed in the nineteenth century. The replacement retablos are of a neo-classical style that does not integrate with the spirit of the building. This type of situation occurred in the past when there was little awareness about the importance of historical accuracy—certainly a contrast to contemporary thinking. Cuitzeo's church, built of solid, thick walls, has only one nave. In the apse of the church is a retablo widely considered one of the most beautiful of the entire colonial era. Frescoes in the monastery attest to the wealth of the Augustinian community during the colonial period. This group had extensive landholdings that included African slaves, for which bills of purchase still exist.

PARICUTÍN
REMEMBERING A VOLCANO

WRITTEN BY JOSEPH SCHLARMAN, *México, Tierra de Volcanes* (Mexico, Land of Volcanoes), is a popular book about the country's history. Even though the title was meant to refer to politicians and military men, it could also apply to its geology. Popcatépetl and Iztlaccíhuatl, snow-capped volcanoes near Mexico City, are the most famous landscape features of the country. They are a symbol of Mexico the way that Mount Fujiyama is of Japan. While the majority of volcanoes in Mexico are dormant, some of them still emit steam, a reminder of their existence.

In 1943 the country awoke to the news that a volcano had been born. On the afternoon of February 20, in Michoacán State, a farmer named Dionisio Pulido was working on his land. Suddenly, approximately three hundred feet away, a column of white smoke exploded skyward. Next an earthquake began, the ground started heating up, and a tremendous explosion occurred close to the column of white smoke. The farmer started to run to his house but it was gone. The surrounding fields were on fire and above him was a giant cloud of rock and sand. During the lengthy eruption, the night sky was illuminated by the brilliant glow of a column of fire; enormous rocks shot into the air. On the third night, rocks began to shoot up from deep inside the earth and a lava flow destroyed everything in its path. Dionisio Pulido was one of the few people to witness the birth of a volcano arising from a field of corn. It was given the name Paricutín—the ultimate volcano on a long list in a land of volcanoes.

Seven nearby towns were destroyed by the volcanic debris, which also covered thousands of trees and acres of grassland for many miles around. Thousands of people were evacuated, though there were no deaths or injuries. Paricutín spewed lava for the next nine years, a spectacle that attracted thousands of visitors, among them many artists and photographers. One was the famous Mexican painter Gerardo Murillo, known by his pseudonym Dr. Atl (Doctor Water). He painted during the revolutionary era, traveling throughout the country in his effort to capture Mexico on a cosmic scale; he did not let his disabled leg stop him. Paricutín was a gift to Dr. Atl, and he chose to live as close as he could to the volcano to draw and paint it as if it were his personal model. During his younger years, Dr. Atl had lived a tormented and difficult life with a beautiful but tempermental woman, Nahue Ollin. He left her to search for peace among the mountains, even though, in the case of Paricutín, it was a mountain with volcanic eruptions.

The atrium of Angahuan's St. James the Apostle Church.

facing page
All but the bell tower and upper facade of the old church at San Juan Parangaricutiro are submerged in lava.

Angahuan is a small town that would have been forgotten if not for Paricutín's eruption. Residents of towns in the path of the destruction sought refuge there. An open-air mass was celebrated, attracting the attention of many photographers. These images were widely distributed, as were images of the church itself. As a result, art historians such as Miguel Toussaint came to the town to admire the church. The church, which is dedicated to the apostle Santiago, has a facade of hewn stone made in the Mudéjar (Arab-Spanish) style. The building is both Spanish and indigenous, while being reminiscent of the towns of mountainous northern Spain.

Partially buried in the middle of the lava fields created from the volcanic eruption is a church with its entire bell tower and part of its facade still visible. This is the only thing that remains of the town of San Juan Parangaricutiro. It's possible to visit this site on horseback coming from the nearby town of Angahuán, an excursion that traverses a forest whose surface is covered with black ash. The actual volcano is still emitting bubbling spouts of vapor. San Juan Parangaricutiro's citizens were able to save an image of Christ, known as Señor de los Milagros, from their church. A local artist created this work, made of carved wood and corn pulp. Today, San Juan residents carry this image throughout the region during religious processions—their destination, the new town of Parangaricutiro.

NURÍO
CATHEDRAL OF THE SIERRA

Santiago Nurío is a town on the Meseta Tarasca in the center of Michoacán State; the indigenous Tarascos, or Purépechas, are its residents. This is a pre-Hispanic tribe that managed to survive and maintain its independence even though it existed in close proximity to the powerful groups populating central Mexico. Today, the Tarascos live in a range of communities and preserve both their language and their traditional way of life.

Santiago Nurío is virtually unknown among Mexico's many towns. But a group of Mexicans and foreigners who love the country's art wanted to "adopt" it, and with their contributions they have been able to rescue marvelous places like Santiago Nurío.

Spanish friars gave the Tarascan town the name Santiago, an important saint in Spain. Santiago de Compostela, at the northwest tip of the Iberian Peninsula, is a major place of pilgrimage in Europe to this day. Santiago, who had been a peaceful Jewish apostle in Spain, was converted into Santiago Matamoros, a killer of Moors and Arabs. Oddly enough, Santiago became one of the most popular saints in indigenous Mexico, and throughout the country there are many pueblos named in his honor.

Santiago Nurío Church was completed in 1693. It was built with thick stone and mud walls and had a carved stone facade. Upon entering the church there is a splendid *sotocoro*—polychromatic carved wood whose central piece is decorated with plant motifs intertwined with cherubim. The wooden ceiling has admirable representations of musical angels. The baptistry is also at the entrance and has a baptismal font designed as a ship carrying the apostles under the watchful eye of God the Father surrounded by angels. The roof of the church itself is made of polychromatic wood, a design unique to Mexican architecture.

An altarpiece and array of flowers in St. James the Apostle Church.

facing page
La Purisima Chapel's exquisitely detailed ceiling.

Three baroque retablos, one from the end of the sixteenth century with a beautiful painting of the Virgin Mary, are also contained within. The retablo behind the altar features an odd image of the patron saint of the church and of the town, a war-weary-looking Santiago Matamoros, who is mounted on his horse and is charging toward an imagined enemy. Max Aub, the Spanish-German writer, offered an interesting theory about the fascination the indigenous towns have with Santiago. According to Aub, it is not based on the apostle's life or miracles, but the horse on which he is always mounted. With the arrival of the Spanish, a horse became the most treasured property that a Mexican could have.

The decorated wooden ceiling of the hospital chapel is an example of Michoacán's indigenous art. It is dedicated to the Virgin Mary, who is at the center of the composition above the altar, and its color scheme is predominantly white and red. It is a naïve depiction of heaven, where the Virgin Mary, saints, apostles, and doctors of the Church, as well as the necessary archangels and cherubim, are gathered. Images of suns, stars, flowers, shields, and religious symbols reflect the baroque style of painting every square inch of space. Santiago Nurío's chapel decoration was completed in 1803, evidence that the baroque survived as a preferred style among the indigenous population of Mexico long after it had lost favor in Europe.

Vasco de Quiroga, one of the most charismatic personalities from the beginning of the colonial era, was a lawyer and Spanish nobleman who came to New Spain with a passion for the indigenous peoples and for defending them. After becoming the Bishop of Michoacán, the ancient land of the Tarascos, he put into practice many of his ideas, among them teaching diverse crafts-related skills. These skills have endured, and today, each town has a particular specialty. For example, Nurío produces high-quality wool. Don Vasco de Quiroga also insisted that each church have a clinic. The clinic at Nurío is very modest, but its chapel is a veritable artistic treasure; its roof has a pictorial decoration and the main altar has been carefully preserved. The type of woodwork found there is known as the Mudéjar (Arabic-Spanish) style.

REGINA PATRIAR

99

PÁTZCUARO
VASCO DE QUIROGA'S UTOPIA

THIS TOWN HAS AN ABUNDANCE OF RICHES INCLUDING A LOVELY LAKE AND INTERESTING ARCHITECTURE, replete with charming details that perfectly blend native and Mediterranean styles. It also has a tasty local cuisine, a wealth of local crafts and an exuberant folklore expressed in its many fiestas, especially the famous "Day of the Dead." Pátzcuaro also has pleasant weather and it attracts tourists who are interested in the arts.

But to top it all, its main plaza is one of the most magnificent in Mexico and is large enough a romantic visitor is likely to feel it is as big as the night. Pátzcuaro is surrounded by small villages both along the shores of the lake as well as among the nearby farms.

Perhaps the greatest figure in Pátzcuaro's history was its founder, Vasco de Quiroga. He was a Spanish lawyer whose honesty impressed Emperor Charles V. The emperor had become alarmed by the terrible abuses of the conquistadores in the new World and de Quiroga was sent to impose law and order in new Spain. He tried, however, to implement nothing less than the Utopia dreamt of and written about by Sir Thomas More. In this ravaged land, he led the first project of urban development in the New World and succeeded in convincing the frightened natives to go along with his ideas. He became the Tata, or father, "Tata Vasco." He designed Pátzcuaro and some of his ideas are still very much alive there.

The town has numerous palaces and houses made in a part Spanish, part native style. The most spectacular example is the "Casa del Gigante", though the "Casa del Portal Chaparro is also a favorite. The most important building is the Colegio de San Nicolas, while the beautiful hospital is also noteworthy. Pátzcuaro is a place where you can walk and then relax in the enormous and yet intimate grand Tata Vasco Plaza.

There are several enchanting towns near Pátzcuaro, such as Erongarícuaro which is a beautiful, marshy town that has attracted many foreign artists such as the French poet Andre Breton who declared Mexico to be the perfect Surrealist country. In this town, local artisans work largely with wood and there is also a noteworthy Franciscan church. Zirahuén is a small nearby lake with enchanting colors and is known for the mythical presence of a siren.

Fishermen using "butterfly" nets on Lake Pátzcuaro.

facing page
Remains of arcades at the ancient Nuestra Señora de la Salud sanctuary.

Pátzcuaro's main building is the basilica where Nuestra Señora de la Salud (Our Lady of Health) is honored. Made by a local sculptor in a soft material, the image of Mary is always dressed like a queen. Though homely and slightly chubby for modern tastes, La Salud nevertheless reigns over Pátzcuaro. Our Lady of Health is one of Mexico's most popular devotions, a reason this town has become a major destination for many pilgrims.

Pátzcuaro was not only designed as a social utopia but is also a very charming town filled with arts and crafts. The most attractive spot is La Casa de los Once Patios (House of the Eleven Patios), nowadays a true bazaar of native, old, and modern crafts. On certain days the main square becomes a huge marketplace for the work of artisans. The state of Michoacán, where Pátzcuaro is located, maintains a strong and well-preserved tradition of native culture.

Fourteen miles from Pátzcuaro is the town of Santa Clara del Cobre. Copper has been mined in this area since pre-Hispanic times to make masks, breastplates, and small bells. For this reason, Don Vasco de Quiroga decided that copper would be the artisan craft practiced in nearby villages as well. So, in Santa Clara he established a great foundry which served for two hundred years until it was burned down and thus both foundry and town disappeared. Pátzcuaro is a very folkloric place with many local dances like the Los Viejitos, for example.

above
The facade of the Sanctuary
of Guadalupe in Pátzcuaro.

left
A local crafts seller in Santa
Clara del Cobre.

below
These colorfully costumed performers entertain a
crowd with the traditional "dance of the elders."

TLALPUJAHUA
INDEPENDENCE AND SPIRIT

TLALPUJAHUA IS A SMALL TOWN LOCATED IN MICHOACÁN STATE. In pre-Hispanic times, the farming Mazahua people lived there. But in the final centuries before the conquest, this community found itself in a rather difficult position between two warlike and imperialistic groups, the Tarascos of Michoacán and the Aztecs, whose capital was the great Mexico-Tenochtitlán.

Curiously, the Spanish conquest itself had little immediate impact on Tlalpujahua, which remained a peaceful place. But in 1560, almost forty years after the conquest, gold and silver were discovered and the town was converted into Real de Minas de Tlalpujahua. Eventually fourteen mines would be discovered and would generate great fortunes, though these would be largely ephemeral.

Just as for the miners, the entire life of Tlalpujahua itself shifted between boom and bust, and its destiny would be proof of this. A fire at the beginning of the eighteenth century destroyed part of the town. Much later, Tlalpujahua went on to suffer from a very unusual accident. Many years before this event, an earthen dam was built using the discarded dirt from the mines that accumulated and became mud. One night, on the Thursday of the feast of Corpus Christi, the dam collapsed and an avalanche of mud buried the town. The only thing that was not covered was the upper portion of the bell tower of the Carmen church. Survivors worked for three months to dig away mud so they could enter the building. They rescued the valuable retablos and, more importantly, an adobe wall where the image of the Virgin of Carmen was painted. Afterward this image was placed in the magnificent church that exists today.

Tlalpujahua also suffered during the war for independence from Spain because it was the hometown of insurgent heroes. Its famous López Rayón brothers had their headquarters in town. Tlalpujahua's sixteenth-century Franciscan monastery is a modest building with no artistic importance. Later, when the Carmelites arrived, they built a monastery and a magnificent church—the one buried in mud—which was reconstructed in a high, dry place. This new church is among the most beautiful provincial churches in Mexico. In front it has an enormous atrium with an unusual cross adorned with a flintlike knife. The facade is comparable in quality to Tepotzotlán or the *sagrario* (shrine) of the cathedral in Mexico City. Its shape is that of a large inverted shield and contains a magnificent stone retablo with niches in which there are statues of the saints, among them the apostles Peter and Paul. A sculpture of Saint John the Baptist crowns the facade.

A view overlooking the small town of Tlalpujahua.

facing page
The detailed facade of the Sanctuary of the Virgin of El Carmen.

In addition to its religious festivals, Tlalpujahua honors the exceptional López Rayón family with an annual celebration. Five López Rayón brothers were heroes in Mexico's revolution and built a fort on a hill outside of town named the "rooster." Francisco López Rayón joined Miguel Hidalgo y Costilla's uprising and shared in the victories and defeats. But in the north, when Hidalgo y Costilla left for the United States, López Rayón separated himself from the other followers and continued the fight. Eventually he was captured and executed by a firing squad. His brothers Ignacio, Ramón, José María, and Rafael all survived. Tlalpujahua remembers them with a fiesta organized on the hill from which they fought the Spanish.

After the Carmen church was buried, one of the richest men in New Spain—a miner of French origin, Joseph de Laborde (known in Mexico as Borda)—offered to pay for the construction of a new church. Though a generous offer, Tlalpujahua's citizens, proud of the richness of their mines, imposed certain terms and conditions. Disgusted, Laborde left Tlalpujahua and began a new mining venture in Taxco, whose silver mines doubled his fortune. This allowed him to build, without impediment, one of the most beautiful churches in Mexico, with imaginative architecture and opulent gilded retablos. Tlalpujahua's loss was certainly Taxco's gain.

Tlalpujahua also has a history of love. It is here that the most famous couple in the history of Mexico, Andrés Quintana Roo and his wife, Leona Vicario, were united during the fight for Mexican independence. He was a lawyer and met her while working in her uncle's office. They fell in love but they were not permitted to marry. Quintana Roo left Tlalpujahua with the brothers López Rayón; she sent them money from Mexico City. She was discovered and imprisoned but later escaped. Quintana Roo would become an important government official, ambassador to London, and a popular poet. The Mexican state, Quintana Roo, is named in his honor. Tlalpujahua was declared a *pueblo mágico* by the Mexican government. It has a quiet charm thanks to red-roofed houses among the landscape of pines, the municipal palace with its arcade and white facade, its churches, and the solitary bell tower, all of which serve as reminders of the day when the pueblo was almost completely buried by a mud avalanche.

above
What remains of the former church of El Carmen after the mud avalanche.

left
A panoramic view of the picturesque town.

below
The domed roofs of the Sanctuary of the Virgin of El Carmen.

107

TZINTZUNTZAN
MYSTERY EMPIRE

THE GRAND HISTORY OF THE AMERICAS is an unknown territory in which great mysteries gradually appear. Each day we become more removed from that distant time of the early civilizations. Discoveries from the plains of North America to the mountains of Peru reveal mysterious figures and incredible technical revelations. Along with more advanced academic archaeology, there's also a fantastic archaeology that focuses on extraterrestrials or great migrations. The Mexican painter Diego Rivera, a collector of pre-Hispanic art, spoke often of the amazing similarities between certain aspects of Mexican and Chinese culture. During the several-year-long voyage on Kon-Tiki, Thor Heyerdahl proved that it was possible that communication between South America and the South Pacific had occurred. The New World is full of mysteries.

The Tarasco people, sometimes called the *purépechas,* are one of Mexico's mysteries. This tribe lives mostly in Michoacán State and has preserved its language and traditions. It may seem like the Tarasco were just another tribe that appeared from northern Mexico, but a number of linguistic and cultural indicators suggest that they came to Mexico from South America. They first crossed through Mayan territory, then went to Veracruz where examples of their architecture can be found. From there they went into central Mexico. Finally, around A.D. 1200, they established themselves in the area of Michoacán in western Mexico.

In Michoacán they founded Pátzcuaro. Through alliances and war their dominion gradually grew. Their leader was Tariácuri, and he became divinized as "the priest of the wind." Like the Aztecs, the Tarasco became great conquerors and their territory in western and central Mexico was as extensive as that of the Aztecs. The Tarasco also sought to extend their empire into the northwest; they fought the Zuni in New Mexico, where there are linguistic traces. The Aztecs called the Tarascan king *Caltzontzin,* meaning "the lord of many lands and houses." It is certain that the Tarascan language sounds distinct—to western ears almost like a gentle and musical form of Japanese.

Tarasco people were metalsmiths, not only creating jewelry but making tools, primarily from copper. Their religion was originally lunar but later focused on the sun and the god Curicaveri, an older sun god who, when dying, gave his power to his son who was a result of his union with the moon. His son would become the god of the dawn and of war. The most significant accomplishment of the Tarasco was their capital, Tzintzuntzan.

The convent of San Francisco.

facing page
Tzintzuntzan town with the Yacatas archeological site in the background.

The Day of the Dead celebration is a major event in the region. Even though the feast day of November 2 is a Christian celebration, the ritual itself has a pre-Hispanic flavor. During the night, the Tarasco go to cemeteries where they visit their dead ancestors with offerings of flowers and food, which the families consume as if the dead were eating with them. People return home from places as far away as the northern United States to participate in the celebration. In the more formal tombs there are altars to the saints as well as beloved figures in the community such as Lázaro Cárdenas, who nationalized the petroleum industry and who, many years after this action, is considered the grandfather *(Tata)* of both Michoacán State and Mexico.

The Tarasco's great addition to pre-Hispanic Mexican architecture was the *yácata.* Its form was very different from the conventional pyramid. It had a base topped with a large rectangular platform that had circular forms above it; there was a staircase to climb to the upper part, which had a temple. The temple was topped with a straw roof, a contrast to the way Mayan pyramids were covered. *Yácata* means "place of the hummingbird." The young sun (the sun of the early morning), fought and was victorious over the stars, a victory incarnated symbolically in the hummingbird. The archaeological site of Tzintzuntzan is extensive but only partially studied. The town itself is lovely and offers a wide variety of artisan goods in its markets.

CACAHUAMILPA
MAGNIFICENT CAVERNS

SOUTH OF MEXICO CITY IN THE STATE OF GUERRERO CAN BE FOUND CACAHUAMILPA'S CAVERNS. These are the most famous caverns in Mexico and certainly among the most beautiful in the world. The remains of a temple found at the entrance to the caverns, as well as one inside, indicate they were in use prior to the conquest. During the colonial era, the caverns appear to have been forgotten. In 1834 the caverns were rediscovered by a rich local landowner who was fleeing from the authorities and took refuge in them. In 1920 the caverns were opened to the public; in 1936 they were declared a national park.

Many legends surround Cacahuamilpa, the most famous being that of the dethroned minor king of the town of Tetipac. He was the true discoverer of the caverns and long before the conquest, he employed a beautiful woman to help him recover his throne. He presented her to the people as a goddess in hopes of scaring those who had overthrown him. Using sound and light in the caverns, the goddess threatened both the destruction of Tetipac as well as eternal damnation for the rebels; as a result, they restored the king to power. Whether or not this actually happened, one thing is clear: the magic of the caverns makes it appear that any miracle or apparition is possible.

Only some portions of the caverns are accessible to visitors, but these areas are enormous. The public is able to visit twenty large caverns connected by a gallery one and a quarter miles long. The height of the caverns varies between 98 and 230 feet and it would be possible to construct a building of over twenty stories in the largest one. Even though many of the caverns have not been explored, many experts believe they are the largest in the world.

The first cavern visitors enter is egg-shaped and about 164 feet long, 147 feet wide, and 164 feet high. It is called *chivo* (the goat) because the primary rock formation is reminiscent of a male goat.

The next cavern is entered through a corridor almost 327 feet long and famous for its alabasterlike rock formations. Another cavern is named *La Aurora,* because its luminosity is reminiscent of the first hours of the morning.

A carriage at the Hacienda Vista Hermosa.

facing page
One of the many majestic spaces found in the Cacahuamilpa caves.

After the caverns of Cacahuamilpa had been rediscovered, they began to attract many distinguished visitors. Among them was Charlotte, the tragic empress of Mexico who left a plaque there to commemorate her visit. Over the years, many memorable events have taken place in the caverns. One was a concert organized by the aging ex-Mexican president Porfirio Díaz, given in honor of the famous composer Juventino Rosas. His waltz, *Sobre Las Olas,* was a worldwide hit at the end of the nineteenth century. This type of event was repeated in contemporary times with a concert of Stravinsky music or even the recent recital of Andrea Boccelli.

Cacahuamilpa is in a tropical area where sugarcane haciendas (plantations) have prospered since colonial times. Among the most affluent and important are San José de Vista Hermosa, San Carlos Borromeo, Chiconcuac, Santa Inés, and San Gabriel de las Palmas. For centuries sugar was a veritable "white gold" that attracted ambitious empire builders to colonial America. Many of the haciendas were converted into actual palaces. These *casas grandes* were richly decorated and each had to have a private chapel as well as its own flourishing sugar mill. Today, some have been converted into luxury hotels or mansions for millionaires.

Finally, in the cavern known as *La Fuente* (the fountain), two large stone cups look as if they are emitting a stream of eternally frozen water. The capricious rock formations of Cacahuamilpa have a magical quality.

TAXCO
TOWN OF SILVERSMITHS

MINING TOWNS ARE UNIQUE IN MEXICO: They can be found set deep within ravines, as in Guanajuato, or rambling across hilltops, as in Taxco. Taxco is the silver-mining heartland of Mexico, and it experienced its first great mining bonanza in the eighteenth century. It was not until well into the twentieth century that a modern highway connected Taxco with the rest of the country—until then, a trip to Taxco was a real-life mountainous adventure. But upon arriving, a visitor would quickly discover a town full of interesting vistas and pathways. Among these could be found capricious streets that turn, climb, descend and then suddenly drop. Fortunately in Taxco, there are no stairways as in other mining towns but rather ramps that were built to accommodate the hauling of rocks. The main street in Taxco is the Calle Real Vieja, but each street has its charm, a surprise or a legend. One such regards Dona Elena de Anorga, a rich colonial mine owner, who ordered that the street be covered with bars of silver when she came into town.

Taxco is a city of plazas. The main plaza has huge trees that give refreshing shade but do not block the view of the church. This main plaza is both the traditional site of the market as well as a meeting place. Among other smaller plazas is Plaza Veracruz, with its Italian cypresses. Plaza of the Roosters where in spite of all moralizing to the contrary, cockfighting regularly takes place with all of its attendant gambling and rowdiness. Strolling the streets looking for the stores of silver artisans and discovering interesting architecture and splendid views is an enjoyable way to spend time here.

The great lover of Taxco was the grand historian of colonial Mexico, Manuel Toussaint, who felt that Taxco was reminiscent of a hill town from Italy. Toussaint loved to travel to the forgotten towns of Mexico, travels that were popularized in his writing and led many readers to undertake the same adventurous trips.

Though many fortunes were both won and lost in Taxco, none equaled that of the its most famous resident: Joseph de Laborde, who was born in Gascony, France. Following in the footsteps of a brother who was a miner in Taxco, he inherited silver mines that made him one of the richest men in the colony. Borda, as he is known in Mexico, was not a miner by vocation, but rather a great administrator interested in serving the community. A generous man, he also established humane working conditions and paid his miners well—both rare at that time.

Though he owned mansions in both Mexico City and in Taxco—Casa Borda—Laborde preferred to live in a simple house close to both his mines and to the many philanthropic works he undertook in the community.

Santa Prísca's magnificent baroque facade.

facing page
Santa Prísca's impressive gold-covered altarpiece.

The church of Santa Prísca is for many—including the acerbic British writer Evelyn Waugh—the most beautiful church in Mexico. Its construction was personally directed by Borda. The rich miner built this church intended for his priest son to worship and preach there. It was built in an ultra-baroque style out of pink hewn stone, and it is famous for its two beautiful bell towers and the shining, colorful tile coveres dome. Rich silver altarpieces and an imposing organ graces its interior. It is a jewel.

Santa Prísca's beauty is a result of the love and the fortune of Don Joseph de Laborde. It was built quickly, in seven years, and because of this it is unified and pure in its design. It's altarpieces are particularly beautiful. Like all altarpieces, these have a dominant theme—in this case the Immaculate Conception of Mary. In general, the altarpiece provided a magnificent context to gather together the multitude of angels and saints that were favorites during the Counter-Reformation. Brought to Mexico after the conquest, altarpieces were very much in keeping with Mexican taste, and Taxco would not be the same without its rich and luxurious visual forms. Obviously, the best altarpieces were built in the rich cities such as mining towns, with their generous patrons such as Joseph de Laborde. Among the church's other treasures are a number of paintings by colonial masters.

Taxco was founded by a now-forgotten indigenous tribe, the Tlahuicas. These indigenous people became important to Hernán Cortés when he discovered they had been paying tribute to the Aztecs in silver and gold. This ignited Cortés's greed; he claimed one of the mines for himself, and it was not much later that the people of Taxco were working there. From the beginning there was native Taxco and a Spanish one. Cortés's mine was the first of many mining companies to follow. The conquest of Taxco took place in 1531, ten years after the fall of the Aztec empire. Its golden era, however, can be dated from the eighteenth century and the building of the marvelous Santa Prísca. Taxco, a city of miners that preserved its traditional ways, attracted a veritable revolutionary designer, William Spratling. He was responsible for the simplicity and elegance for which the silver of Taxco is known, and today a museum is dedicated to him.

below
The town's main plaza.

above
Taxco's charming
cobblestone streets.

left
The city at sunset.

ATOTONILCO
THE FLAG OF INDEPENDENCE

Santuario de Atotonilco is not far from the well-known town San Miguel de Allende. Though it may look sleepy, it is one of the treasures of popular Mexican colonial art. The interior walls of the church are covered with murals and the church itself contains beautiful works of art.

The murals were painted by an indigenous artist, Miguel Antonio Martinez de Pocasangre; it took over thirty years to complete them. He labored largely in semidarkness.

He was painting in the eighteenth century when Mexico was still in the grip of the late baroque; after this neoclassicism arrived and was embraced by some in hopes of cleaning up the visual excesses. This new movement was favored by the aristocracy but did not speak to the indigenous and mestizo communities, whose heritage was closer to that of the ornate and excessive.

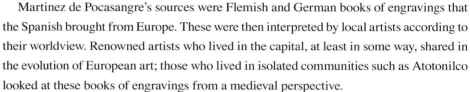

Martinez de Pocasangre's sources were Flemish and German books of engravings that the Spanish brought from Europe. These were then interpreted by local artists according to their worldview. Renowned artists who lived in the capital, at least in some way, shared in the evolution of European art; those who lived in isolated communities such as Atotonilco looked at these books of engravings from a medieval perspective.

A mural created by native artists inside the sanctuary.

facing page
Atotonilco's sanctuary dedicated to Jesus of Nazareth.

The Santuario de Atoltonilco was the work of a mystic, Father Luis Felipe Neri de Alfaro, who each Holy Week personally carried a heavy cross in the procession that re-enacted the Passion of Christ. This was the origin of the annual pilgrimages the faithful embark on to this day. Father Alfaro looked at Atotonilco as a distant echo of Jerusalem with the Santuario as a replica of the Church of the Holy Sepulcher. Included among the paintings in the sacristy of the Santuario are two oils that are meant to express the similarities between the landscapes of San Miguel de Allende and Jerusalem—the latter a place the painter had never visited. The images of Jerusalem are a work of caprice and imagination; the images of San Miguel, a wonderful visual document of how the city looked in colonial times.

Father Alfaro wanted to build a church whose design and art reproduced two places in Jerusalem: Mount Calvary and the Church of the Holy Sepulcher. His church was designed in the form of a Latin cross, with six side chapels and various devotional side altars. The Santuario de Atotonilco is the dream of a mystic who lived Christ's Passion and of a painter who dedicated his life to giving form and color to that dream.

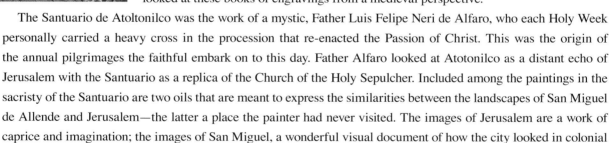

Atotonilco is a place of religious pilgrimage similar to other sites in Mexico that attract thousands of people each year, who often walk great distances—sometimes from hundreds of miles away. In Atotonilco, the most important time is Holy Week; pilgrims flagellate themselves and fast during this spiritual retreat. This tradition not only has roots in the indigenous communities, but Spain as well, and it is one carried out in many cities and towns around Mexico, including Taxco, where people re-enact the Passion.

Atotonilco had one great moment when it became immersed in the drama of Mexican history. In 1810 there was a sense of nervous anticipation throughout Mexico because of developments in Europe. Napoleon's military ambition led him to invade Spain; as a result, Spain's king abdicated. This prompted a rebellion and then civil war, while in the Spanish colonies it inflamed a desire for liberty. In the nearby town of Dolores a local priest, Miguel Hidalgo, proclaimed the independence of Mexico and began a popular rebellion using a peasant army. But this improvised army had neither uniforms nor a flag. When they passed through Atotonilco, Hidalgo appropriated the image of Our Lady of Guadalupe from the church and used it as his army's flag.

DOLORES HIDALGO
CRADLE OF INDEPENDENCE

IN PRE-HISPANIC TIMES, DOLORES HIDALGO, LOCATED THIRTY-THREE MILES FROM GUANAJUATO, was an Otomí town named Cocomacan. After the conquest, a religious group named Nuestra Señora de los Dolores gave its name to the town, but it had little importance until the eighteenth century when prosperity struck. Its fame and place in history was set in 1810 when a local priest—Don Miguel Hidalgo y Costilla—proclaimed Mexico's independence from the town.

Hidalgo y Costilla lived in passionate times. Born in 1753, he was the son of a large landowner of Spanish origin. Orphaned at the age of twelve, he was sent to Valladolid (today Morelia) to study with the Jesuits. With the expulsion of the Jesuits, Hidalgo y Costilla's studies were interrupted but he entered the seminary of Valladolid instead. In 1770 he received a degree with high honors; he received another degree in Mexico City. Upon returning to Valladolid, he dedicated himself to his ecclesiastical career and was ordained in 1778. His genuine interests were academic life and languages. He spoke Latin, French, and Italian, as well as three indigenous languages. However, his personal life was not exemplary: he had at least two female companions, fathered a number of children, and loved gambling. But he also had a practical and enterprising mind and he brought progress to the towns in which he served. An unexpected inheritance made him reasonably wealthy, allowing him to associate with important people of his time. He expressed controversial religious opinions that led to his denunciation before the Inquisition but eventually led nowhere. In 1802 he was named pastor of Dolores.

Meanwhile in Europe, Napoleon Bonaparte was expanding his empire by invading Spain. He forced King Charles IV to abdicate and crowned his brother, Joseph Bonaparte. Among the consequences of this act was a common perception in the Spanish colonies that the legitimate royal power had been abrogated, naturally leading to the idea of independence. Among these thinkers was Don Miguel Hidalgo y Costilla, who entered into a plan that eventually led him to proclaim the independence of Mexico. During the night of September 16, 1810, he gathered his parishioners and cried out these famous phrases: *¡Viva la Independencia!, ¡Viva la América y Muera el mal gobierno!* Thus began the fight for Mexican independence with Hidalgo y Costilla as head of the movement and Ignacio Allende as its military leader. This stage of the revolution moved quickly, was largely accidental, and ended with the capture and death of Hidalgo y Costilla in the summer of 1811. However, the independent movement continued untill 1821 when the Spanish army was finally defeated.

GUANAJUATO
ART, ROMANTICISM, AND SILVER

ONE OF THE MOST FAMOUS TOWNS IN MEXICO, Guanajuato was recently named a World Heritage site by UNESCO. But it has long been an important destination for travelers drawn to its romantic atmosphere. This is an ancient town first populated by the Tarascos, who named it Quanaxhuato, meaning "the place of the frogs" (to this day frogs are a local symbol). It was only after the Spanish conquest in 1541 that its silver mines were discovered. In 1570 the town of Santa Fé de Guanajuato was founded; it became the provincial capital in 1786.

While the Mexico independence movement began in nearby Dolores Hidalgo under the direction of a local priest, Miguel Hidalgo, the first military conflict occurred here. Leading an improvised army, he took the city as well as the famous *Alhondiga* (public granary) which he later fortified. This improvised redoubt was taken thanks to a miner known as Pípila who, while covered with a large stone to protect himself from gunfire, burned down the entrance door. These events occurred in 1810.

It was not until the end of the nineteenth century, during the dictatorship of Porfirio Díaz, that Guanajuato entered what became known as its golden age. At this time the Teatro Juárez, the market, and many parks and avenues were built following the French style popular at the time. After the revolution, Guanajuato gradually became seen as an authentic Mexican environment where the ideas of both the colonial and the romantic were found.

Guanajuato was built on a gorge, and its streets are capriciously laid out. One hidden street—Father Belaunzarán—takes the visitor to the heart of the city. Among the many narrow streets is the famous Callejón del Beso (Street of the Kiss), where two lovers kissed each other from their own balconies—one balcony across from the other. In some plazas and gardens, fountains and large street lamps can be found as in the Plaza of San Roque, where in 1952 open air theater performances began to be celebrated. Here, light comedies of Miguel de Cervantes or other classic Spanish works are performed. These shows were the beginnings of what is now the International Cervantino Festival, the most important cultural festival in Mexico.

Celebrated every October, the festival invites international artists from opera, music, dance and theater to perform.

Nightlife unfolds at Teatro Juárez.

facing page
A romantic view looking down on the city's San Diego Church.

Teatro Juárez is delightfully designed. Begun by an enterprising governor in 1872 as a rather austere project, by the time it was finished thirty years later it had a style that can now only be described as a delirious mix of Moorish, French, and Greek influences. One stairway leads to a portico supported by Greek columns decorated with lyres and topped with sculptures of the muses. The interior is even more fantastic with its foyer and smoking room in which carved furniture is mixed with sculptures of famous artists such as Dante and Mozart as well as the little-known Portuguese poet, Camoens. To give a more oriental flavor to the theater, the stage curtain has a representation of Constantinople. It's simply one more enchanting aspect of Guanajuato.

Guanajuato is a walking town, especially with its lengthy streets called *callejones*. Visitors can start from the cathedral in the Plaza de la Paz, the location of the Conde de Rul, one of the most beautiful houses in Mexico. Or one can start from the Jesuit church, with its important art gallery. Guanajuato is the birthplace of artist Diego Rivera and on one street you can find his family home and a museum of his work. On another street is the famous corn exchange and the market, both of which are worthy of visits. At the highest point in the city, one gets an impressive panoramic view, along with a view of the famous sculpture of Pípila, the military hero.

The first university in Guanajuato was founded in the eighteenth century by the Jesuits, who were later expelled. After independence, a state college opened on this site.

above
The University of Guanajuato.

left
A panoramic view of sprawling Guanajuato.

below
One of the many *callejones* that crisscross the city.

123

SAN MIGUEL DE ALLENDE
A HERO'S TOWN

ONCE KNOWN AS SAN MIGUEL EL GRANDE, this colonial town was destined to play a significant role in Mexico's history. It was here that a disquiet formed; by 1810, this unhappiness would lead to the Declaration of Independence by Nueva España, today known as México. And it was because of the leadership of a young local official, Ignacio Allende, who played an important part in these revolutionary affairs, that San Miguel today is called *de Allende* not *el Grande*.

San Miguel was transformed into one of the most enchanting small towns of Mexico and became an oasis for the arts. Situated in a valley in the mountains of central Mexico, it combines an ancient agricultural past with that of robust tourism. The main church may seem somewhat out of place due to its Gothic style, but there is a reason for this. For the church was not built in the French or English formal style, but rather developed into an enchanting and eccentric example of the country itself. Originally, San Miguel had a parish church, which was built in the Baroque style by a famous architect of the period.

At the beginning of the twentieth century, a local priest decided to modernize the town's baroque-style church with a new facade. He placed Zeferino Gutiérrez in charge of creating it. Zeferino, undaunted by the incongruity of his design, transformed the facade into what we now see, with its feel that is both false and overweight, ingenious and happy. The bricklike facade appears as a festive toy-version of the Gothic style. Directly in front is the town plaza, where the gardens are enjoyed by locals and tourists. At the corner of the paza is the elegant colonial home where Miguel Allende was born. Nearby is the beautiful theather Angela Peralta. This remarkable building was built in 1871.

A wonderful example of colonial architecture is the neighboring palaces of the Condes de la Canal. It is well known that this noble family was devoted to Our Lady of Loretto and because of this, they ordered the construction of a small dressing room in the nearby Santa Casa Church. This chamber was designed to provide a feminine and elegant atmosphere to change the liturgical clothing of the Madonna. The nearby convent and garden, Immaculate Conception, has a cupola reminiscent of Des Invalides in Paris.

Over the years, San Miguel has become a thriving artists' colony for Americans, which is driven by the presence of an important art school, the Instituto Allende. This town is a great place to enjoy a relaxing getaway weekend spent in the style of Ignacio Allende's San Miguel.

A statue of Ignacio Allende.

facing page
The town's central plaza lined with arcades and with majestic San Miguel Church as its focal point.

The town is situated beneath rolling hills, and it is centered around the vibrant plaza facing the fantastic Gothic parish church devoted to the archangel Saint Michael. Elegant colonial houses line the plaza. But beyond the beautiful buildings, the essence of San Miguel is in its private homes. The town's secret life can be glimpsed through the flower-filled patios, as well as the fondness for artisans and arts and crafts.

Many of San Miguel's old houses have found new life: they have been renovated into boutique hotels. Some of them where originally built in the sixteenth century. San Miguel de Allende's hotels combine an enchanting colonial ambience with that of sophisticated modern conveniences. The food served in the town's small luxury hotels is a fusion of both Mexican and international flavors. Interesting boutiques can be found, though the more adventurous can still find bargains at the local markets.

One of the most wonderful characteristics of San Miguel de Allende is its tranquility which you can breathe in its streets. Walking along these stone-paved streets beneath a blue sky and surrounded by beautiful colonial homes really reflects the unique and enchanting style of this Mexican town. It is a style that includes a touch of the profound Spanish roots that were a gift of the conquest. Thanks to the presence of so many foreigners in San Miguel, the local cuisine is full of variety offering the gamut of syles from from typical Mexican food to French haute cuisine as well as Italian, Spanish and Argentine fare. Meanwhile, as clouds fill the afternoon sky, San Miguel invites its visitors to enjoy a coffee in the plaza or dine by candlelight in an unforgettable, hidden place.

above
A cobblestone alley in town.

left
Approaching San Miguel de Allende.

below
A view of the main square.

YURIRIA
A MONASTERY STRONGHOLD

THIS TOWN'S FIRST MISSIONARIES ARRIVED IN 1535, and in a mere five years a prosperous town had been established, thanks to cattle raising. Construction began on a large fortified monastery ten years later. The fortified monastery, an architectural style unique to Mexico, was required because of the very specific conditions that existed there in the sixteenth century. The primary event of Mexico's conquest was the fall of the Aztec capital Mexico-Tenochtitlán to the forces of Hernán Cortés and his indigenous allies in 1521. In fact, this was only the beginning of a very lengthy process that in some places lasted as long as two hundred years. Many indigenous tribes did not integrate into the new civilization because they fled to inaccessible mountain and jungle regions. The sixteenth century was a time of conquest, evangelization, and defense against these tribes, some of which wanted to retake lands from the conquerors. Because of this animosity toward the Europeans, fortified monasteries were a necessity.

Stylistically these buildings were a combination of old medieval Gothic forms and new ideas from Renaissance Italy. These styles were then adapted to Spanish taste, which still maintained elements of the Arabic artistic tradition.

Evangelization of Mexico in the sixteenth century primarily was undertaken by three religious orders: the Franciscans, the Dominicans, and the Augustinians. Each one of these orders stamped its particular style on the area of Mexico in which it worked.

Monastery strongholds did not develop capriciously. It was the first (and one of the best) viceroys of Mexico, Don Antonio de Mendoza, who gathered together the superiors of the three religious orders to determine the design of Mexico's churches and monasteries. It was decided that each structure should have three parts: a large space open in the front that would be called an atrium, the church itself, and a monastery where the friars would live. The atrium had to be very large because it had to accommodate large numbers of indigenous people who were undergoing conversion, as well as provide space for ecclesial processions. At the center of the atrium would be a stone cross generally decorated with indigenous designs that would give it an exotic feel. Each church would face east with the main altar inside; behind the altar would be gilded-wood retablos with sculptures and paintings. The church would be connected to its monastery, which generally faced south; the cloister with its patio would be at the center of the monastery. Friars lived on the second floor while the ground floor was reserved for the refectory, the kitchens, and the stables. Yuriria's fortified monastery follows this model.

The patio of the former Convent of San Agustín.

facing page
The detailed facade of the former Convent of San Agustín.

Yuriria's cloister, which is no longer used, is a typical sixteenth-century design with a strong medieval feel that is created by its large beams and Gothic traces. This monastery has a somewhat extravagant feel, because the Augustinians were not bound by the same vows of poverty as the Franciscans. There are remains of frescoed walls as well as fantastic gargoyles that can be admired in the patio with the fountain in its center. Sadly, an act of arson at the end of the colonial period destroyed the church retablos. Yuriria is also famous for its artificial lake—a notable colonial-era hydraulic work built to irrigate the fertile farmlands.

Yuriria's monastery was built for the Augustinian order between 1556 and 1567 by the architect Pedro del Toro, whose likeness, as well as that of his wife, are sculpted above its entrance. Its church is extraordinarily strong and many times served as a refuge for the entire community during rebellions. The structure does not have the traditional nave; instead it has two that form a Greek cross. It also has a strong, solid bell tower with more of a military than ecclesiastical feel. Its facade is one of the best examples of the native plateresque style—a Mexican interpretation of an Italian style. Primary motifs on the facade are inspired by vegetation, and the quality of the sculpture is outstanding. On top of the facade is an image of Saint Augustine, a bishop and philosopher, as well as the founder of the order.

BERNAL
POWERFUL ROCK, ENCHANTING TOWN

THIS CHARMING TOWN IS LOCATED IN A TERRITORY THAT FELL UNDER the domination of the Spanish very late—it wasn't colonized until the mid-seventeenth century. It is part of an immense northern territory called La Gran Chichimeca, which was an easy way to refer to the part of Mexico populated by uncivilized native tribes. This distinction dates from pre-Hispanic times, when the great cultures of Teotihuacán or Tajín also referred to the north as "savage." The civilized pre-Colombian cultures were all located in the center or the south of the country.

According to Aztec text, "the Chichimecas lived the life of hunters, they had no houses, no lands and their clothing was not cotton but animal skins and cloaks of hay. They ate the fruit of cactus and wild roots." They did not work with stone or metal, and they did not have the social structure of the advanced cultures of ancient Mexico. In addition, unlike advanced cultures they did not have a developed religion. They did not have stone idols and did not practice human sacrifice; instead, they worshiped the sun, the moon, and the stars. It was a religion focused on the cosmos and in which certain places were sacred. One of these sacred spots is Peña de Bernal, a massive monolith close to the town that rises up from a semi-desert plain. It is considered to be the third largest monolithic rock in the world after the Rock of Gibraltar and Sugar Loaf in Rio de Janeiro. It is 1,120 feet tall and is thought to emit energy.

Many travelers come to this area in search of this energy, just as the Chichimecas did hundreds of years ago. March 21, the day of the spring equinox, is the most popular time to visit; according to ancient tradition this is when "the sun visits" all the great archaeological sites such as Teotihuacán and Chichén Itzá.

Aside from some New Age and magical beliefs, there is a scientific explanation for this energy emanation from the rocky monolithic mass. The rock can synthesize the strong electromagnetic rhythms of the planet, and the mineral deposits inside them—quartz, obsidian, and fluoride—are highly conductive. It is ironic that in the territory of the "savage" Chichimecas, there is a place that resonates with people today because of unique physical properties first recognized by them. The Rock of Bernal, an awe-inspiring natural wonder, can be seen from many miles away.

Founded late in the colonial period, Bernal's first Spanish settlers arrived in 1647, more than 125 years after the fall of the Aztec's great capital, México-Tenochtitlán. This is considered the beginning of the colonial period, which lasted exactly three hundred years.

Bernal has been identified as a *pueblo mágico* because of its enchanting colonial atmosphere. Its paved streets crisscross a quiet town surrounded by houses with patios and arches that have survived for centuries. The most interesting site in Bernal is a place called the "castle," which was built in the seventeenth century for military purposes. Today it has a more romantic appearance with a clock tower that slowly marks the passage of provincial time. San Sebastian is the main church, and also important is Portal de la Esperanza; both are somewhat notorious because of the ghost stories associated with them. These include the tale of the Charro Negro, a horseman who appears silently at night seeking forgiveness for his sins.

Dominating the town of Bernal like a huge protector, or like a perennial and subtle threat, is the rock, which is part of everyone's daily life. Although it attracts rock climbers and rappelers, conquering it is not easy. At a height of 1,120 feet, it presents a real challenge—even for professionals. The first inhabitants of Bernal were soldiers sent as an advance garrison to the territory of the Chichimecas. They built a barrack, which was the origin of the pueblo and provided protection so that the first colonists could farm and raise cattle.

JALPAN
THE INDIAN MISSIONS

JALPAN IS LOCATED IN THE STATE OF QUERÉTARO IN CENTRAL MEXICO. The Sierra Gorda is the state's most important region—a beautiful yet hard-to-reach mountainous area that is considered a biosphere reserve. Hidden in this lovely area are five fully restored Franciscan missions dating from the eighteenth century: Santiago de Jalpan, Nuestra Señora de la Luz de Tancoyotl, San Miguel Concá, Santa María del Agua de Landa, and San Francisco del Valle de Tilaco.

For many years, the Sierra Gorda was used as a refuge by indigenous tribes seeking to escape the oppressive authority of the Spanish. Among these were the Chichimecas, who were labeled as barbarians. It was not until 1742, very late in the colonial period, that the Spanish captain José de Escandón organized an expedition to conquer the Sierra Gorda. During the fatal battle of Media Luna, Escandón encircled this tribe and nearly exterminated them.

Father Junípero Serra, an extraordinary man, came to Jalpan in 1750. He was a Franciscan friar who was born in Majorca in 1713, and it was there that he entered the order of Saint Francis. He earned a doctorate in theology, but the academic world was not for him. In 1749 he was sent to Veracruz and from there he walked on foot to Mexico City. His superiors sent him to pacify Sierra Gorda by establishing missions; it was work that he did brilliantly. This enterprising friar calmed the indigenous population using Franciscan doctrine; this proved to be consolation for the evils they had suffered.

But Serra's real saga began in 1767 when the Spanish king expelled the Jesuits from his dominions and forced them to abandon their enormous missionary territory. This area included the entire northern part of Mexico as well as the southwest of what is now the United States, including California. It was also in 1767 that the viceroy of Mexico, the Marquis de Croix, asked the Franciscans if they would try to evangelize this territory. It was Father Junípero Serra's destiny to spearhead this work. He left to attend to the missions in California, accompanied by twelve other friars. In 1769 Serra founded the mission of San Fernando en Villicalá, and in 1770, San Diego. In later years, he and the other missionaries would establish San Antonio, San Luis Obispo, San Juan Capistrano, and Santa Clara. His companions on the expedition established missions in Los Angeles and San Francisco. Junipero Serra was canonized as a saint for his work.

A detailed lintel of the Señor Santiago Church in Jalpan.

facing page
The facade of Tilaco's San Francisco Church.

Baroque missions featuring the native style place a decorative emphasis on certain themes and present an enchanting visual equilibrium. Their rich decor mixes many forms. Architectural elements were transformed by the baroque imagination into fanciful figures far removed from their classical origins; examples are vegetation carved in stone as well as symbols such as the Franciscan shield on which the arm of Christ crosses over that of Saint Francis—both atop a Latin cross. In general, religious art has a visual language that you have to know to read well, for which is the case of another shield in a different mission church that symbolizes the five bloody wounds of Christ.

While José de Escandón represented the brutal face of the Spanish. Junípero Serra represented the best of European idealism as well as the religious beliefs of Saint Francis. It undoubtedly took a great deal of work to convince the natives that the conquest represented more than death and exploitation. To accomplish this he lived among the natives and preached to them in their native languages. From an architectural perspective, the missions of the Sierra Gorda represent a unique concept: a baroque style interpreted for natives—in other words, an indigenous Baroque. San Francisco de Tilaco is the best of the five churches, with its tall, nicely formed tower and its magnificent facade, a retablo finished with an image of Saint Assisi sculpted by a native whose work was accepted by the benevolent friars.

EL CHICO
AN INDISPENSABLE ELEMENT

GOLD WAS EXTREMELY PRECIOUS TO EUROPEANS, in sharp contrast to the way it was viewed by the peoples of Mesoamerica. They considered gold to be of value but much less so than jade stones or the plumes of the quetzal bird. Cacao was used for money, not gold. For this reason, in spite of the abundant mineral riches of the continent, mining was very limited.

A view overlooking Mineral del Chico.

facing page
The lovely central garden of Immaculate Concepcion.

After the conquest, however, mines opened across New Spain; the focus was the extraction of gold, silver, lead, copper, zinc, iron, sulfur, barium, and fluorite. In rich Hidalgo State, abundant deposits were discovered in towns such as Mineral del Chico, Real del Monte, and Pachuca.

Mines had surprisingly little association with the Royal College of Mining, the root of many invaluable scientific discoveries. This organization was presided over by Fausto de Elhuyar, the respected discoverer of the chemical element tungsten. Also at this institution was Andrés del Rio, an excellent chemist and disciple of Antoine Lavoisier, the father of modern chemistry, as well as the Abbe Haüy, considered the father of crystallography.

Del Rio explored the deposits of Hidalgo, and in 1810 discovered a new element he called *eritrono* (erythonium). Del Rio sent samples of his discovery to the notable Prussian naturalist and scientist Alexander Von Humboldt. While initially doubtful that it was a new element, he sent samples around Europe.

Thirty years later, the Swedish chemist N. G. Sefstrom announced the discovery of vanadium. But later studies indicated that vanadium was the same element as the eritrono discovered by del Rio. Though the scientific community proposed that the new element be named rionio in honor of del Rio, it was given the name vanadium in spite of del Rio's desire to name the new element after a mexican deity.

Del Rio went on to make three significant contributions: he published many books on mining, including a book on mineralogy in the Americas; he taught literally hundreds of miners; and he produced the first Mexican steel. The discoverer of vanadium never could have imagined that the new chemical element found in Hidalgo would one day be considered indispensable to modern existence—it turned out to be crucial for the chemical formation of black gold, or petroleum. In industry as well, it is important for producing steel, which led the iconic automaker Henry Ford to say, "If vanadium didn't exist, there wouldn't have been a car."

Mineral del Chico is a beautiful mining town nestled among leafy forests of pines, oaks, and oyameles, all within the El Chico National Park. Exploring the natural beauty of the park on foot is enjoyable. It is also possible to go mountain climbing, rappelling, fishing, and horseback riding. Attractions of the region are the *peñas*—huge, oddly shaped rock formations located at over nine thousand feet, of which Las Monjas is the most famous. There are picturesque cascades and ample wildlife. Perhaps the greatest treasure of this mining town is the incredible panorama, like a piece of silver placed in the heart of the country.

In contrast to Hidalgo's mostly melancholy landscape of weeping-willow valleys, entangled cashew trees, and agave cacti for making pulque, El Chico is an enchanting mountain town in the clouds featuring splendid forest vegetation. The sinuous rock-paved streets come together in the elegant central plaza, which is surrounded by beautiful buildings from the mining era as well as a simple church with red cupolas. The architectural style of this picturesque town is based on adobe and stone construction integrated with wood and metal. El Chico is a good place to enjoy Hidalgo State's interesting cuisine, which integrates pre-Hispanic elements such as the exquisite ant larvae as well as *chinicuiles*, all accompanied by the rarely found alcoholic beverage known as pulque.

HUASCA
A SILVER BONANZA

DURING THE CONQUEST OF MEXICO, the intense economic activity generated by the mining towns required the development of an efficient system to provision the workers. It also required an efficient plant to treat and transform the silver after being mined. These plants were called *beneficios de minerales*. Huasca was founded to meet these two needs for the prosperous mines of Real del Monte and Pachuca in Hidalgo State. Before the discovery of silver, the haciendas here were devoted to agriculture and cattle ranching.

Even though the silver veins in this area were very rich, relatively little pure silver was extracted. Smelting proved too costly; as an alternative to increase productivity, the miners introduced a revolutionary system called amalgamation, a "system of patios," to treat the silver. Fine-ground silver was spread on top of paved spaces (patios), and then mercury, water, and salt were added. The silver was then left undisturbed for months. Gradually the silver thickened and afterward was washed in large tanks where circulating oars separated the dirt and impurities from the mercury and silver; the final product was pure silver. Later, the mercury was removed and recycled. Thanks to this method, mining productivity was extremely high in New Spain.

Because of its unrivaled land and climate, four large haciendas were established in Huasca in 1760 to implement this complex process. Their names were all under the surname Regla but were individually known as Santa María, San Francisco Xavier, San Antonio, and San Miguel. The owner of the mine was Don Pedro Romero de Terreros, Count of Regla, thus the name Regla. He was a friendly entrepreneur responsible for the explosive growth of the region, as well as an important national figure.

Among other accomplishments, he founded the Nacional Monte de Piedad (National Pawn Shop), in 1775. In its first year, seventeen thousand transactions took place, equal to a quarter of the population of Mexico City at that time. Today it continues to help 25 percent of the people of Mexico with more than twenty million transactions annually.

Another important person in Huasca was Romero de Terreros, the richest man in New Spain. He was a constant source of money for the viceregal government. Over the years he donated sufficient money to build over twenty orphanages, convents, schools, and hospitals. To honor him, King Charles III presented him with a warship with eighty cannons that was used against the English during the Battle of Trafalgar. Don Pedro Romero de Terreros died in 1781 in his Huasca hacienda, San Miguel Regla.

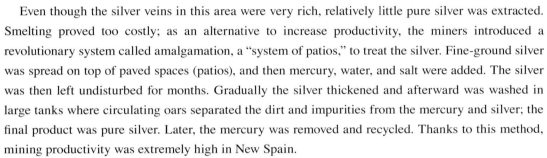

Remains of silver-treatment basins at the former Hacienda of San Miguel Regla.

facing page
A lone mining stack stands like a sentry on Cruz Lake.

The beautiful Hacienda de San Miguel still maintains its regal ambience. Preserved there are the grand arcades that were part of the patios and ovens where silver was treated, as well as the remains of earthenware vessels. The hacienda has been converted into a hotel surrounded by forests and lakes. Nearby is the equally beautiful Hacienda de Santa Maria de Regla, the home of Don Pedro Romero de Terreros. It was the first place to treat silver and later became a distillery. Here, amidst a labyrinth of patios, ovens, and large earthenware jars rises a tall tower. Also preserved at the hacienda is a beautiful baroque chapel.

Huasca is a beautiful town with slope-roofed stone houses. But above all, the town is known for its interesting natural feature—basalt prisms that are embedded in a nearby gorge. These incredibly uniform columns of basaltic rock are washed over by waters from the nearby San Antonio dam. The first examples are a geological phenomenon of singular beauty. Only a few of these fascinating formations—a result of the rapid freezing of volcanic lava—exist around the world. The basalt columns in Mexico were discovered by Alexander Von Humboldt, an explorer who is considered by many to be the father of modern geography. It is possible to fish near Huasca and to partake in excursions to Pena del Aire and the Metzitlán region, where the magnificent Ex-Convento de Los Santo Reyes is located.

MINERAL DEL MONTE
SILVER LABYRINTHS

REAL DEL MONTE'S RICH MINERAL DEPOSITS OF GOLD AND SILVER were discovered by the Otomíe indigenous people, who understood their potential and established trading routes that crisscrossed the region between Hidalgo and Mexico-Tenochtitlán. During the conquest, the colonizers focused attention on these deposits. Mineral del Monte, the highest town in Mexico at nearly ten thousand feet, was created to aid in the extraction process. At first, the mining went slowly because the tunnels were constantly being flooded; many mines were abandoned.

Later, at the end of the seventeenth century, Pedro Romero de Terreros, the Count of Regla, reactivated the mines after the construction of a tunnel for draining water. When he discovered how rich these deposits were, he applied efficient methods of production; in a short time he amassed the largest fortune in colonial Mexico. After his death, mining activity slowed at Real del Monte. In the nineteenth century the mine was leased to a British company, and 350 workers from Cornwall, England, came to the wilds of Hidalgo to mine. At that time Cornwall was considered the international capital of copper mining, producing two-thirds of the world's output.

Production at Real del Monte returned to its original level thanks to the capable Cornish miners. Moreover, they enriched the culture of the town. They performed plays in the plazas, where the characteristic English sense of humor was in evidence. There was even an increase in the number of clowns. The most famous clown was Ricardo Bell, who was not only considered a symbol of the era because of his brilliant acting but also because he was a favorite of Mexico's president Porfirio Díaz. Soccer also came to Mexico because of the Cornish miners; Real del Monte was the location of the first soccer game ever played in the country. These miners also brought traditional foods, including Cornish pasties, their delicious lunchtime fare of puff pastry turnovers filled with meat and potatoes. Today, pasties are a part of the regional cuisine, though they have been enhanced with a variety of Mexican additions including red and green *mole* sauces, *picadillo*, *frijoles*, and sweets like *creme* or *arroz con leche*.

The town of Mineral del Monte entered the twentieth century at a new high point. In the midst of the turbulent social struggles during Mexico's revolution, the mining activities continued to expand and by the 1930s, Mineral del Monte became the biggest silver-producing town in the world. It is estimated that it has been responsible for 6 percent of all the silver that has been mined worldwide in the last 450 years.

Sitting atop a hill one can see the tall chimneys of the Acosta mine, today part of a museum. A beautiful panoramic view of Mineral del Monte—including its plazas and its parish church—can be enjoyed from this vantage point. The parish church is named in honor of the Virgin of the Assumption. Construction began in the sixteenth century, but it took years to finish and features a late baroque style. The town, which has been named a *pueblo magico* of Mexico, features another curiosity, the rather nostalgic English cemetery. According to tradition, the tombs are oriented toward the east—that is, toward Great Britain. Without a doubt, a visit to Hidalgo, a state known for its vast mining activities and for the beverage *pulque*, would be incomplete without a stop in this beautiful place, which came to be Mexico's primary silver producer.

Today's Mineral del Monte was formed because of the silver bonanza. Labyrinthlike paved streets rise and fall haphazardly across the hills that connect the mines to the picturesque town with its red-tile-roofed multicolored homes. Side streets and stairways lead to beautiful plazas and gardens made lush due to the frequent rains. Time seems to have stood still here, a feeling emphasized by the remnants of the previous century that can be seen daily, including burros delivering goods and residents gathering together to celebrate their traditional festivals of Silver and Sweets. Talented artists create surprisingly beautiful creations using silver, wood, clay, and textiles. The sound of pickaxes and shovels can still be heard in the mines; and to this day, miners still enjoy their traditional lunchtime food, Cornish-pastylike turnovers with a Mexican flare.

T U L A
MESSENGERS OF THE SUN

Tula, or Tollan as it was called by the natives, means "place near the tules." It is located in the state of Hidalgo in central Mexico. Tula is an important archaeological site, especially because the city existed many centuries before its formal founding in A.D. 900. According to great interpreter of Mexican culture Laurette Sejourne, Tula was the final city in the great Toltec tradition. This civilization was based on the cult of Quetzalcóatl, who was unlike other gods but was fundamental to all ancient-Mexican religions.

While the other gods incarnated natural forces such as the earth, the sun, and the rain, Quetzalcóatl was an extremely human deity. Contradictory myths surround him—from being a creator of the universe to a Christlike figure and benefactor of humanity who gave us the gift of corn. According to another myth, Quetzalcóatl was a white man with a beard who came from the east as a victor over his enemies and who, after leaving his land, promised to return. During the colonial era, certain Christian clerics tried to link him with the apostle Thomas who had come to preach the gospel, but the archaeological evidence does not support this theory. Astronomically, Quetzalcóatl is identified with the planet Venus, the morning star.

His name meant the "plumed serpent," a symbol of the union between spirit and matter: the beautiful quetzal bird represented the former and the serpent the latter. A deity who was a great teacher of the arts and of civilization, he was also the founder of ancient Tollan, which some compare to Teotihuacán. There is a beautiful temple in his honor at the site. Quetzalcóatl is the god of the spirit and a great civilizer who confronted his rival, the malevolent Tezcatlipoca, a capricious god of chance and a devil-like spirit. While Tezcatlipoca was in favor of human sacrifice, Quetzalcóatl rejected this practice and in its place preached spiritual perfection through artistic creation. This is why "Toltec" also came to mean a good artist who was following the directives of Quetzalcóatl. Even though he was primarily venerated in central Mexico, the cult of Quetzalcóatl was later integrated into Mayan culture. The Mayans called him Kukulcán; his presence transformed Mayan art, as can be seen at Chichén Itzá.

The Palace of the Columns with Tula beyond it.

facing page
Impressive stone sculptures of warrior figures known as "Los Atlantes."

Tula's Palacio de las Columnas and the Palacio Quemado were not used as residences but had an administrative function or were markets. It is noteworthy that there were two ball courts, an atypical feature among ancient Mexican cities, which usually had only one. This indicates the importance of this game in Tula. The players represented the "Lord of the Night" who challenged the sun to play. He was victorious and beheaded his victim, interring the head at the west. The sun, represented by a rubber ball, had to pass through a vertical ring that represented the devouring mouth of the earth. There was also a *Tzompantli*, or altar, on which victims were to be sacrificed. This *Tzompantli* revealed the decadence inherent when human sacrifice triumphed over Quetzalcóatl's doctrine.

At a less mythic level, the conflict between Quetzalcóatl and Tezcatlipoca could symbolize the eternal fight in Mexico between the agricultural tribes who civilized central Mexico and the constant invasions by the savage tribes who came from the north. It was a fight between civilization and barbarity, between knowledge and ignorance.

Tula was the capital of a large and extensive empire. Toplitzin, its founder was a priest of Quetzalcóatl. There are a number of buildings that date from Tula's high point: the Templo de los Atlantes, or the "House of the Lord of the Morning Star", which consists of a five-level temple with beautiful sculptures. At the upper section of Quetzalcóatl's building was a covered temple whose columns have survived and were similar to the famous atlantes or caryatids. Representations of the god Tlahuizcalpantecutli, these columns are nearly sixteen feet high and are adorned as celestial warriors. Their arms hang down straight at their sides, holding their weapons, including dart throwers and arrows. They are ornamented with breastplates in the form of stylized butterflies, as if they were messengers of the sun with crowns; on their backs are solar discs.

MALINALCO
HOME OF THE EAGLES

MALINALCO HAS TWO REMARKABLE SITES—ONE HISTORIC, THE OTHER ARTISTIC. The former is an archaeological area called Cuauhcalli ("house of the eagles") dating from the Aztec empire; the other is a monastery and church dating from the conquest. Cuauhcalli has a curious construction that is unique in pre-Colombian architecture. It was built as a covered temple and the interior has a type of semicircular sidewalk with a jaguar in the center and eagles on either side. In the center of this enclosure is another eagle with a carved-out depression where the hearts of sacrificial victims were placed.

Even though the temples of Malinalco are not as spectacular as the pyramids found in other places, the primary temple with its rock-eagle depression is exceptional. The Aztec practice of human sacrifice was a central aspect of its religion, a practice far removed from the humanism of Quetzalcóatl—the god of Teotihuacán. Aztecs believed that their gods had to be fed with flesh and precious fluids, which made the human heart and human blood of supreme value. It is this belief that transformed the Aztecs into an imperialist culture bent on war.

An important part of an Aztec warrior's strength came from being part of a military order, similar to those of Europe such as the Knights Templar, the Teutonic knights, the Knights of Malta, or even the Japanese samurai. In these elite units, members had to undergo initiation ceremonies. It is believed that Malinalco may have been one of these initiation sites. It is regrettable that we have no record of the rituals that changed young warriors into a military aristocracy. The "warriors of the eagle" and the "warriors of the jaguar", each with their typical helmets sculpted to symbolically represent the animal they "imitated". These warriors were people of privilege in a society where religion and war were so closely linked.

The Aztec state was headed by an emperor but it is clear by the constant state of war that it was not primarily about increasing the imperial territory; even during times of peace there were wars, fought solely to obtain prisoners to be sacrificed to the Aztec gods. In the classical era when Teotihuacán was the cultural capital, sacrifice was only spiritual in nature and artistic expression was the principal teaching of the god Quetzalcóatl, the plumed serpent.

A view of Santa Maria Chapel.

facing page
The exceptional painted Franciscan dining room at the former San Miguel Convent.

Malinalco is located in a magnificent mountain setting, close to a national park and a popular religious pilgrimage destination, Chalma, where a "miraculous" Christ is celebrated. Though the Spanish conquest interrupted Aztec expansion, the archaeological remains here are a testament to Aztec power. Malinalco is surrounded by mountains so it was not well suited for a major city to develop. Its isolation, however, favored its development as a cultic site constructed to carry out esoteric ceremonies of initiation for warriors of the jaguar and the serpent.

A monastery, completed around 1580, has several magnificent frescoes that incorporate as decorative elements important plants and animals of the region deftly intermixed with Christian symbols. These frescoes include important medicinal and traditional plants of the indigenous culture. Medicine was a rather advanced science in the pre-Hispanic world and herbs, flowers, and curative roots were used. This science was sufficiently advanced that Mexican doctors are now studying its traditions. Included in the frescoes are characteristic animals of Mexico including parrots, lizards, and monkeys climbing through the trees.

TEOTIHUACÁN
CITY OF THE GODS

NEAR THE TOWN OF ACOLMAN ARE TWO MARVELOUS PLACES WELL WORTH VISITING: the archaeological site of Teotihuacán and the Augustinian monastery. Each place represents the best art from its respective era—Mexico's distant past (Teotihuacán) and the culture brought to Mexico by the Spanish conquest (San Augustin de Acolman monastery).

Depiction of the Crucifixion in Acolman's convent.

facing page
Teotihuacán's glorious Pyramid of the Sun.

Teotihuacán is one of the most sacred sites anywhere in the Americas, equal to that of Machu Picchu in Peru. Without a doubt, it is the philosophical and cultural center of Mexico and began to flourish as an imperial city from about 200 B.C.; at its zenith it had around one hundred thousand inhabitants. It was abandoned around the year A.D. 800. The Aztecs arrived in central Mexico about three hundred years after Teotihuacán was abandoned and considered it to be a sacred place. It was also in Teotihuacán that the divine benefactor of humanity—the god Quetzalcóatl—lived.

Teotihuacán has a ceremonial area that is built around a grand celebratory north-south–running boulevard—the famous Avenue of the Dead. It passes in front of the Pyramid of the Sun, certainly one of the most important in central Mexico, and ends in front of the Pyramid of the Moon. Nearby is the aptly named Grand Plaza, the *Ciudadela* (Citadel), as well as two smaller pyramids dedicated to Tlaloc, the god of rain, and to Quetzalcoatl.

The pyramids of the sun and moon are built on a series of slopes and terraces based on horizontal planes. No vertical lines are visible and the stairways on the pyramids slowly climb upward, narrowing the higher they go. Teotihuacán was built from an astronomical plan and its central feast was the day of the spring equinox. On this day, when "god visited the city," thousands of people came to celebrate the beginning of spring.

San Augustin de Colman monastery was built in 1539 and has an interesting roof dating from that time, which was reinforced in the seventeenth century along with the building's walls. Its facade is one of the most authentic examples of Spanish plateresque style (a style based on early Italian Renaissance traditions).

It is said that an artist was brought from Europe to design and oversee the monastery's construction. The cloister has medieval touches that tie together this period and the Renaissance in a new way. The monastery also has some of the most beautiful murals of the era. These were created based on books brought from Europe, and the results are quite sophisticated. Outside in the atrium is a crucifix—the heart of this space and a key to the evangelization of the local indigenous community.

Though the sun and the moon fought for primacy at Teotihuacán, reigning along with them was also a redemptive god, the great benefactor of humanity, Quetzalcóatl, who was a patron of the arts and a great moral teacher as well. To understand Teotihuacán's greatness and significance, it is important to understand the myths of Quetzalcóatl, whose name meant the "plumed serpent," a powerful symbol of the unity between spirit (the plumage of a bird) and matter (the serpent), a combination that resolves the fundamental philosophical problem of the union of opposites—and a symbol which, in turn, represented the harmony of the world.

Quetzalcóatl's pyramid in Teotihuacán is one of the most important monuments in Mexico. It is next to the great plaza named "the Stronghold"; at thirteen-hundred square feet, it is one of the largest spaces built in the pre-Columbian era. The pyramid is made up of a series of sculpted panels that show a serpent in motion as well as large panels of the god Quetzalcóatl and of Tlaloc, the god of the rains. Tlaloc was one of the principal gods personified as a natural phenomenon both in the Mayan world as well as in the center of Mexico. The symbolism of the god Quetzalcóatl is extremely complex; *cóatl* means "twin of a serpent," while *Quetzalcóatl* is the divine twin of the planet Venus, the morning star. It is because Quetzalcóatl disappeared into the sea prior to his ascension to the skies to become the "morning star" that various marine symbols such as seashells are included in Teotihuacán's sculptures.

TEPOTZOTLÁN
COLONIAL-ERA BUILDINGS AND ART

THIS TOWN TO THE NORTH OF MEXICO CITY HAS A MAGNIFICENT NATIONAL MUSEUM FEATURING COLONIAL ART. It is housed in what was once the seminary of the Jesuit fathers, whose history is intimately bound with the best of Mexican religious art. The Jesuits arrived in Mexico in 1572 and were among the three great religious orders—the Franciscans, the Dominicans, and the Augustinians—who worked to convert the native peoples of Mexico (there was a period of fifty years between the conquest of Mexico and the arrival of the first eight Jesuit fathers). In 1580 five Jesuits founded a house of studies in Tepotzotlán to teach indigenous languages.

San Francisco Xavier Church and the National Museum of the Vice-Royalty in Tepotzotlán.

facing page
An extraordinary baroque altarpiece in San Francisco Xavier Church.

In 1606 a wealthy admirer of the Jesuits donated money that enabled them to construct a novitiate in what was the Patio of the Cisterns. They were also able to build their first chapel where a retablo, an image of a saint painted on a flat wooden panel—in this case a copy of a Roman painting of the Madonna attributed to no less than the Apostle Luke himself—was installed. This was the beginning of the incredible collection of art the Jesuits assembled in Tepotzotlán.

Construction of the local church began in 1670. In the meantime, a rich priest from nearby Querétaro gave them money to both enlarge the novitiate as well as construct a seeming curiosity, the Casa de Loreto. It is believed that this is the house in which Jesus and his family lived in Nazareth; it was converted by the first Christians into an oratory.

In A.D. 320, the Empress Helen—mother of Constantine—built a large basilica above the house. But when the Turks took control of Jerusalem in 1291, it is said that the angels miraculously delivered the house to a more secure location in what is now Croatia. But this place was not deemed safe enough and, once again, the house was delivered to a forest in Italy—a place that became the town of Loreto. Initially the popes viewed this miracle with skepticism, but eventually it was accepted and this sacred house was later re-surfaced in marble and decorated with statues by the great Donato Bramante.

Because the Jesuits were also devoted to Our Lady of Loreto, they decided to build a replica of this sacred house in Tepotzotlán in 1733. The construction of the church with its rich facades and tower was completed in 1762, but the Jesuits were not to enjoy their new church for long; in 1767 the Spanish king expelled them from all his territories and Tepotzotlán was abandoned.

Tepotzotlán's national museum of colonial art is one of the most important in Mexico, with collections of paintings, sculpture, and a wide variety of sacred objects. But the church's cloisters and chapels are where the most beautiful art can be found. Featured inside are works by the most famous colonial painters such as Cristobal de Villalpando and his scenes from the life of Saint Ignatius, as well as pieces by Miguel Cabrera, José Padilla, José Ibarra, and Juan Rodrígues Juárez. The changing room of the Virgin merits special attention. This room is a special place dedicated to changing the liturgical vesture of the statue of Our Lady of Loreto.

The retablo is the high point of the late-Mexican baroque, and the most beautiful examples are found in Tepotzotlán. The central retablo is dedicated to Saint Francis Xavier. Other prominent spots are occupied by the Virgin Mary, Saint Joseph, and Saint Anne. The retablo contains seventy-nine heads of angels and saints, fifty-two complete angels, and other images that add up to one hundred thirty-eight sculptures in total. Another retablo is dedicated to the Virgin of Guadalupe, while the Epistle side has a statue dedicated to Saint Ignatius Loyola. Baroque artists were able to sculpt angels and seraphims as if they were birds flying in paradise. The lateral walls have two other notable retablos— one dedicated to Saint Joseph, the other to the Virgin of Light. These were the last to be constructed and influences from the French rococo of Louis XV are evident.

VALLE DE BRAVO
A VALLEY AND ITS LAKE

THERE ARE MANY MEXICOS IN THIS COUNTRY. Of course, the country is called Mexico and the capital is Mexico City, although Mexicans refer to their capital as México. To add to the confusion, there is also a state named Mexico with a capital, Toluca. Valle de Bravo is in the state of Mexico. In English, as well as in other languages such as German or Italian, the same word is used for the city and the state, and the places are distinguished by adding the word city—or *stadt* or *citte,* in German and Italian respectively. Only in French is the clear difference made between Le Mexique, the country, and Mexico, the capital city. I imagine no one wants to complicate life further by referring to the "state" of Mexico.

But the state of Mexico surrounds the city of México, which is, like Washington, D.C., actually a federal district. Due to its immense urban sprawl, areas to the west, the north, and the east, as well as a significant portion of the capital itself, are actually part of the state of Mexico—not the city. This vast urban area has little in common with the state proper, since the state itself is one of the most varied and beautiful in the country. Located within its borders are tall mountains, forests, archaeological zones, colonial monuments, and interesting towns like Valle de Bravo.

Many different tribes populated Valle de Bravo, which bordered the Tarasco empire, until 1432 when the Aztec emperor Axayácatl conquered the region. The best examples of Aztec architecture, such as the magnificent Tenayuca pyramid, are in the state of Mexico. This area contains the only complete remains of the Aztec's powerful architecture, much of which was displayed in the Aztec capital, Mexico-Tenochtitlán, and later destroyed by the Spanish. In Mexico-Tenochtitlán the Spanish razed the Aztec buildings so they could build their colonial town on top of the remains of the old empire. But surviving structures reveal that, in contrast to Mayan or Oaxacan architecture, Aztec buildings were very simple.

For centuries, life in Valle de Bravo was typical of other towns in the region. However, it was heavily bombarded during the revolution. Three armies—those of Villa, Carranza, and Zapata—all fought for control of it at various times. The town was almost completely ruined, but in 1937 the government became interested in building hydroelectric dams. It initiated a project near Valle de Bravo that created a five-thousand acre artificial lake. Completed in 1946, the project changed the destiny of "the Valley," as locals call it. The lake complemented the beauty of the area. It was the town's good fortune that the lake became an attractive tourist destination for the residents of nearby Mexico City, who loved this *pueblo mágico.*

A view overlooking scenic Valle de Bravo.

facing page
A panorama of Valle de Bravo and its lake.

Apart from the many sports activities offered, Valle de Bravo's charm is a big draw. Its peaceful provincial atmosphere is reminiscent of Mexico's other mountain and forest towns. Its traditional architecture, combining stone walls and adobe with wood and red-tile roofs, has been re-interpreted respectfully by its new rich, modern inhabitants who have built retreats with large gardens as an escape from the hectic life of Mexico City. These mansions have minimized the excesses of modern architecture to better blend in with the traditional atmosphere of the Valley. These mansions combine old and new: traditional crafts and rustic furniture are mixed with the occasional contemporary objects, creating a felicitous look.

Valle de Bravo combines two very attractive points. It has a traditional feel, with its mountain architecture and natural serenity, but the Valley is also a place to participate in modern sports activities that have developed both on the lake as well as in the mountains that surround the town. Nearby Peña del Príncipe is a place to enjoy a magnificent view of the lake, and it is also where people parasail over the Valley. However, the preferred sport here is sailing. There are eighteen nautical clubs at the lake for different types of sailing. It is also possible to fish, water ski, wind surf, and jet-ski. Avándaro is near Valle de Bravo; the lake is complemented by its forests and waterfall, and it adds to the pleasant atmosphere of the region.

COYOACÁN
THE HOME OF FRIDA AND DIEGO

Mexico's heartland is known as the Valley of Mexico. The Aztecs arrived there in the fourteenth century and built a floating city (it was built above a lake), which would later become Mexico City. In 1332 a tribe from the region arrived in the southern part of the valley and founded a pueblo named Coyoacán. The Aztecs hadn't arrived at the time it initially was founded and the city prospered. By the time the Spanish conquistadores came there were around six thousand homes and various pyramids built for religious purposes.

After the conquest, Coyoacán was chosen by Hernán Cortés as his temporary capital. Cortés built his first house there and established it as the first formal, official city in Mexico. A grand plaza was built and for several years Coyoacán was the capital. In colonial times, Coyoacán was converted into a charming village visited by affluent residents of Mexico City. During the nineteenth and twentieth centuries, Coyoacán maintained its individual identity but was eventually subsumed by Mexico City. But Coyoacán has fought hard to defend its atmosphere of a privileged town. Today, numerous artists, writers, and intellectuals live there, making it a charming bohemian enclave. Among the foreigners who sought refuge there was Leon Trotsky, who was unable to escape assassination by Stalin's agents.

Calle Real, once the main street of Coyoacán, is today called Francisco Sosa. It is here that the most important buildings are concentrated, including palaces such as the Casa Alvarado and the Casa de Ordaz, as well as smaller houses that have been converted into museums. The street leading to the main plaza is spectacular, and it is this plaza that is the heart of town, with it cafés, bookstores, theaters, and open-air markets. Saint John the Baptist, built by the Franciscans, is the principal church and is also located on the plaza. Cortés's house—one of the first Spanish homes constructed in Mexico—is near the church.

Coyoacán is a great walking city, with many streets to explore and wonderful plazas to encounter, such as La Conchita and Santa Catarina. Close to the main church is the national museum of popular culture. In the neighboring Churubusco area one also finds an interesting museum: the Museum of the Interventions. Built in an old monastery, this museum is dedicated to remembering the aggression or invasions throughout Mexico's history and detailing the country's political evolution.

The doorway of La Casa Azul, the home of renowned painter Frida Kahlo.

facing page
A view of San Juan Bautista Church from Centenario Garden.

One important relationship seems to dominate Coyoacán: the creative and tempestuous one between Diego Rivera and Frida Kahlo. Rivera gave Coyoacán the magnificent Anahuacalli Museum, designed and built in an Aztec style. It was supposed to house murals that he was eventually unable to paint. Today it displays a collection of close to sixty thousand archaeological remains. Kahlo's beautiful home is here. It is painted with vibrant Mexican colors and is filled with her furniture and artwork.

A must-see is the nearby University City, known in Mexico as CU. Construction began in 1950 on a twenty-eight-hundred-square-mile field of lava. The most important architects in Mexico participated in its construction, which took four years to complete. In its time, the CU was considered the most attractive modern campus in the world. Among its most important featured works is Juan O'Gorman's fabulous grand mosaic built from colored rocks, which decorates the enormous walls of the central library. Diego Rivera designed mosaics for the stadium.

TLAXCALA
JEWEL OF THE MEXICAN BAROQUE

TLAXCALA, WHERE THE BEAUTIFUL OCOTLÁN CHURCH IS LOCATED, is one of the most interesting places in Mexico. Prior to the conquest, Tlaxcala was a free state. It was founded in the fourteenth century as an independent republic and was governed by four senators who reached decisions by consensus. This political organization was unique to Mexico, in stark contrast to the absolute monarchies of the Aztecs. Tlaxcalans fought the Aztecs to maintain their independence and were always victorious. While gaining great fame as warriors, the Tlaxcalans were also well known as artists and musicians.

In 1519, however, Hernán Cortés arrived and quickly decided to conquer the Aztec empire, then ruled by the powerful Montezuma. Cortés formed alliances with the leaders of coastal tribes and organized a mixed army of indigenous peoples and Spaniards. Arriving at the border of the Republic of Tlaxcala, Cortés sent an ambassador to invite the Tlaxcalans to form a military alliance. The Tlaxcalan senate deliberated, but decided to fight the Spanish instead. While the war had both high and low points for both sides, the superiority of European weaponry was eventually decisive. To seal the alliance, several important Tlaxcalans were baptized while several Spanish captains married natives. Cortés continued his march to the Aztec capital, where with the help of the Tlaxcalans, he defeated the Aztecs. The Spanish gradually converted this place into a beautiful colonial city.

In 1537 one of the first of four monasteries built in Mexico—Saint Francis—was constructed there. This monastery has a beautiful carved roof and is one of the best-preserved examples of Mudejar, or Arab, design in the country. It has a uniquely Mexican feature—an open-air church. These were constructed because the large numbers of converts could not be contained in a normal church, and instead Mass was celebrated in the open air. The venerable municipal palace is a stolid building maintaining an atmosphere reminiscent of the era of conquest.

Pre-Columbian murals in Cacaxtla.

facing page
Majestic Our Lady of Ocotlán Church with locals selling their wares in the plaza.

Tlaxcala is one of those towns whose history must be known if it is to be fully appreciated. For many Mexicans, the Tlaxcalans were justified in allying themselves with the Spanish to fight against their traditional enemies, the Aztecs. For others, this decision by the Tlaxcalans was an act of treachery against their country, though in fact this concept was European for the indigenous only though in terms of their tribes. However, it was only later that some of the native realized the danger that had arrived. Today, however, Tlaxcala is a tranquil and pleasant place where the dramatic past bothers no one. Today, the legacy of the Indians flourishes in their art work full of life and color such as the beautiful women's dresses.

In 1975 an archaeological site was discovered at Cacaxtla, near Tlaxcala. It dates from between A.D. 700 and 900. Cacaxtla consists of a series of buildings built in the indigenous style: new buildings were simply built on top of older buildings, a technique that was used both for regular buildings as well as pyramids. As a result, many objects that had been hidden have survived, as have the remains of murals. To preserve the entire adobe-constructed archaeological area as well as the murals, a metal structure was built to cover the entire site.

The late-baroque style was well-received in Mexico; as a result, the most exceptional examples are found in towns with large indigenous populations.
This is true of Ocotlán, built on a hill overlooking Tlaxcala. The church there, Our Lady of Ocotlán, is the work of an exceptional artist, Francisco Miguel. Ocotlán reaches the highest level of visual richness found in the Mexican baroque. The interior contains retablos of gold-covered wood; the magnificent facade, flanked by two high bell towers, is not made of stone, as it appears, but instead is constructed of brick and mortar.

CUERNAVACA
CORTÉS'S PALACE AND GARDENS

A portion of the Diego Rivera mural in the Palace of Cortés.

facing page
The imposing cathedral in downtown.

TODAY CUERNAVACA IS A FAVORITE WEEKEND GETAWAY FOR MEXICO CITY RESIDENTS, many of whom have second homes here. While quiet, traditional Cuernavaca lives on, development has imposed aspects of a modern city. Though it is the capital of the state of Morelos, Cuernavaca is most famous for being the "place of eternal spring." It earned this name for both being in the tropics and at an altitude of five thousand feet. It has a mild climate—perfect for growing lush gardens—and is a haven for artists.

Hernán Cortés wrote about the beauty of Cuernavaca in letters to King Carlos V, who in turn ceded him the land. The town itself was eventually named Cuernavaca because Cortés was unable to pronounce the original name of the site, Cuauhnahuac, which meant "a place near the woods." Perhaps a better name would have been the "City of Gardens," because of the famous gardens of Don Manuel Borda, the priest son of the famous miner from Taxco, Don José de la Borda. Now named the Borda Gardens, they were used by the Emperor Maximilian as a refuge from the multiple preoccupations of his ill-fated empire. In 1910, Plancarte—a bishop who loved archaeology—discovered a stratum from the Aztec era. He then concluded he had discovered the mythical Tamoanchan, said to be the site of their paradise.

Cuernavaca has played a role in the national history of Mexico. It is the birthplace of Morelos, one of the heroes of the independence movement (thus the name of the state). Later, the revolutionary hero Emiliano Zapata fought here for the return of land to the indigenous population. Zapata was later betrayed and killed in an ambush, but his ideals live on in Mexican politics.

Cuernavaca is best enjoyed for its hospitality, a place that invites visitors to rest and relax and—if possible—spend time in one of the small hotels decorated with the best of Mexican taste. Cuernavaca is rich in cultural attractions; after the cathedral, the most important building is the Palace of Cortés, one of the oldest public buildings in the Americas. Today, it is home to an archaeological museum featuring splendid Diego Rivera murals. Rivera's fame has been eclipsed by that of his wife, Frida Kahlo, a portion of whose work can be seen in the Robert Brady house located across the street from the cathedral. Brady was an American artist who collected paintings by leading artists such as Kahlo, Rufino Tamayo, and Miguel Covarrubias.

A remarkable building of Cuernavaca is the Cathedral. A revolutionary Bishop—Sergio Méndez Arceo—

The Franciscans arrived in Cuernavaca eight years after the conquest and immediately began preparations to build a monastery. The heart of their complex was to be the cathedral, a convent, cloistered chapels, and an open-air chapel. The cathedral was decorated with murals that suffered the ravages of time, but in 1952 the cathedral was modernized and the original murals restored.

Diego Rivera's murals in the Palace of Cortés illustrate his greatest talents: a gift for fluid design and the use of color. At the same time, these murals reveal several of Rivera's obsessions. Because of his interest in indigenous history, his personal museum, El Anahuacalli, was built as a type of monument to pre-Hispanic art. In Cuernavaca, however, he created murals that express both the encounter of two civilizations and the brutal nature of the Spanish conquest. But curiously, we also see in these murals another interest of Rivera's—Italian Renaissance art.

worked with a young architect who also was a Benedictine monk to create a modern design. The mixture of ancient and contemporary in the cathedral is very unique. The interior was decorated with murals. One of them contains a historical curiosity: a Franciscan martyr who was killed in 1637 while preaching in Japan.

TEPOZTLÁN

A MONASTERY SURROUNDED BY MAGIC

The patio of the former Our Lady of the Nativity Convent.

AMONG THE MONASTERIES IN THE STATE OF MORELOS, La Natividad in Tepoztlán is more famous for the surrounding countryside than for its architecture. The great historian of colonial art—Don Manuel Toussaint— named Tepoztlán the most beautiful place in Mexico. Toussaint came to realize this during the 1930s, when a large part of Mexico was still untouched by progress, highways, urban sprawl and other trappings of modernity.

Toussaint himself was a type of missionary, giving himself the task of rediscovering ancient colonial sites that had been forgotten by his contemporaries; he published his discoveries in Mexico's most important paper under the title "Colonial Journeys." The resurgence of interest in Mexico's colonial past is in large part due to his efforts.

In turn, many artists discovered Tepoztlán. Among them was the poet Carlos Pellicer, who built a weekend house among the hills to which he invited friends. One of them, a landscape painter who had adopted a rather curious artistic name, "Dr. Atl," (Dr. Water) was then one of the great travelers of the Mexican countryside, especially the mountains and volcanoes. Because he was such an expert on the landscape, he was very skeptical of Pellicer's enthusiasm for Tepoztlán and its beauty; the poet frequently invited his friend to spend weekends there but these were declined. When the painter finally accepted, he ended up spending several years there. This is an example of the power Tepoztlán can have over artists.

Perhaps this is because the mountains that surround Tepoztlán and La Natividad are unusual. Mountain peaks and hills are smoothly formed, and they become even more so when covered by vegetation. It is an intimate landscape that exists on a more human scale than is typical of the geography of Mexico.

facing page
An incredible seed-decorated arch at the former convent.

At the end of the nineteenth century a pyramid was discovered among the hills and the entire region enjoys a reputation as a place of magic. El Tepozteco, as the mountain here is known, is a national park and would be sufficiently spectacular even without the famous sixteenth-century monastery nearby.

La Natividad was built by the Dominican fathers, who were known in Mexico for their work as architects and preachers. Construction of the monastery began in 1570 and was completed ten years later. The atrium is enormous and the art notable.

The monastery with its two solid floors maintains a certain military feel. The friars realized that even though the conquest was spiritual, without military support their work had no future. For this reason, the Spaniards of sixteenth-century Mexico were largely occupied by conquering the indigenous people, and it was a particularly bloody time. Later, almost as if an act of healing, the work of the friars—converting the Indians and bringing western culture to the land—brought peace. At least Tepoztlán's friars had one prize for their efforts: when they looked out the windows of their cells they were able to enjoy one of the most beautiful landscapes in Mexico.

Tepoztlán has, if not the most beautiful landscape in Mexico, certainly one with a unique personality.

The church's military ambience is strengthened by its two extremes: fierceness and ingenuity. Its stone castle with battlements accentuates its military character. The facade itself is delicate, and the door frame is of a finely crafted stone. Its central feature is a depiction of the Virgin with child above the moon. They are accompanied by two saints: Saint Dominic with his dog and Saint Catalina, with her heart—the seer and theologian. Together two enormous angels stand nearby like guards. The figure has the enchantment of the plateresque, the style of the Spanish Renaissance and, as its name indicates, the art of jewelers. In the entrance to the atrium is a detailed mosaic made with seeds.

TETELA DEL VOLCÁN
THE MONASTERY OF POPOCATÉPETL

MEXICO IS A VERY COMPLICATED COUNTRY. When one visits a small village it appears to have no significant history yet many civilizations have passed through it—a past that seems even more distant because there are no visible "footprints." To illustrate this point is Tetela del Volcán, originally a settlement of the Olmecs, the first great civilization of Mexico. These peoples flourished almost a thousand years before Christ. They are famous for their monumental stone heads and their cities, the first of which were in Mexico. Though the Olmecs came to Tetela with an important culture, it was the Toltecs, the followers of Quetzacoatl, who brought with them the teaching of this great spiritual master. It was this divine, mythic personality who promised the advent one day of a truly Indian world. And it was the Toltecs who built the nearby city of Teotihuacán with its monumental pyramids. Signs of the Olmec civilization no longer exist.

Shortly after the disappearance of the Toltecs in the early sixteenth century—other peoples who arrived and then disappeared without leaving a trace—the Spanish came. In 1521, even though the residents of Tetela del Volcán put up a heroic resistance against Hernán Cortés, his ferocious captain Pedro de Alvarado carried the day and subjugated the inhabitants for Spain's king.

Tetela is situated on the slopes of the Popocatépetl volcano in the middle of gorges, rivers, and waterfalls. This region is not only one of the most picturesque in Mexico, but it also brims with history. In addition, the village contains one of the most important monasteries along the "Route of the Monasteries," Saint John the Baptist, which was constructed in 1574 by Dominican friars. They were great builders and architects.

Saint John the Baptist is a typical sixteenth-century monastery that served an important role in the spiritual conquest of Mexico, just as the medieval monasteries served for the evangelization of Europe. In addition to being a retreat, it was the place where the new faith was preached so that the native peoples would reject their ancient gods for the doctrine of Christ. Finally, the monastery was a place to teach the values of European civilization as well as put the friars in contact with daily life in Mexico. In their gardens the friars planted both transplants from Europe as well as examples of local plants.

The area around Tetela del Volcán has a range of churches and monasteries, such as Hueyapan, Tepoztlán, Tlayacapan, Totolapan, Xumitepec, Zaualpan, Jonacatepec, Jantetelco and Ocuituco. All these monasteries around Popocatépetl were named UNESCO World Heritage sites in 1994. Many folkloric traditions in dance and in the design of clothing and textiles can still be found in the area.

Image of a bishop, as symbolized by the church he carries in his hand.

facing page
A fresco depicting a young martyr who was killed by spears.

Sixteenth-century Mexican temples and monasteries were generally decorated with frescoes. Taken from figures found in illustrated books, many of these murals were first produced in black and white, color was gradually incorporated. The function of these murals was to teach religion to recent converts. Walls of monasteries of the sixteenth century were usually completely painted—every inch of space decorated. Like all religious art, that of the monasteries used conventional symbols to identify the saints: Saint Peter with his keys and Saint Michael with his sword. Over time, the community gradually learned how to read this visual language.

Monasteries of the sixteenth century were solid and almost militarylike in feel—in their grand simplicity—however, their interior decoration was enormously sophisticated. This is especially true regarding monastery murals. It is almost as if the friars could not tolerate an unpainted surface and so every wall is filled with artistic decoration. In Tetela del Volcán its possible to see and admire murals that have been well restored. Generally done as frescoes, the themes are religious while at the same time being very decorative. Stylistically, this work dates from a time when the medieval was waning and the Renaissance was the preferred style.

XOCHICALCO
THE HOUSE OF THE FLOWERS

BEFORE THE SPANISH CONQUEST THERE WERE MANY EPOCHS AND EMPIRES IN MEXICAN HISTORY. But unlike other nations, Mexico did not have a continuous center of power that dominated the country. Only very late in its history was a "capital" founded; it was the city of Mexico-Tenochtitlán, which was the capital of the Aztec empire (and today the site of Mexico City). During the brutal Spanish conquest, this city was destroyed and left in ruins. Before this event, Mexico-Tenochtitlán included in its domain many cities and ceremonial centers.

While Mexico's history is often divided into certain periods such as primitive, pre-classical, and classical, this does not imply a strict artistic and cultural continuity. Forms of art did not pass seamlessly from older cultures to newer ones; the same was true for religion and the passing down of myths and rituals.

Xochicalco is an example of a civilization that flourished very late, about A.D. 650 and 900. This was later than the magisterial city Teotihuacán and much earlier than Mexico-Tenochtitlán, the imperial capital. We are as ignorant of the reasons for its appearance and growth as we are of its decline and disappearance.

The Xochicalco archaeological site cannot be understood without the context of its illustrious predecessor Teotihuacán, the sacred and magisterial city of ancient Mexico that had been abandoned for centuries. This most important city—the apex of absolute classicism—became a ghost town. It can be thought of as the city where the gods gathered together to create the world, since Teotihuacán was Quetzalcóatl's city. His is a figure that mixes aspects of both Christ and Prometheus and is symbolized by a plumed serpent. Is the synthesis of contraries with the material world represented by the serpent and the spirit by the plumed wings. Quetzalcóatl, the master of the arts and patron of artists, occupies the place of Venus in the heavens, the star and planet of the dawn.

Without Quetzalcóatl it is impossible to understand Xochicalco, an splendid city dedicated to his glory. Xochicalco's architecture was a more modern version of traditional building design, constructed years after the glory days of Teotihuacán.

These cities/ceremonial centers were built for the gods, not for people. People in the community lived outside of the ceremonial center in simple huts; stone buildings were reserved for the deities.

Quetzalcóatl's temple in Xochicalco.

facing page
An aerial view of Xochicalco's entire archaeological site.

On the top of a hill in Xochicalco, a ceremonial center was constructed with temples honoring both Quetzalcóatl and the stars as well as containing an offering room. In the southern part of the plaza there are temple basements and a boulevard that leads to a palace with its ceremonial baths. Close by is a ball court in the shape of an *I*, as well as an observatory. The observatory has a subterranean room with a chimney used to study the movement of the sun. Two days out of every year—in May and July—direct sunlight enters through a vertical aperture; it lights a hexagonal image on the floor.

Xochicalco's best-preserved and principal structure is a basement area covered in beautiful, sculpted flagstones. Its square building was a temple dedicated to Quetzalcóatl. Serpentine figures that seem to come alive adorn the walls. The higher walls have decorated cornices; they depict important people as well as astronomical information, including references to solar eclipses. From this evidence it is possible to deduce that heavenly observation and the measurement of time were great preoccupations of these civilizations. The platform has stairs that rise to the west and lead to the ceremonial center.

YECAPIXTLA
A MOORISH INFLUENCE

Morelos, a small state just south of Mexico City, is one of the most attractive regions in Mexico and features a wealth of colonial art. Known for its "Road of the Monasteries," Morelos has fourteen such buildings that were constructed during the sixteenth century; UNESCO has named these World Heritage sites. To understand the significance of these monasteries, it is important to remember that the sixteenth century was the era of the Spanish conquest in Mexico. After a bloody battle in 1521, the capital of the Aztec empire, the city of Mexico-Tenochtitlán, fell during an assault led by Hernán Cortés.

The Franciscans, the Dominicans, and the Augustinians built churches and monasteries from which they were able to preach to the communities. These buildings were unique, designed as churches and militarylike fortifications; even give this dichotomy, some are actually quite beautiful. The indigenous people understood that their gods had been defeated by the god of the white men, so successfully evangelizing them required sufficient space in the churches for the many new faithful to gather.

Stylistically, the monasteries of the sixteenth century incorporated medieval, Gothic, and Renaissance influences; in Spain this was called plateresque, or the silver style. But to complicate matters further, some of the buildings demonstrated the clear Arab influence of Moorish architecture, prompting comparisons with the Alhambra of Granada.

In a few of churches on the "Road of the Monasteries," such as the one in Yecapixtla, the Moorish influence is evident. The town had been governed by kings known as "the ones of the glittering nose"; they practiced a primitive form of piercing in which they put precious stones in their noses. This community had been very independent and even though it was near the Aztec empire, the great Montezuma had been unable to conquer it. This work was left to the conquistador Gonzalo de Sandoval, one of the more cruel among a group of very violent Spanish conquistadores. The Spanish took Yecapixtla in March 1521. Gomara, the great historian of the conquest, wrote that "the Yecapixtla river was running red with blood." Yecapixtla then became part of the marquisate that King Charles V gave to Hernán Cortés as a reward for his exploits.

To be awarded a Marquisate was one of the few prizes given by the king to the Conquistadores but this land was often not a contiguous territory but included parcels of that were often distant from one another. Its size was over 11,000 square kilometers and was full of enormous riches.

In 1540 construction of Yecapixtla's monastery was finished by Friar Jorge de Avila; during colonial times it was considered to be a magnificent work of art, expertly combining Renaissance and Moorish influences.

A Gothic-influenced rosette in Yecapixtla's monastery.

facing page
The Moorish-style patio of the former convent in Yecapixtla.

The "Road of the Monasteries," alongside which Yecapixtla rises like an Arab fortress, comes to an end amid one of the most impressive landscapes in Mexico—that of the two volcanoes, Popocatépetl and Iztlacihuatl, or "Popo" and "El Istla." These volcanoes are national symbols, just as Fujiyama is for Japan. And even though the "Road" crosses low-lying tropical lands, it is the snowy pinnacle of Popo that remains its enduring image—its crowning glory. In just one day, the "Road of the Monasteries" takes the visitor from the burning sun (El Istla) to perpetual snow (Popo), a landscape that has inspired many Mexican painters

Early on, Yecapixtla had only a simple chapel, but it was destroyed by fire. Hernán Cortés himself ordered the construction of a new church—the magnificent one we see today. It is typical of monastic architecture of the sixteenth century. In the corners of the atrium are "rest" chapels, where the devout could place the Blessed Sacrament (the consecrated host) during long processions. These sections consisted of a simple nave for which the ceiling was a great vault made of wood. But this simplicity was enriched with frescoes executed in the Italian style, covering every square inch of ceiling. In Yecapixtla it is possible to experience a range of influences—the European, native, and Arabian, and those of the Middle Ages and the Renaissance.

CUETZALÁN
A PLACE OF QUETZALS

Puebla State's northern mountains are replete with splendid landscapes featuring lush, varied flora: in pre-Hispanic times it would have looked like a paradise. Cuetzalán is an attractive place but not because it houses colonial treasures typical of many Mexican towns. Its beauty derives from its unique ambience, with stone-paved streets and lanes harmoniously rising and falling across the landscape, and its pure, spontaneous popular architecture.

Cuetzalán originally belonged to the Totonaca society, which existed in the states of Puebla and Veracruz but eventually became part of the Aztec empire through that civilization's imperial expansion. The Aztecs named the place Quetzalan, which meant "place where the quetzal bird is abundant" in the Aztec-spoken Náhuatl language. The quetzal was the most revered bird in the pre-Hispanic world and was a sacred symbol of beauty. Unfortunately, its plumage was highly coveted (Emperor Moctezuma was a fan) and the bird became extinct in this region though it survived in Guatemala. After 1552 the region came under Spanish control, and the Franciscans began evangelizing the native people. At that time, Cuetzalán became San Francisco Quetzalan, the name that endured until the nineteenth century when it was designated Cuetzalán. During the colonial period, the Franciscans used Cuetzalán as the center from which to extend their activities into places such as Zacapoaxtla and Jonotla. Cuetzalán's main church was built in honor of Saint Francis, but it deteriorated badly; in 1790 restoration work began. This nearly interminable job was finally completed in 1942, when a tall clock tower, reminiscent of many provincial French churches, was added.

Cuetzalán made history when many men from the town as well as neighboring Zacapoaxtla went to Puebla to fight the French army. On May 5, 1862, the native army was victorious over the French—an army that was widely considered the best in the world at that time. Napoleon III had ordered military intervention in Mexico in order to prop up the failing regime of Emperor Maximilian of Austria. But this adventure ended in a disastrous French retreat. After this glorious moment for the natives, Cuetzalán returned to its peaceful, nostalgic ways.

Cuetzalán is surrounded by a luxuriant vegetation. The region is famous for its coffee farms and its abundant birds. Cuetzalán was declared a national monument in 1967, a typical city of Mexico in 1986, and a *pueblo magico* in 2002. But more important than these official titles is the simple truth that it is an enchanting town.

The church of the "tiny jars" and its cemetery.

facing page
A lovely view of San Francisco Church with red-tile-roofed buildings in the foreground.

The parish church of San Francisco has a European-influenced design; another church in town is dedicated to the Virgin of Guadalupe, the Indian virgin and patroness of Mexico. It is a copy of Lourdes, the famous sanctuary in France, and it has a faux-nineteenth-century Gothic design. But the building of the church presented a seemingly insoluble challenge: how to construct a tall, elegant tower of cut stone like those created by the Gothic builders in France—yet have it be safe. To avoid a collapse, the builders used earthenware jars cemented together. This is why the church is commonly referred to as the church of the jars.

A minor archaeological site—at least minor compared to those in other parts of the country—is located near Cuetzalán. Yohualichan has pyramids that stylistically are very close to those in Tajín. It was originally a possession of the Otomies. They were beaten by the Totonacas, who then built this city. From these origins a rich indigenous folklore has developed of which dance is an important part. Papantla has its "flying men," and Cuetzalán has the Quetzales, a traditional dance. During the feast of San Francisco on October 4, dancers wear great tufts of multicolored plumes like those of the quetzal bird. The purpose of this dance ritual is to ask the quetzal bird for forgiveness for having hunted it to pay plume tributes to Aztec overlords. The dance is majestic yet the sounds of reed flutes and percussion has a somewhat hypnotic effect.

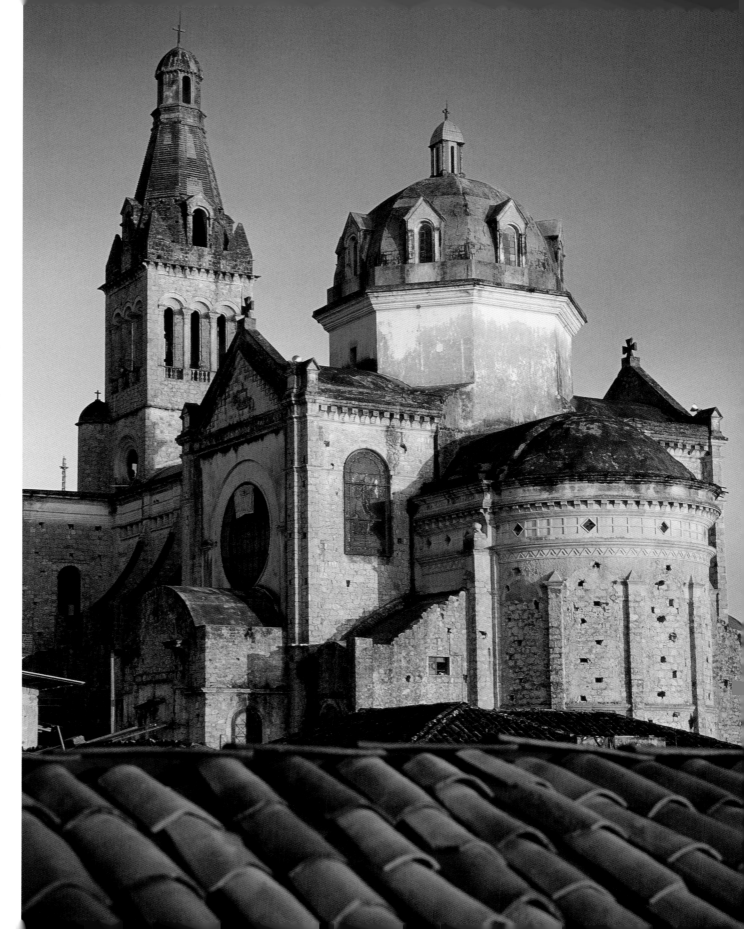

Many people in Cuetzalán wear traditional white clothing, and on market day indigenous people from all over the region come to town. However, in this very authentic place a curious European presence also exists. Even though the municipal palace was built in the twentieth century, it was designed according to a neo-classical style. Moreover, the model for the facade was not some European public building but Saint John Lateran Basilica in Rome. This basilica, the second most important building in the Catholic Church, inspired the genius builder of the municipal palace, who was not concerned about possible incongruities. Unable to crown the facade of a public building with saints, he decided to allot space for only one statue. To fill this space he chose as the subject the last Aztec emperor, Cuauhtémoc—the first Mexican hero who was tortured and executed by Cortés. Some would say it is pure surrealism; others would say it is typically Mexican.

above
Agustín Márquez Plaza
with its kiosk.

left
A romantic night view of
Cuetzalán's charming
stone-paved streets.

below
The Municipal Palace and
San Francisco Church.

CHOLULA
LAND OF TEMPLES

CHOLULA WAS ONE OF THE MOST IMPORTANT CENTERS OF CIVILIZATION IN ANCIENT MEXICO. It is said that the Cholulans were one of the seven tribes that came from the north in pre-historic times to populate and civilize the center of Mexico. These seven tribes came from a mythic place named Chicomoztoc and after a great deal of wandering finally arrived at this high plateau. The Toltecs arrived in Cholula in the eighth century, converting it into a sacred city; they built a pyramid that would be the tallest building in all of Mesoamerica. It was said that Quetzalcóatl lived in Cholula, where he took refuge from the conflicts in Tollan, the other Toltec city.

Quetzalcóatl supposedly left on his mythic journey to the sea—from which he would rise to the heavens and become the morning star, the star we know as the planet Venus—from Cholula. Mexico tends to mix myth and history and Quetzalcóatl appears to have been both a king and a spiritual master, or simply one of the most important gods of ancient Mexico. For this reason Cholula also means "the place from which he fled," in memory of Quetzacóatl's journey to his celestial home.

Cholula was converted into a religious center covering a large swath from the Gulf of Mexico to what is today southern Mexico. Apart from building the largest pyramid in America, the Toltecs also built 365 minor pyramids, one for each day of the year. It is not difficult to understand how this important city and successor to Teotihuacán would be threatened by the rise of the Aztecs, who were latecomers to the region and were building their own city not far from Cholula. The violence of the Aztecs was known and feared.

An interior view showing the unusual forty-nine domes of the former San Gabriel Convent.

facing page
Looking out over Cholula from Los Remedios Church.

Spanish explorer Hernán Cortés arrived in Cholula in October 1519 and, as he hoped, turned the Cholulans into allies. The Cholulans fought with him, bringing about the destruction of the Aztec city, Tenochtitlán (later to become Mexico City). But the Cholulans were not interested in continuing their alliance with Cortés, which became apparent when Cortés turned to the Cholulans for provisions to continue his military advance. They denied his request, and this convinced Cortés of their lack of goodwill. He organized a party for them in a town plaza. During the party, Cortés led a bloody attack on his allies killing, thousands of them. This massacre marked one of the darkest chapters in an already violence-filled conquest. Curiously, the conduct of the conquistadores did not end the alliance and the natives who helped conquer Tenochtitlán went on to help conquer the entire country.

Cholula's churches represent every style from the Gothic to the neo-classical at the end of the colonial period. The most important example is the Franciscan monastery San Gabriel built in 1529 with a Gothic rib-vaulted roof. Nearby is the unusual Royal Chapel, one of the most unique religious buildings in Mexico. Originally it was an open-air church built without a roof, reminiscent of a mosque like that in Cordoba in Andalucia, with nine naves and thirty-six columns. For a while it was covered by a wooden roof, but later the wooden arches and cupolas that we see today were constructed. One of the characteristics of the churches of Cholula is that their cupolas have ceramic coverings, giving them a beautiful brilliance.

Cholula supposedly had a temple for every day of the year, but the truth is more modest. Upon their arrival, the conquerors either covered over or built a church atop each one of these temples, which is the basis of the legend that Cholula had 365 churches. In the town itself, thirty-four churches were built; another seventy-six were constructed in neighboring pueblos. Including the chapels in surrounding haciendas, the total number of churches is 159—still an enormous number. The most important is La Virgen de los Remedios, which was constructed atop the grand pyramid, Tlachihualtepetl. This church was a symbol of the spiritual conquest of Mexico.

Rising in the distance close to Cholula is the largest pyramid in the Americas. Dedicated to Quezalcóatl, it is 1,150 feet at its base and 216 feet tall. Like all Mexican pyramids, this one was built atop others constructed before it. The original temple, dating from around 500 B.C. was uncovered, and measured 350 feet at its base and was 59 feet tall. This temple was then covered by another. Smaller buildings surrounded this pyramid; in turn, these were covered over by the current pyramid and its walls and stairways. Archaeological remains from nine separate periods were uncovered revealing that the pyramid of Cholula was a witness to at least two thousand years of civilization.

above
A majestic view of Los Remedios Church built over the Great Pyramid and mountains in the distance.

below
An interior view of Los Remedios's dome.

left
A panoramic view of Cholula.

HUEJOTZINGO
THE MONASTERY OF THE MURALS

The Poza Chapel of the former San Miguel Convent in Huejotzingo.

THE CONQUEST OF MEXICO WAS A RATHER STRANGE EVENT. Rather than a planned invasion by a conquering army, it was more like a series of accidents. In the beginning the focus was on exploring the coast of the Gulf of Mexico; the conquerors departed Cuba for Mexico with the sole idea of opening a commercial port. Moreover, the expedition was a private business undertaken under the direction of a rich farmer named Hernán Cortés. Originally, the governor of Cuba had given his permission for the voyage but then had withdrawn it. This then forced Cortés to begin his adventure to explore Mexico illegally. It was a country of which he knew nothing.

Cortés had his first encounter with the Mayans when he reached the coast at Yucatán. Later, he arrived at the point where he would establish his base, the port of Veracruz, and there he organized a vote to legitimize his leadership. His contact with the natives, including his new lover, convinced him to develop a strategy to conquer the Aztec empire, which was at the height of its power and covered an enormous territory. It was both an act of courage and madness to undertake the project, but Cortés went ahead and entered the Aztec lands. He formed alliances with the indigenous tribes who hated the Aztecs for their bloodthirsty practices.

One of the tribes with which Cortés allied himself was the Huejotzingas, who lived in what is now the state of Puebla. After his victory against the Aztecs, Cortés decided to found a European-style city where his allies could live; this was the origin of Huejotzingo and its monastery, one of the first constructed in Mexico.

facing page
A Franciscan-style dining room in the former San Miguel Convent.

The town of Huejotzingo was founded on two axis points that form a cross in whose center the monastery was placed. The building is enormous, with a cloister of more than 150,000 square feet; at its center is the missionary cross. Even though it is of European origin, it is indigenous in character. The cloister was built before the Franciscan church in plateresque style. This style, named after the silversmiths, is unique to the oldest buildings dating from the conquest. These churches were built in a Renaissance style that was elegant and florid yet easy to defend against attack. Huejotzingo is famous for its frescoes painted with a technique that has survived more than five-hundred years. The intention behind these murals was to give the natives visual lessons of bible history, stories and images of the saints and reveal the reason why the friars had come to dedicate themselves to the evangelization of the Indians.

Huejotzingo's oversize atrium was designed to hold enormous crowds and is distinguished by the beauty of its side chapels; these served as "rest stops" for those who carried heavy crosses or carved figures during religious processions. The processions began at the high altar and then went into the atrium where the first rest stop was located. Then the devout would walk along the wall to the second stop, then the third and fourth. At each stop prayers would be said and songs would be sung. Each rest stop was dedicated to a particular saint: John the Baptist, Saint James, The Virgin Mary and Saints Peter and Paul. It would also be worthwhile to visit Calpan, a monastery just a few miles from Huejotzingo, is best known for its beautiful rest chapels.

Saint Michael's monastery is dedicated to the patron saint of Huejotzingo. Construction started in 1526 and was finished almost fifty years later. At the beginning, there were few friars—only twelve Franciscans had arrived at the beginning of the conquest. The monastery has survived largely intact and its interior features many works of art—Mexican and Spanish masters were commissioned by the friars to create pieces. It also contains many carved wooden objects. The architecture of the monasteries combines various styles among which it is possible to note a Gothic influence as well as traces of the Italian Renaissance. Monasteries built immediately after the conquest had both an undeniable simplicity and military strength. These "castles of God" are among the most important remains of Mexico's colonial heritage.

TONANTZINTLA
AND ACATEPEC
BAROQUE SPLENDOR

THE BAROQUE PERIOD WAS BORN IN ITALY IN THE SPIRITUAL CLIMATE OF THE COUNTER-REFORMATION, the reaction of the Catholic church to the arrival of Protestantism. It was a complex phenomenon and the only aspect to be mentioned here is that in the visual arts, the Baroque was a style of excess, drama, and movement. But even though the Baroque was transplanted from afar, the indigenous communities adopted it willingly.

The Mexican aesthetic is not classical and restrained but exuberant and colorful. From the temples of the Mayans to the murals of the revolution, Mexican artistry is full of rich forms, symbols, colors, and textures. So it's not surprising that Mexicans embraced the baroque style. The designs of many grand buildings, churches, and palaces were inspired by its elegance and opulence.

Two churches close to the city of Puebla represent the Baroque era in all of its excess: San Francisco Acatepec and Santa Maria Tonantzintl. In both places voluminous forms and spaces are covered with decorative design. You can find the shaft of a column contorted into a spiral that is the most extreme example of this decorative impulse. One's eyes cannot rest because of the thousands of details.

In Acatepec everything is covered with tile and it is even used to inlay mirrors. This creates an atmosphere that rather than tasteful elegance has instead a charming, almost naive quality to it. Like all baroque churches, these too are replete with saints. There is a veritable celestial court, as if the church was designed to be a miniature replica of heaven. At Acatepec, the pulpit is made of marble lined in white and laminated with gold. It is covered with images of doctors of the Catholic church such as Gregory, Jerome, Ambrose, Augustine, Thomas Aquinas, and Dominick, with Saint Francis at the highest point. Of course, one not only encounters the saints, but also the most baroque of subjects, the angels. This is especially true in Tonantzintla where these angels have taken possession of every surface of the church, like a gleeful invasion of birds and butterflies.

In 1939 Acatepec lost its golden altarpieces—features that made it one of Mexico's most famous churches—to fire. They were later completely restored in plaster and stone and then fully covered both in vibrant colors as well as in gold. The Mexican Baroque is a style profoundly expressing the pleasure a community takes in building small altars where candles are eternally lit, for example, and around which prayers for the saints and family members are said. Of course, an image of the Virgin of Guadalupe is also included since she is the patroness of the country.

The dramatic belfry of the Immaculate Conception in Santa Maria Tonantzintla.

facing page
The exquisitely painted interior of the popular baroque church in Santa María Tonantzintla.

San Francisco Acatepec expresses baroque taste through its use of ceramic Talavera tile, made in nearby Puebla. Tile in combination with red brick and carved marble covers every surface of the church. The result is spectacular—perhaps made more so because the community is so small and top artists had to be hired to create it. This tile is no doubt of Arabic origin and we can see its use throughout southern Spain as well as in Portugal. In Mexico this decoration covers cupolas that shine in the sun with their vibrant colors. But the facade of Acatepec is unique, and no other place in Mexico has this rich mastery of design.

Santa Maria Tonantzintla Church has a relatively simple, modest red-tile exterior—but the interior is deliriously decorated. The church is dedicated to the Immaculate Virgin Mary, and it is interesting to note that *Tonantzin* was the name the indigenous peoples gave to their mother goddess, their "little" mother. It is quite possible that, unconsciously, the place occupied by the Virgin was also that of an ancient deity. Building a church here at Tonantzintla in honor of the Blessed Virgin to commemorate her for all times is an expression of the same impulse that occurred with the Virgin of Guadalupe in Mexico City, where a temple was also built in her honor. With these playful angels we are far removed from the more austere, serious style that can be seen in other churches.

The Italian Baroque was exported from Spain to its colonies, where in Mexico it was adopted quickly due to the native aesthetic that showed a preference for the excessive, dramatic, and decorative. The maternal character of the patroness helps understand the rather childlike and pleasant interior in Santa Maria Tonantzintla.

above
Detailed decorations featuring angels and cherubs, recurring motifs in Tonantzintla.

below
The union of angels and plants, a distinctive aspect of Baroque style.

right
A splendid native-influenced facade-retablo in San Francisco Acatepec.

COATEPEC
COFFEE CAPITAL

COFFEE IS ONE OF THE MOST IMPORTANT PLANTS IN THE WORLD. The beverage created from its seeds (or "beans") is not only a physical stimulant, but the beans themselves are very important to the economies of the countries where coffee is grown. While coffee is the second most highly traded commodity in the world—after petroleum—it is also the primary source of employment for many of the world's poorest people. In rural areas of the world, coffee is the agricultural product that produces the most money and jobs. Many underprivileged people are involved in the process of cultivating, cleaning, picking, and preparing coffee beans. Moreover, the cultivation of coffee helps conserve nature, and coffee plantations often promote sustainable development.

Mexico is one of the five principal coffee-producing countries in the world. The charming town of Coatepec is internationally renowned as Mexico's coffee capital. Its lovely ambience is enhanced by its wonderful colonial-era architecture, which gives it a magical nostalgic feel. Walking along the town's stone-paved streets past colorful houses with red-tile roofs is an enjoyable way to get a sense of the place.

Only fifteen minutes from Coatepec is the city of Xalapa, home to an important treasure: the Museum of Anthropology. This major collection covers nearly thirty centuries of pre-Columbian history and contains more than twenty-nine thousand pieces. A modern museum, it is a fantastic place to gain an understanding of the three great civilizations that inhabited the Gulf of Mexico: the Totonacs, the Huastecs, and the Olmecs. The Olmecs are considered the cultural source of all Mesoamerican civilizations and among its most valuable artistic legacies are colossal stone heads. These sculptures are characterized by thick lips, flat noses, penetrating eyes, and elaborate, incredibly carved headdresses. Of the seventeen heads that have been discovered, the seven most ancient are specially preserved and are memorably exhibited among the museum's beautiful patios and rock gardens. The most important of these, the imposing Head Number 1, is six feet high and weighs almost twenty tons. Other extraordinary Olmec pieces include *El Señor de las Limas*, innumerable *caras de niño*, earthenware figurines of infants, as well as jade masks, and enormous steles.

A panoramic view of Coatepec.

facing page
A quiet street in Coatepec with the dome of San Jerónimo Church rising above it.

Cloudy skies above and exuberant plants and vegetation below characterize the location in which Coatepec is situated. The region has the ideal altitude, humidity, and temperature for coffee cultivation. This remarkable habitat is rich in trees, orchids, insects, mammals, reptiles, and amphibians—all of which enable the area to grow and cultivate this crop, which is done according to the strict parameters established by environmental groups. This beautiful region is the origin of Café Coatepec, a variety of coffee plant known for its smooth flavor. Nature enthusiasts will enjoy the Clavijero botanical gardens as well as some of the important coffee haciendas in the area. Excursions can also be arranged to climb Cofre de Perote or the imposing Pico de Orizaba, the tallest mountain in Mexico.

The Totonacs built two principal ceremonial centers: the dazzling Tajín and Cempoala. There are several outstanding examples of this civilization in the museum collection including the murals *Las Higueras*, as well as earthenware female figurines. From the Huastec culture there is a huge collection of phyto- and zoomorphic vessels. In addition, there are earthenware figurines and images of deities.

With its beautiful cupolas and clock tower, San Jerónimo is a picturesque church that dominates the main plaza of Coatepec. Overlooking the esplanade is the municipal palace as well as beautiful homes where traditional coffees and ice creams are sold. Nearby is María Cristina, the famous orchid garden, and not far out of town is the very interesting former Hacienda el Lencero. Built in the sixteenth century, the main house is surrounded by a lake and beautiful gardens filled with ancient trees, among them a fig tree that is more than five hundred years old. This hacienda was the home of the eleven-time president of Mexico, Antonio López de Santa Anna. Also worth visiting is the small village of Xico. It is known for its beautiful waterfalls, which were made famous by the actor Michael Douglas in the movie *Romancing the Stone*.

LOS TUXTLAS
INFUSED WITH TOBACCO'S SMELL

ON THE COAST ALONG THE GULF OF MEXICO is a plain near the High Sierras in the region of Los Tuxtlas. Santiago Tuxtla and San Andrés Tuxtla are the two towns here that comprise Los Tuxtlas. The region is extraordinarily rich in natural resources and it was the heart of the first great culture of Mexico, the Olmecs. In many ways the Olmecs were the least known of the ancient peoples because they existed so long ago. But evidence of the civilization can be found throughout Mexico, including regions far from Los Tuxtlas.

Based on architectural finds it is thought that the Olmecs appeared in about 1500 B.C., three thousand years before the conquest of Mexico. The tribe's principal cities—at least those that have been found thus far—are La Venta, Cerro de las Mesas, and Tres Zapotes. Along with urban centers, these sites contain the famous Olmec sculptures, including monumental heads as well as ceramic figures and jade jewelry. An Olmec site has the same features of other ancient archaeological sites found in Mexico: massive pyramids, plazas, and buildings aligned along the axes of the earth. But the most famous discoveries are the monumental heads, two of which were discovered in Tres Zapotes, close to Santiago Tuxtla, where the archaeologist Matthew W. Stirling worked from 1939 to 1941.

At other sites, altars have been discovered with a figure that supposedly is of the Olmecs' principal god, the "baby face jaguar"—part jaguar, part human to whom sacrifices were offered. The jaguar was very important in the tropical religions of Mexico and was considered the "heart of the mountain," an earth deity.

How the colossal heads made of basaltic rock were transported from the nearby mountains to a marshy area remains one of the mysteries of archaeology. These heads have exaggerated Mongoloid- and Negroid-race features, with fat bodies and heads in the form of a pear. Slanted eyes, projecting chins, and thick lips are also depicted. They have some sort of plaster cranium or headpiece, and a number have jaguarlike expressions. It is thought that these are representations of the jaguar god even though no other representations have been found. It is also believed that these are the precursors of the great Mexican gods such as Tláloc, Chac, or Cocijo in Oaxaca.

Some scientists believe the Negroid features indicate a possible African presence in ancient America; others believe these colossal heads are simply representations of jungle ghosts, spirits, or dwarfs.

Whatever they were depicting, these sculptures are remarkable works of Mexican art.

The huge Olmec head of Cobata in Santiago Tuxtla.

facing page
Raúl Colí rolling a cigar.

Tropical Los Tuxtlas is a fertile region where the Universidad Nacional Autonoma de Mexico has established a biology station to study biodiversity. Lake Catemaco is also located there as is the nearby town of Catemaco, famous throughout Mexico for the efficacy of its witches and wizards. Many people come here seeking cures and cleansings, or freedom from a curse or bad luck. Witchcraft has existed in Mexico for centuries. In pre-Hispanic times it was combined with a magical way of thinking that was intertwined with religion. But it became a clandestine activity after the conquest.

Hernán Cortés was attracted to the region of Los Tuxtlas, and it became one of many areas he took as his personal property and controlled. Cortés introduced the cultivation of sugarcane and brought slaves from Africa to work the land. He also introduced cattle ranching, which changed the ancient way that cotton, corn, and rubber trees were grown. Although tobacco had been cultivated since pre-Hispanic times, it was not until the nineteenth century, during the dictatorship of Porfirio Díaz, that tobacco was widely grown for commerical purposes. Díaz wanted to modernize Mexico at any cost. Los Tuxtlas tobacco is the highest-quality product found in Mexico, and connoisseurs say it is on par with Cuba's best. Workers in these towns make high-end cigars by hand using the best leaves of the plant.

PAPANTLA
WHERE VANILLA ORIGINATED

THIS TROPICAL TOWN IS RICH IN FLORA AND FAUNA, AND IT IS BORDERED BY TWO RIVERS. Known as the place that scented or perfumed the world, Papantla is where vanilla comes from. Vanilla originated along the Gulf Coast of Mexico, where its most important genetic source can be found. The vanilla-making process was perfected in the eighteenth century and it was in the nineteenth that vanilla became world-renowned and popular, bringing prosperity to Papantla; previously the same thing had happened with chocolate.

Vanilla requires a special combination of sun and humidity to flourish, as well as a laborious cultivation process: it takes three years from the first planting for the seed to mature.

As is often the case in Mexico, there is a story about the origin of vanilla. According to the legend, there was a young virgin who had dedicated herself to the god of sowing, but she was seduced by a young man. They tried to flee but first a monster and then the priests of this god detained them. Both were sacrificed and the place where her blood fell to the ground became a vanilla flower and then the plant itself.

Papantla was founded around the year 1200 B.C. and was inhabited by the Totonacos. This group originated in the seven caves, a mythic place in northern Mexico called Chicomostoc where it is said all of the principal tribes of central Mexico came from. Like many other tribes that arrived from the barbarous north, the Totonacos easily assimilated to a life of farming in central Mexico.

The Totonacos formed a small empire, which not only had its own golden era but survived until the conquest. It was among the principal cultures of Mexico. Its jewel was the city of Tajín, which was also known as the "city of thunder" for the powerful tropical storms that were commonplace.

The city was founded around the year A.D. 100 and reached its cultural zenith between the years 800 and 1150, when it became closely connected to other cultures in central Mexico. After a series of wars, Tajín was abandoned, and, as is typical with many tropical Mexican ruins, thick jungle vegetation grew over it, and it disappeared.

Though the ruins were discovered by the Spanish captain Diego Ruiz, it was a German baron, Alexander von Humboldt, who first noted their real importance.

He was a great traveler who visited the Americas at the end of the eighteenth century and wrote about its geography and society.

Steps leading to the top of the Pyramid of the Niches.

facing page
The amazing Papantla Flyers performing in the town square.

Tajín's principal structure, the Pyramid of the Niches, is one of the most important archaeological ruins in the Americas. It is very different from the majority of Mexican pyramids and is a strong expression of Totonaca art. The pyramid is a quadrangle measuring 117 feet on each side. Six stepped levels, gradually narrowing, reach a height of 59 feet. Each level has a sloped wall on which rests a panel with niches; these are crowned by a flying cornice. On the eastern side of the pyramid is a large ceremonial staircase decorated with designs resembling a finely stylized serpent. The pyramid has 365 niches, suggesting a relationship with a solar cult. It is possible that during certain festivities the Totonacos placed incense-burning thuribles in these niches, giving the pyramid an air of the fantastic.

The Danza de los voladores or "dance of the fliers" is one of the most spectacular surviving rituals, requiring an eighty-two-foot pole with a post and frame at the top, four fliers, and a priest. The post represents a connection between the earth and the sky, and each of the four cords attached to it represent an umbilical cord. Four fliers ascend the pole first, sitting on a frame at the top of the post where they fasten themselves to the cords with a belt. Next, the priest ascends. He dances and plays the flute in tribute to the four directions of the universe. The fliers then hurl themselves into the air and circle the pole thirteen times in memory of Venus and its astronomical cycle of fifty-two days.

A large platform separates the Pyramid of the Niches from a section
known as Lesser, or Little, Tajín where the Building of the Columns
is located. Many mounds in the hills that surround Tajín are worth
exploring; together with the archaeological site itself these make
Tajín one of the largest cities in ancient Mexico.

above
Building No. 5 and the
Pyramid of the Niches.

left
A view looking across the Tajín
archaeological site in Papantla.

below
A fortress wall at Tajín.

TLACOTALPAN
A HAPPY PLACE OF COLORS

TLACOTALPAN IS A COLORFUL TROPICAL TOWN SITUATED ON THE GULF OF MEXICO; the Papaloapan River, or "river of the butterflies," runs alongside it. According to the ancient indigenous religions of Mexico, heaven, called Tamoanchan, was a tropical paradise with an abundance of water, vegetation, flowers, and butterflies. In contrast, hell was situated in cold lands or blazing deserts such as those early peoples had crossed on their way to North America.

Colorful boats docked at a pier on the Papaloapan River.

facing page
A decorative kiosk in the main square.

The town was founded at the beginning of the twelfth century by the Toltecs. When the Spanish arrived in the sixteenth century, Tlacotalpan was converted into an agricultural area with the best lands being awarded to the conquistadores. Because of the persistent wars between Spain and England, Tlacotalpan suffered regular attacks by British pirates who pillaged, sacked, and burned many Caribbean and Gulf Coast towns.

In 1714 a natural disaster struck when the Papaloapan River overflowed; at the end of the eighteenth century, a fire destroyed this town of wooden structures. After this, all houses were built of brick or stone and roofed with tiles. These structures give the town its unique character. Homes have pillars and arches, and are painted in bright colors. Because of its tropical charm, Tlacotalpan was named a World Heritage site by UNESCO in 1998.

The Plaza de Armas is the heart of town. In its center is a tropical garden with tall palms trees. Nearby is the nineteenth-century Municipal Palace and the white-painted parish church. Surrounding the plaza are walkways with elegant porticoes.

Tlacotalpan is the birthplace of Agustin Lara, Mexico's most popular composer, who wrote innumerable boleros, a musical form of Spanish and Cuban origin. The bolero is Mexico's great national genre, comparable in its importance to American blues or French chansons. His work is well known in the entire Spanish-speaking world and there is a monument dedicated to him in Madrid. Another famous artist of Tlacotalpan is the painter Salvador Ferrando, a romantic painter whose work is preserved in his home, today a museum. Very few Mexican towns have paintings of this luxurious quality, but it is because romanticism, a very European style, was interpreted in tropical Mexico in a particularly enchanting way. The museum contains portraits of his contemporaries.

For the majority of its history, Tlacotalpan was a port town, making it an important economic center. It was not until the beginning of the twentieth century, with the arrival of the railroad, that water-based transport faced competition. It was here in Tlacotalpan that Mexico's first president, Guadalupe Victoria, opened the country's first naval school. While some shipbuilding occurred, Tlacotalpan was not destined to become a great port, a role reserved for the nearby Veracruz. But Tlacotalpan maintains the atmosphere of a small port town and is a lovely destination for visitors.

Its location on the Gulf of Mexico
and its tropical feel creates a
feeling of ease and relaxation;
as a result, a more joyful folklore
developed. This was even true
in pre-Hispanic times where
the art was human, happy, and
sensual. Mexico is a paradise for
botanists, and the Plaza de Armas
in Tlacotalpan—where one can
hear tropical music—exemplifies the
natural abundance; any space can
be transformed into a garden.

Popular Mexican architecture is partly based on Spanish and Mediterranean influences as well as ancient pre-Hispanic traditions. While the materials vary, adobe and brick predominate; wood is rarely used. To keep houses cool, the windows are always open but are protected by iron bars. The walls of the houses are carefully painted every year—whether in cool white or more vivid, dramatic colors. Residents are proud of their pretty town with its playful aesthetic.

above
A streetscape featuring vibrant colors.

left
Tlacotalpan's beautifully landscaped and maintained central square with kiosk.

below
Brightly colored house facades in this UNESCO World Heritage site.

The interplay of light and water on the Mexican Caribbean.

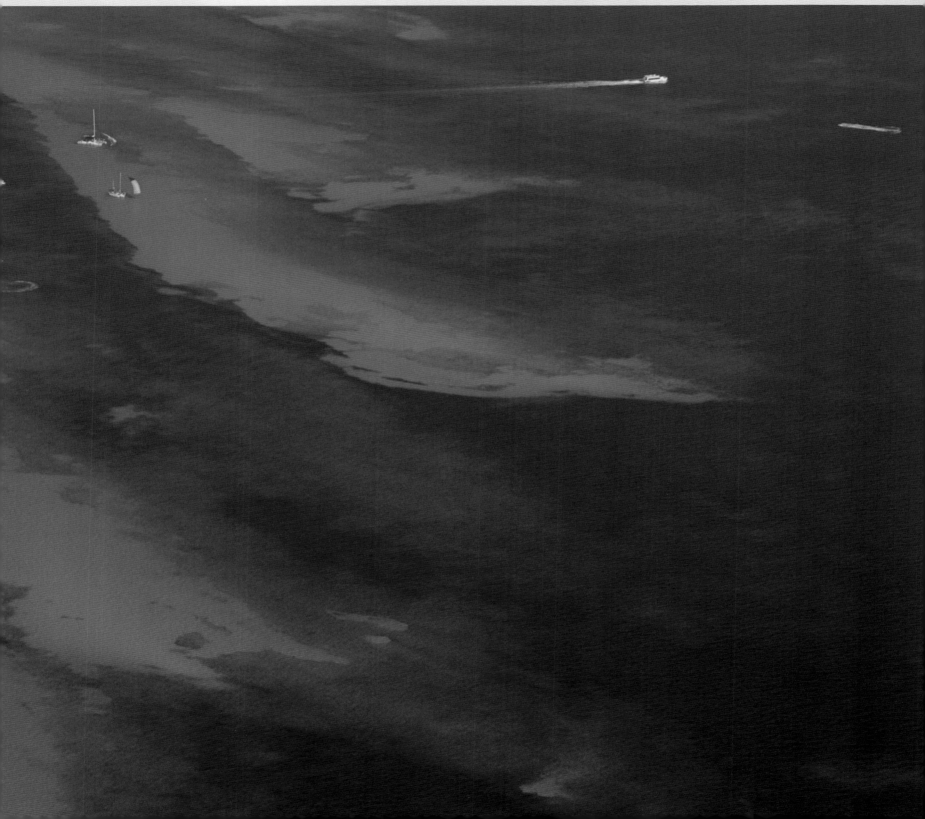

CUILAPAN
MAGICAL BEINGS AND LEGENDS

An *Alebrije*, a fantastic creature carved from wood and painted in vibrant colors.

facing page
An archway with a view into Saint James the Apostle Convent.

CUILAPAN'S CHURCH, WHICH IS ONLY ABOUT SIX MILES FROM THE CITY OF OAXACA, is one of the most unusual in Mexico. Cuilapan was an important Mixtec settlement and, during the conquest, the Dominicans were responsible for evangelizing this area. These friars were great builders, constructing marvelous churches in Yanhuitlán, Tlacolula, Tlacochahuaya, and Teposcolula.

At Cuilapan they designed and built an extremely ambitious work that, despite the friars' enormous abilities and patience, they were not able to finish. A roof was never built. But some experts believe the church was left open intentionally.

If Cuilapan was left open and roofless on purpose, this may be related to an architectural practice of the sixteenth century. Because the evangelization of the natives led to massive conversions, it was necessary to have large open spaces where they could be taught and preached to, and where liturgies could be celebrated. Consequently, there are many churches in Mexico for which the main building has an attached outdoor church with a large open-air atrium. An example of this type of building—there are at least a dozen in Mexico—is also found in nearby Teposcolula. Typically these buildings are very simple with arches surrounding the space and a large balcony.

The buildings at Cuilapan are very ambitious with an enormous church containing three naves with interior arches and strong columns to support the vaulted roof. It is in the basilica style, which is based on Roman churches that had multiple naves. During the sixteenth century the basilica plan in Mexico was primarily used for cathedrals and not for churches of religious orders that generally had only one nave. So Cuilapan could have been an exception, or it could be the most ambitious and original open-air church in Mexico.

The principal argument against this theory is that, in general, an open-air chapel had open spaces so the faithful could see everything that was happening. The columns in a normal basilica would have prevented this; additionally, an open-air space holds many more people than a building can.

It is more likely that the builders were unable to finish their work. The reason could be as simple as money. Many of the great churches in Mexico, such as the cathedral in Guadalajara, took centuries to complete because of lack of funds.

Or in the case of Cuilapan, where there are frequent earthquakes, the builders may have thought it more prudent to leave the church and its three naves open to the *air*.

The strange legend about the devil building Cuilapan's church is an example of the importance of the devil and the supernatural in Mexican life and art. The devil can be a terrible figure but then converted into a comedic one. He is represented in red with horns and a pointed beard. While there was no concept of the devil in pre-Hispanic religion, there was a god, Tezcatlipoca; similar to the devil in Mexico, he is always beaten by spiritual superheroes such as Saint Michael the Archangel. This puts the devil's abilities in doubt. Though seemingly fantastical, the devil is part of an important current in forms of popular Mexican art, such as the *alebrije*.

There is an interesting legend about Cuilapan. The prior of the convent there was Father Domingo de Aguinaga, who in his youth had studied architecture and wanted to build a great church. In 1574 Father Domingo allegedly received a visit from a very unusual person, an aristocrat dressed in black with an intense gaze; they conversed for many hours. One day, Father Domingo ordered the friars to return to their cells early. That night the sounds of voices, guffaws, and blasphemies were terrible; then suddenly, with the crowing of a rooster, the clamor subsided. During the night Cuilapan Church had been built. Before dying, Father Domingo confessed that the church had been built by the devil disguised in peasant attire, whom the rooster had crowed at before the break of dawn.

IXTLÁN
LIBERALS AND DOMINICANS

An altarpiece with holy oil in Santo Tomas Church.

facing page
An incredibly detailed baroque altarpiece in Ixtlán.

LOCATED ABOUT FORTY-TWO MILES NORTH OF THE CITY OF OAXACA, Ixtlán de Juárez is reached via a mountainous road that climbs through a forest. Ixtlán is famous because the nearby village, San Pablo Guelatao, is where the Mexican hero Benito Juárez was born in 1806. He was baptized in Ixtlán; many tourists visit the church's marble baptismal font each year. Benito Juárez is Mexico's greatest hero and his life reads like a novel. Juárez, of pure Zapotec stock, was orphaned at a young age; he lived first with his grandparents and then with an uncle for whom he worked as a shepherd.

Later he was working for a friar who taught him Spanish and encouraged him to enter the seminary to receive an education. Just before being ordained a priest, the young Juárez decided to study law and became involved in Mexico's extremely contentious politics. He had a remarkable political career as a member of the liberal party. Soon after entering politics he became the governor of Oaxaca, a job at which he was extremely adept. After a serious political reversal in which the liberals lost power, he went into exile to avoid capture. He fled first to Cuba and then went to New Orleans, where he survived by working as a tobacco-leaf roller. When the liberal party triumphed, he returned to Mexico and was named minister of justice. He proposed laws to limit the power of the Church.

In 1858 he became the liberal president of Mexico. But there was also a conservative president. Once again he had to leave the divided country at war, later returning to Veracruz. He continued his fight against the Church and nationalized its enormous holdings, especially in the capital, while also getting assistance from the United States.

Mexico's civil war between liberals and conservatives was bloody. Conditions deteriorated to the point that the conservatives wanted a member of European royalty to become Mexico's emperor. Maximilian of Hapsburg (an Austrian) accepted the offer with the aid and support of Napoleon III of France. At the same time, Spain, England, and France sent fleets to invade Mexico to begin collecting on debts. But only the French landed, largely to sustain Maximilian's throne. Juárez had to fight both the conservatives and the French, so he began traveling around Mexico as a representative of the rule of law. The war went his way and the French abandoned Maximilian. Maximilian was later captured in Querétaro. Juárez resisted European pressure to pardon him and ordered him to be shot before a firing squad. With the republic restored, Juárez was re-elected president, a position that he held until his death in the National Palace in 1872.

Two great forces present in Ixtlán forged Mexico's national history. One is the baroque church with its retablos, which are symbols of the riches of the Church. The other is the man, Benito Juárez, who fought against the Church and diminished its power in Mexico. During the colonial period the church had total control of the spiritual realm, sending heretics and Jews to the stake to be burned. At the same time, with the support of the Spanish state, the church had total control over life and thought while simultaneously accumulating enormous riches. Juárez's liberalism was the wave of the future and gradually grew in popularity in Europe and the United States. Conflict with many other forces was inevitable.

Ixtlán's church was built by the Dominicans in the eighteenth century when the baroque style was still in vogue. Originating in Italy, it was the preferred style of the Counter-Reformation. The style expressed the Church's vision of the world and flourished in Catholic countries including Spain, Portugal, and Austria. The Spanish brought the Baroque to Mexico during the conquest, and it was well received by the indigenous population. Even in a small town like Ixtlán, a magnificent baroque church was built with extremely rich retablos. This church is dedicated to the apostle Thomas who is represented on the facade. The retablos, especially the example behind the altar, are from the ultra-baroque period; the central section is dedicated to Christ and the side to the saints. Retablos dedicated to the Dominicans' saints are on the side walls of the church.

MITLA
A CITY IN RED

MITLA'S ARCHAEOLOGICAL ZONE IS LOCATED ABOUT TWENTY-SEVEN MILES FROM OAXACA and boasts the longest continuous human presence anywhere in Mexico. The remains of various work-related items have been found and date back to at least five thousand years before Christ, and Mitla was still inhabited when the Spanish arrived at the beginning of the sixteenth century. The city probably flourished between A.D. 1000 and 1521.

Mitla means "Place of the Arrows" or "Place of the Warriors," elements or symbols that this culture's mythology placed in the eastern cardinal point, whose symbolic color is red. As a result, red was the predominant color used on the city's buildings. Originally, Mitla was a Zapotec city, as was Monte Albán. But in the final years of the pre-Hispanic period, a new power appeared on Oaxaca's horizon: the Aztecs. They were an imperialistic people, who sought to dominate all of central and southern Mexico, as well as Soconusco, Guatemala, which was rich in products such as cacao and jade that were important to the Aztec economy.

In the final years of the pre-Hispanic era, these ancient, relatively tranquil ceremonial places bore witness to a history that was dominated by militarists. These overlords simply built palaces to live in while at the same time fortifying their cities as much as possible, a situation reminiscent of medieval and Renaissance Italy.

In Oaxaca the two dominant local groups were able to put aside their ancient rivalries and co-exist. From an artistic point of view, this led to a style that mixed various forms, and Mitla is a great example of this. Architecture reflects the austerity of the Zapotecs, while the decoration shows the preferences of the Mixtecs. It is seen in the panels on temples that are covered with a fret design of thousands of carefully cut and assembled stones put together like a mosaic. This motif, which is an extremely stylized version of a fretted serpentine design, has become a symbol of Mitla. This fretwork enabled the builders to round a corner with a design without losing its continuity. Eventually there was a fusion—this one brutally forced on it by history. It occurred when stones from the site were used to superimpose a church on original structures in honor of Saint Paul the Evangelist.

Mitla has a very interesting museum which like many in Mexico reflects the love of an individual collector, in this case that of Erwin R. Frisell. He bought a rather old house which is a fine example of the popular architecture of the region which earlier had served as a "posada", or hotel. Frisell turned the hotel into a museum. Later, the collection was enriched by the addition of the collection of Howard Leigh, a noted collector of Zapotec art.

The petrified waterfall in Hierve del Agua.

facing page
Red domes punctuate the top of the convent built on the Zapotec ruins in Mitla.

Hierve el Agua is close to Mitla. Though the name indicates the presence of some type of thermal waters, it actually refers to fossilized saline cascades that appear in the middle of a semitropical landscape. Their "frozen" appearance is a remarkable sight. Between A.D. 700 and 1350, the region had an advanced water system unique in Mexico. It supplied around six hundred plots of land, though the only way to get the water to the land was circuitous. The system itself depended on building several miles of canals. The best place to appreciate it is from the Anfiteatro.

Mitla's importance grew as that of Monte Albán declined. This situation helped unite the two great cultures of Oaxaca, the Zapotec and the Mixtec. This fusion is shown in various groups of connected buildings: de la iglesia, de las Columnas, del Sur, de los Arroyos and de los adobes. De la iglesia consists of two quadrangles: the northern one has a patio surrounded by rooms, while the southern one serves as a basement for the Catholic church. The group of columns supports a principal building, El Palacio de las Columnas, with a grand salon that is 123 feet long and a little over 21 feet wide. Its roof is supported by six ingeniously constructed columns designed to withstand the seismic dangers of the region. Underneath this building are tombs designed in the form of a cross and covered with magnificently carved gravestones.

MONTE ALBÁN
TOMB OF TREASURES

IN A SPECTACULAR LOCATION, these ancient remains are found near the city of Oaxaca on a ridge rising thirteen hundred feet above a tropical valley. This site was once was the great city of the Zapotec civilization, though during its final throes the Zapotecs were pushed aside by their rivals, the Mixtecs, both of whom would continue to live on in the area that is today Oaxaca State. Monte Albán was the last name of one of the Spanish landowners who discovered the site. Monte Albán's Zapotec name is unknown, although some speculate that it was named Dauyacach, meaning "ridge of the precious stones" (others think it means "ridge of the jaguar").

The origin of the Zapotecs is unknown, though they considered themselves to be descended from the jaguar, or from trees or rocks. Nevertheless, they were an ancient tribe that existed in Oaxaca for at least two thousand years. Archaeologist Alfonso Caso has divided the tribe's cultural development into five distinct phases. Phase one was when a civilization appeared that had great similarities to the Olmecs, the most ancient Mexican peoples. They had sophisticated ceramics and rock sculptures, usually of the "Baby Face Jaguar," the Zapotec god of rain. In phase two, known as Monte Albán II, sculpted ceramics were the predominant art form, though it was in this period that the first covered tombs were built.

Monte Albán III occurred between A.D. 500 and 1000. This is the classic Zapotec era, when jade jewelry made its appearance. Jade was a precious material—a Zapotec symbol of the spirit. They also produced beautiful earthenware funerary urns with characters sitting with crossed feet, as well as luxurious jewelry, sumptuous vestments, and sophisticated anthropomorphic figures. Monte Albán IV (A.D. 1200–1300) was a period of decline, when the Zapotecs abandoned Monte Albán.

Monte Albán V (A.D. 1300–1521) was predominantly the period of the Spanish conquest. But prior to the arrival of the Spaniards was a period of great cultural splendor when much jade, quartz, and gold jewelry was created, when turquoise mosaics were used as decoration, and when hieroglyphic writing was painted on deerskins. The discovery of the famous Tomb Seven, which dates from this period, ranks among the most significant in the archaeological history of the Americas. Nine human skeletons were unearthed in this tomb, each surrounded by treasures such as gold jewelry, massive gold masks, pearl necklaces, jade sculpture, turquoise mosaics, and alabaster and amber ornaments—all precious objects to the Zapotecs. Eventually, more than five hundred pieces were discovered, all of which are on permanent display at a museum in Oaxaca.

A court where sacred ball games were played.

facing page
A sculpted Zapotec stele with decorative details.

In Monte Albán various plazas, platforms, and a unique structure that was necessary for a great ancient Mexican city—a ball court—was constructed. Monte Albán's court has been well restored and is located to the left of the entrance of the Grand Plaza. Its lengthy court is walled on two sides by two rectangular buildings with sloped walls. The structure to the west has a sculpture on its upper part that represents a locust, while the eastern wall has two commemorative steles. The ball game played was not strictly a sport but instead a sports-related ritual with cosmic importance.

Not only is Monte Albán famous for its architecture but it is also renowned for other treasures, such as its stone steles. On these columns are glyphlike standing figures with inscriptions that signify mountain; another glyph with an inscription over its head signifies heaven. Some of the steles appear to commemorate important historical dates or astronomical events, indicated by dates and numbers that use pre-Hispanic numerology. These steles feature elegant ornamentation and decoration and utilize certain recurring motifs such as squared spirals with curved corners and the depiction of serpent heads with stylized human faces. Also famous are tablets that represent full-size human beings in strange positions, called dancers; they are unique to ancient Mexican art.

Monte Albán is an enchanting place that gives visitors the impression of being at the top of the world. In essence it is a vast horizontal and sacred space that has the most important buildings in Mexican architecture. The heart of Monte Albán is the Grand Plaza—980 feet long and 650 feet wide. Aligned in this plaza area are the Northern Platform, the Handball Court, the M mound, the Southern Platform and System IV. Other parts of the plaza include the Palace and the famous Tomb Seven. Monte Albán is a place where one can trace the footprints of a lengthy historical and cultural development that was constantly evolving. The vast remains of this ancient city are reminiscent of the complexity and diversity of the Roman Forum with its ruins from various epochs.

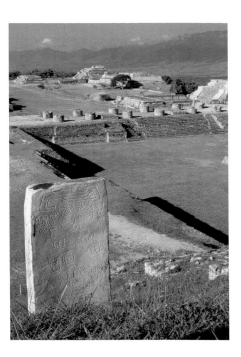

above
The M mound and a stele.

left
A view looking across the expanse
of the archaeological site.

below
Looking down from
the J hillock.

OCOTLÁN
COLORFUL PAINTERS AND MARKETS

OCOTLÁN DE MORELOS, ABOUT EIGHTEEN MILES FROM THE CITY OF OAXACA ON THE ROAD LEADING TO THE SEA, is an indigenous pueblo where the Dominican friars arrived in 1555. They came at vespers on the feast of the founder of their order, Saint Dominic Guzman. This is why the town was called Santo Domingo Ocotlán. The name endured during the colonial era but was changed to Ocotlán de Morelos in honor of the second most important hero of the independence movement, José María Morelos. He was a priest who became an excellent military leader and was beloved throughout southern Mexico. Soon after the friars arrived, construction of a church and friary began; however, as is rarely the case in Mexico, the work did not continue. Builders abandoned the project to work in the nearby mines where they hoped to find their fortunes. Unfortunately, they only encountered death caused by brutal exploitation at the hands of the Spanish.

For many years completion of the project went nowhere and the friars simply installed a straw roof to prevent damage to the walls. Work on the church resumed a century later but proceeded slowly. It was not finished until 1823, after Mexico gained independence. This explains why Ocotlán, both church and friary, are unique examples distinct from the many Dominican foundations in Oaxaca and around Mexico, which are generally quite sophisticated and built and decorated according to European traditions.

The church is a popular attraction. Its ornate facade is painted blue and yellow with plant motifs, and its thick columns and rough capitals are cheerful and fun. The interior of the friary is beautifully painted and is decorated with frescoes dominated by floral motifs within a luminous atmosphere. To really appreciate Ocotlán's beauty, however, it is important to learn about an important local, Rodolfo Morales, who was born there in 1925. He was the son of a carpenter and teacher. Eventually, he moved to Mexico City where he studied art at the famous San Carlos Institute. While there, he made a modest living as a high-school art teacher, a place where he painted a mural but remained unknown. A friend urged him to go to Cuernavaca—near Mexico City—where the great artist and fellow Oaxacan Rufino Tamayo exhibited his work. Tamayo took an interest in Morales's work and became his great guide and protector. Soon after, national and international exhibitions followed and the modest art teacher began to earn a lot of money. He returned to Ocotlán and dedicated the remaining years of his life to his native town.

Using his money and his artistic genius, Rodolfo Morales became the protector of his town—especially the Dominican church and friary. The restoration works reveals the hand of the painter himself. This is especially true in the friary, which was rescued from its previous use as a prison. Today it is a charming cultural center exhibiting works of religious art as well as photography. Morales painted its tall columns. Oaxaca's artistic traditions, a mix of the pre-Hispanic, the popular, and the contemporary, influenced his work, as well as that of artists such as Tamayo and Toledo. Morales's work has a gentle quality to it, employing women, dogs, the flowers of Oaxaca, and its towns, which he painted with all inhabitants present, including ghosts.

The cloister of the former convent in Ocotlán.

facing page
An intricately detailed and brightly colored facade of the Santo Domingo Church in Ocotlán.

Oaxaca is famous for its market days—called *el tianguis*—when people throughout the region gather with their products. A tianguis, an institution dating from pre-Hispanic times, is where you find regional specialties such as mezcal, the typical drink of the state. Like tequila, mezcal comes from the cactus plant. In pre-Hispanic times, the only part that was consumed was pulque, also derived from the cactus but only consumed by the affluent. After the conquest, the Spanish introduced stills, which were an Arab invention and were used to produce mezcal; the drink became popular in southern Mexico. It is strong and aromatic, and the highest-quality product has a white worm in the bottle. The worm assures that artisans distilled it.

San Bartolo Coyotepec is a town about
five miles from the city of Oaxaca and
is famous for its specialty, brilliant black
earthenware ceramics. Potter Rosa Real de
Nieto discovered this particular ceramic-
making process accidentally when she
rubbed the surface of a piece of black
pottery with a quartz stone. Doña Rosa's
son, who is quite elderly, continues to
perfect his technique, creating expensive
ceramics of exceptionally high quality.
Many famous people, including Nelson
Rockefeller and Jimmy Carter, have visited
her shop. Her ceramic pieces are purely
decorative. Their production uses ancient
pre-Hispanic techniques of a base of two
large concave earthenware plates, one
supporting the other; a wheel is not used.
Making this pottery takes between twenty
and thirty days from the molding to the
decoration, usually consisting of flowers
and birds.

above
The famous black clay pottery
of San Bartolo Coyotepec.

left
With its wood-beamed ceiling and painted
walls, this room at the Museum of the
Community has a rustic ambience.

below
The Hall of Columns created
by painter Rodolfo Morales.

SANTA MARÍA DEL TULE
GREAT ANCIENT TREE

Dominating the main square is Santa María del Tule's enormous and ancient conifer tree.

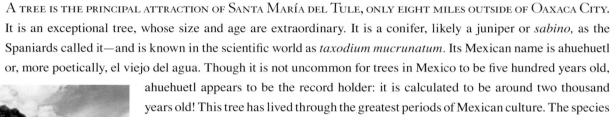

facing page
Named *ahuehuetl*, Santa María del Tule's remarkable tree is approximately two thousand years old.

A TREE IS THE PRINCIPAL ATTRACTION OF SANTA MARÍA DEL TULE, ONLY EIGHT MILES OUTSIDE OF OAXACA CITY. It is an exceptional tree, whose size and age are extraordinary. It is a conifer, likely a juniper or *sabino,* as the Spaniards called it—and is known in the scientific world as *taxodium mucrunatum.* Its Mexican name is ahuehuetl or, more poetically, el viejo del agua. Though it is not uncommon for trees in Mexico to be five hundred years old, ahuehuetl appears to be the record holder: it is calculated to be around two thousand years old! This tree has lived through the greatest periods of Mexican culture. The species itself has existed since the Mesozoic Era, which means the conifer has been present between one and two hundred million years. It is found in every region of Mexico, no matter what the climate; it just needs to be near water. This conifer is particularly hardy, being resistant to the diseases that are fatal to other species.

Santa María del Tule's conifer has impressive dimensions. Its diameter at the middle of the trunk is forty-five feet and its circumference is nearly 150 feet. It would be difficult for fifteen people standing around the tree touching finger to finger to fully encircle it. It is thought to have a volume of nearly twenty-five thousand cubic feet and weighs more than five hundred tons. Some botanists believe the tree is really three trees growing together that are totally intertwined. Its ancient trunk has inspired many fantastic names among Santa María del Tule's residents, including The Elephant, The Lion, The Deer, and The Three Magi. Whether saint or deity, this remarkable tree is honored with an annual fiesta on the second Tuesday of October.

Since this particular species grows almost everywhere in the country, it has been connected with any number of dramatic historical anecdotes and poetic stories. Thus, for example, King Netzahualcóyotl, known in pre-Hispanic Mexico as the poet king, created an enormous garden where he planted conifers, a garden that in 1938 was named a national park. Another historic conifer is named La Noche Triste and is found in Mexico City. It is said that beneath its shade conquistador Hernán Cortés sat and wept when pursued by the Aztec troops, who were furious with the Spanish. The Spanish had organized a slaughter in order to rob important people during a fiesta. At that moment, Cortés thought he had been beaten and would have to abandon the conquest of Mexico. But his native allies urged him to continue the fight and so it was that the future of the country was decided beneath a conifer tree.

Santa María del Tule is a typical Mexican town whose center is the main plaza. Religious and government buildings line the plaza. The plaza is part of an urban-design concept brought from Spain. In pre-Hispanic times, the main plaza usually served as a large space in front of a pyramid. But King Philip II decreed that the towns founded in the New World would be formally designed and that the principal space in the town would be reserved for the plaza. Santa María del Tule's main plaza is spacious with a variety of gardens and with a large monument representing plant life. In front of this is a lovely church and the municipal palace with its high palms.

Trees were important symbols in the religious thought of pre-Hispanic peoples. The Aztecs placed a tree facing each of the four directions of the universe and another in the center. Aztec priests would use red sap combined with small seeds to form a heart-shaped offering to the gods in order to save the life of a maiden. The Mayans placed a silk cotton tree in each of their cosmic directions. The tree's color corresponded with each direction: red for the east, white for the north, black for the west, and yellow for the south. To the Mayans, the silk cotton tree was sacred—the mother of life. In some places, a machete was used to create a cavity in the trunk of the silk cotton tree into which a male baby's umbilical cord was placed. They thought it was a way to ensure that the boy would grow up to be strong and tall like the tree.

TLACOCHAHUAYA
THE MONASTERY OF SILENCE

MEXICO IS A COUNTRY OF GREAT CONTRASTS. While much of it is practically uninhabited—one can travel for hours without seeing a town—in other areas the towns are virtually piled on top of one another. In a category all its own is the capital, Mexico City, one of the largest megalopolises on the planet. One of the areas with a large concentration of closely spaced towns is the area around the city of Oaxaca. The state as a whole, one of the most indigenous in Mexico, is subdivided into 570 municipalities, each with its own local government. Oaxaca State has an incredible cultural diversity as well as a varied geography with high mountains, temperate valleys, and tropical forests.

Church of San Jerónimo.

facing page
Main altar with attractive frescoes and oil paintings in the Church of San Jerónimo.

From the capital city of Oaxaca travelers can plan a trip to nearby towns, each with its distinct personality. Tlacochahuaya is a good place to begin. About fifteen miles from Oaxaca, this town was founded in A.D. 1100 and became the first place in the state to have an *encomendero*—a Spanish landowner who was given Indian lands with the idea that he would preserve the value of the land. These lands ended up in the possession of the Spanish crown instead. A small Dominican monastery was established in Tlacochahuaya at the behest of the Spanish king, who had given this religious order the task of evangelizing Oaxaca. It was named after Saint Jerome, an unusual saint who lived in the desert in isolation save for the company of a lion. Here he undertook the enormous task of translating the entire Bible into Latin. This version, known as the Vulgate, became the official biblical text of the Catholic Church. This Bible would not be translated into the European languages until the famous German Bible of Martin Luther. This monastery's location in a remote corner of Oaxaca reveals the friars' desire for as much isolation from the world as possible, so they could live in complete silence, meditate, and practice mortification.

Ironically, this especially religious place is an enchanting example of the indigenous interpretation of European art. It is colorful and imaginative. The church itself contains a range of artwork, including a painting of Saint Jerome by Juan Arrue, whose inspiration came from models of European Renaissance art. He is one of the few native painters who gained recognition for his work; the vast majority remained anonymous. In contrast to a rather primitive retablo are the frescoes, which present a rich indigenous interpretation of religious motifs mixed with floral designs—the result of a playful imagination. Saint Jerome Church in Tlacochahuaya also has a musical jewel, an organ constructed in the sixteenth century.

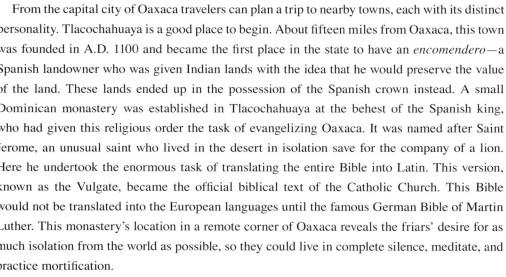

Saint Jerome is the patron saint of Tlacochahuaya. This saint from the time of the Dominican desert hermits is represented a number of times listening to the voice of God through a trumpet. It is said that whether awake or asleep, he was always listening for the trumpet call that would announce the Final Judgment. To honor the patron saints of the communities of Oaxaca, each year magnificent fiestas are held; they are overseen not by the community but by a patron. This member of the community is chosen and pays all of the expenses of the sometimes eight-day-long fiesta, which includes food, drink, music, and fireworks; however, the honor sometimes brings financial ruin to the generous person.

Joyfully imagined indigenous colonial art can be found in numerous churches near Oaxaca. The Baroque in Mexico lasted longer than in Europe, and this style is featured in Santo Cristo de Tlacolula Church; in its side chapel one finds one of the most beautifully decorated cupolas in Mexico. It is octagonal and mounted on rings supported by angels. At the pinnacle of the cupola, typically where there is an opening to permit the sun's light to come through, there is an unusual Jesus carrying his cross surrounded by imaginative stars; the octagonal divisions contain figures of saints. It is a fascinating mix. In neighboring Teotitlán del Valle, the architecture is poor but the local textiles are nationally famous and its rugs combine a primitive ingenuity with great simplicity. One of Mexico's most remarkable features is that it is possible to find colonial towns near, or even on top of, archaeological sites. Dainzú, near Tlacochahuaya, is an example of this. A Zapotec town founded in about 600 B.C., at about the same time as Monte Albán, it had been continuously populated for 650 years. Its most significant archaeological site is a ball court, one of the oldest in Mexico. Additionally, there are other structures with reliefs of figures of ball players in motion. This sacred sport was also played at Yagul, another nearby archaeological site.

YANHUITLÁN
A CHURCH OF IMPRESSIVE DIMENSIONS

ONE OF THREE RELIGIOUS ORDERS THAT BEGAN THE EVANGELIZATION OF MEXICO, the Dominicans were founded in Toulouse, France, in 1215 by the Spaniard Domingo de Guzmán. The order had both a benevolent side in its vocation of preaching and one that was less so: it was in charge of the Inquisition. Dominicans arrived in Mexico in 1526; after a difficult start, they gradually gained a toehold and began evangelizing Oaxaca, where the Zapotecs and Mixtecs lived.

They established many small churches and undertook their missionary activities using indigenous languages; as a result, they had to write dictionaries and grammar books. This was an incredible challenge as there were more than seventy indigenous languages in Mexico.

It is certain that the Dominicans were responsible for the document that Pope Paul III wrote recognizing that the indigenous peoples were fully rational, which limited the actions of the conquistadores and prohibited their enslavement. It was the famous Dominican bishop Fray Bartolomá de las Casas, a lawyer by profession, who was converted into a great defender of native groups. He wrote a famous history of the conquest in which he denounced Spanish atrocities and condemned European colonialism—one of the first historians to do so. He became a hero in Mexico.

The principal nave of the San Pedro y San Pablo Teposcolula.

facing page
An imposing former Dominican convent in Yanhuitlán.

Yanhuitlán was a Mixtec region that was easily subdued by the Spanish, who came to Oaxaca shortly after the fall of the Aztec empire. Francisco de las Casas, one of Cortés's relatives, was the first person given control of the area; he left money in his will for the construction of a modest temple. Later, Yanhuitlán began a period of prosperity when a Dominican monk introduced silkworms as well as plants that could be used to color the silk.

Construction of the church and monastery began in 1548; these would become buildings of impressive dimensions. Yanhuitlán's church is 246 feet long, 48 feet wide, and 82 feet high. Its mass dominates the town. Construction took about twenty-five years to complete and employed an enormous workforce of six thousand native people. The conditions were primitive and the bishop of Oaxaca complained about what he had to pay the workers and the distances necessary to transport them. Europeans also arrived to direct various aspects of the project. Because of Yanhuitlán's massive size and that fact that so many trees were cut down to make room for it, its construction affected the ecological balance of the region. But the result—an enormous stone church that rises above the landscape of red clay—is spectacular. The church's interior matches the grandeur of the exterior.

Yanhuitlán's monastery is constructed of cut stone and is an excellent example of architecture that utilizes both medieval and Renaissance forms. The cloister has an Italian-style vaulted stone roof, but the overall essence of the monastery is medieval. At the top of a huge staircase is an excellent painting of Saint Christopher, here a giant saint protecting a diminutive child Jesus, a common subject of colonial artists.

San Pedro y San Pablo de Teposcolula was a prosperous colonial town with magnificent homes. While the town's heyday has long since passed, the monastery and convent are exceptional. Especially interesting is the elegant, recently restored open chapel, a type of structure unique to Mexico and needed to accommodate the numerous converted natives. Nearby Coixtlahuaca is also worth a visit.

The church and monastery were named in honor of the founder of the Dominican order, Saint Domingo de Guzmán. The church has a large nave without a transept, with the main altar facing the east and the principal entry facing the west. It is possible that the doorway, which is not very distinctive, was modified to follow the style of other Dominican churches. In contrast, the northern door is a splendid example of the plateresque style. This door is surrounded by high columns that are reinforced with powerful buttresses—essential structural components given the area's frequent earthquakes. Gothic influences are represented in the beautiful arched window as well as the interior windows. Because the apse began to crack, an Italian was brought in to create two strong arches that harmonize well with Yanhuitlán's powerful design.

COMITÁN DE DOMÍNGUEZ
FASCINATING DIVERSITY

An evocative nighttime view of the lighted San Jose Church.

An evocative nighttime view of the lighted San Jose Church.

facing page
International Lake with its brilliant blue hues at Montebello Lagoons National Park.

COMITÁN DE DOMÍNGUEZ IS A PLEASANT TOWN IN THE HIGHLANDS OF CHIAPAS STATE, one of the most diverse states in Mexico with a range of climates as well as surviving ethnic groups. Although the area originally was Mayan, when it was colonized it was subsumed by the province of Guatemala and other Central American countries. After Mexico gained independence, the people of Chiapas were given the choice of becoming part of Guatemala or Mexico; they chose Mexico. This helps explain why Chiapas has its own personality with a fascinating mix of cultures. As an example, Chiapas is one of the few places in the country with German immigrants; they came because they were interested in growing and selling coffee.

Comitán, on the border with Guatemala, was founded at the beginning of the conquest. During colonial times it was a peaceful place. Its architectural inheritance is reminiscent of Spain, and its religious buildings are well executed. Saint Dominic Church has a facade inspired by mudejar, an Arab-Spanish style found only in the first buildings constructed after the conquest.

Calm in Comitán was interrupted in 1824, three years after Mexico became independent. It was the place where Chiapas's act of independence was signed. The act, which allowed Chiapas to integrate into the newly created Republic of Mexico, was signed immediately after the failed imperial experiment headed by the unusual Agustin de Iturbide, who wanted to be crowned emperor just like his hero, Napoleon Bonaparte.

A virulent epidemic of cholera threatened to wipe out the population of Comitán in the nineteenth century. This illness, unknown in Mexico and brought by the Spanish, had almost annihilated the indigenous population after the conquest. But Comitán survived due to the intervention of a lesser-known saint, Caralampio. To give thanks to Caralampio for his help, the town built a beautiful church in his honor in 1852 and each year remember him with festivities that take place in February.

Rosario Castellanos, the most famous modern Mexican writer, was born in Comitán. She was educated in Mexico City and Madrid and received her doctorate in philosophy. She both promoted the indigenous culture of Chiapas and developed an important literary oeuvre. This included a novel, *Balún Canán*, that describes with great sensitivity life in a small town like Comitán and the inequalities between the Europeans and indigenous peoples. She died while serving as ambassador to Israel. Comitán continues to preserve its charming architecture, and its main plaza still has the flavor of the Mexican provinces.

Lagunas de Montebello National Park, on the border with Guatemala, is less then an hour's drive from Comitán. There are fifty-nine lakes in this park; half are in Mexico, the other half in Guatemala. Well-maintained roads provide easy access to ten lakes; the rest are for travelers seeking a bit of adventure. Lagunas de Montebello's most attractive feature is its diversity. Some of the lakes are green, some are blue; the atmosphere is tranquil; and the air is pure and calming. Comitán is also near twenty other deep, crystal-clear lakes called de Colón.

Comitán de Domínguez is named in honor of its most notable son, Belisario Domínguez, who was born there in 1863. He was sent to Paris to study. He came back to Mexico City where he published a book, *Chiapas,* in which he denounced the misery and inequality in his state. After he returned to Comitán, he opened a free clinic. In 1911 he was elected mayor of Comitán, and in 1912, a senator of the republic. Later, during a bloody coup led by Victoriano Huerta, the democratically elected president, Francisco Madero, was taken prisoner and assassinated. Belisario Domínguez wrote a speech against Huerta, which he was planning to read in the senate. He published it and for this he was arrested and assassinated, causing great political turmoil. Later, Mexico commemorated him by establishing the Belisario Domínguez Medal, the highest honor for civic valor.

The road from Lagunas de Montebello passes by Trinitaria, a town where the best accommodation in the region, the lovely Santa María Hotel, is located. The town has a jewel of a museum; though small it exhibits sacred art including sculptures and a splendid collection of oil paintings from the colonial period by the most prestigious artists of that time such as Correa, Pardo, and Morlete, as well as others from the Chiapas school. While Marian themes predominate, there is an interesting black Christ on a cross. Travelers should also visit Chinkultic, a large Mayan ceremonial center constructed during the classic period and dating from around A.D. 600 to 900. The principal building—the acropolis—has a base with four structures mounted on it, a stairway, and a temple at the top. There is also a ball court. The combination of the ruins, the park, and a lake make Chinkultic well worth a visit.

above
A view of Pojol Lagoon.

left
Comitán de Domínguez's
romantic town square at night.

below
An interior exhibition space at the
Parador Santa Maria Museum.

215

CHIAPA DE CORZO
THE ART OF THE MOORS

CHIAPAS IS ONE OF THE MOST BEAUTIFUL STATES IN MEXICO. Along with neighboring Oaxaca, Chiapas has a large population of indigenous groups who have preserved their languages, rituals, and traditions. The geography of Chiapas is a fascinating mix of cold highlands, tropical jungles, and the warm Pacific-coast area. It also has a large number of excavated archaeological sites, as well as many waiting to be explored and unearthed. There are many enchanting towns in Chiapas, and Chiapa de Corzo is one of them.

Impressive Sumidero Canyon from above.

facing page
Chiapa de Corzo's town clock and its colonial mudejar-style fountain.

Chiapa de Corzo is located close to Tuxtla Gutiérrez on the banks of the Grijalva River. Its history dates back to the year 1400 B.C., the classic period in Mayan history. Around the year A.D. 1000, the Chiapanecas invaded the region, displaced the Mayans, and imposed their own government. The first Spaniards arrived in 1524 and conquered the region. In 1528, under the leadership of Captain Diego de Mazariegos, this town was established. The original Spanish name for the town was Chiapa de la Real Corona (Chiapa of the Royal Crown); because of the dearth of economic activity in the area, the town depended on financial support from the Spanish king. In 1824, in response to the independence movement, the state of Chiapas chose to become part of Mexico rather than Guatemala; with this decision, Chiapa became a Mexican town.

Because of the persistent conflicts between liberals and conservatives, Chiapa had an eventful history during the nineteenth century. The liberals achieved victory in 1863 when Angel Albino Corzo was elected governor of Chiapas, the man in whose honor the name of Chiapa was changed.

Located in the heart of the town is the plaza with the famous La Pila fountain, which resembles a baptismal font. Nearby are the city's major buildings, including city hall, Angel Albino Corzo's house, as well as an ancient tree that is considered sacred by the locals and is linked with the founding of the city.

There are eight barrios, or neighborhoods, in Chiapa de Corzo, a division inherited from the original natives. Six of these barrios still use the original Indian names, such as Cacú or Shanguti, and each barrio preserves its artisan customs. Santa Elena retains its traditional architecture, including San Sebastian Church. The design of the church combines Renaissance, Arab, and baroque influences.

El Cañón del Sumidero is one of the most beautiful natural attractions in Mexico. This canyon is near Chiapa de Corzo and covers an area of more than seventy-seven square miles. It is a deep canyon with walls extending as much as 3,280 feet; a range of vegetation and fauna live there. The climate is tropical, in sharp contrast to the dry climate that characterizes Mexico's famous Copper Canyon, found in the northern state of Chihuahua. El Cañón del Sumidero can be toured by boat—departures take place from Chiapa de Corzo—or by following a roadway along the edge of the canyon with convenient rest stops and scenic viewpoints along the way. At the end of the canyon is one of the most impressive feats of Mexican engineering, the immense Chicoasén hydroelectric dam. But on the whole, it is the natural landscape that is most impressive.

It was converted into a fort during the continuous wars of the nineteenth century, but today is an excellent vantage point to enjoy a view of the surrounding area.

La Pila fountain is Chiapa de Corzo's most famous place and symbol. Its design is unique in the panorama of Hispanic-American colonial art, while at the same time being the ultimate example of Hispanic-Arabic art. Spain was conquered by the Arabs as part of Islam's great expansion and was occupied for almost eight hundred years. During this time, there were repeated attempts to re-establish authority, but this was not achieved until the Catholic kings ruled Spain. From an art-history perspective, the mixture of Arabic and Spanish influences resulted in a hybrid style known as *mudejar*, employing elements of both cultures. Interestingly, a marvelous example of this style is found in Chiapa de Corzo, a Mayan village. Its octagonal fountain was constructed with tile in the Arab style and covered by a Renaissance-inspired cupola.

216

PALENQUE
A JADE MASK

facing page
Temple of the Inscriptions at Palenque.

PALENQUE, ONE OF THE GREAT ARCHAEOLOGICAL SITES OF MEXICO, was originally named Otulum, which means a "strong house"; during its height, it dominated its geographical region. Palenque was likely founded in the fourth century B.C., but the period of its greatest splendor was between the seventh and eighth centuries A.D. Afterward it was abandoned and Palenque's first appearance in modern history was not until the end of the eighteenth century. At that time, a report about it was sent by an army officer, Ordúñez de Aguilar, to a captain in the colonial army. This report was not published until the end of the nineteenth century; by that time, Palenque had a number of "discoverers," including Waldeck, Dupaix, and Maudslay.

However, the most important of these arrivals were the British painter Frederick Catherwood and the American diplomat John L. Stephens, an odd pair who were the authors of a beautiful book about the region and Palenque itself, *Incidents of Travel in Central America, Chiapas and Yucatán*. A local landowner offered Palenque to them as a father would offer a wedding gift to his daughter, but Catherwood and Stephens courteously refused.

It was not until the twentieth century that the Mexican Institute of Anthropology took charge of the restoration work at Palenque. In 1952, archaeologist Albert Ruz Lhuillier made one of the world's great discoveries: the funeral crypt in the Temple of Inscriptions, a discovery comparable to similar ones made in Egypt.

Only a small portion of Palenque has been restored. Within these nearly 270,000 square feet are over two hundred structures; the potential rich treasures buried within have not been unearthed. Palenque's buildings contain many inscriptions that have revealed the names of important people and dates of historical significance. Most importantly, it reveals the Mayans' astronomical knowledge.

A number of Palenque's principal buildings have been studied. These include the Temple of the Inscriptions, one of the great architectural works of pre-Columbian culture, as well as the palace, Temple IX, the Temple of the Count, the ball court, Temple XIV, and the temples of the Cross, Sun, Beautiful Reliefs, and Foliated Cross. There is also a notable aqueduct in front of the palace that has controlled the course of a river and was covered with a vault of massive Mayan arches.

The Mayan temples were not places where the faithful gathered as they do in mosques or Christian churches. Priests, who were the only ones allowed access to these places, performed religious rituals in them. The temples were placed atop pyramids that were always located in open spaces. While the temples were small, they are rich in ornamental sculpture. The origin of the temple is found in the typical Mayan house covered with palms. It was re-interpreted in stone with powerful sculptured pillars that separated the rectangular doors. The roof was constructed of slender, finished stalks crested with geometric designs based on the crossed branches of palms.

Discoveries in the Temple of Inscriptions also represent an unequaled artistic treasure with its works of jade, jewelry, and the refinement of its sculpture. Palenque has been declared a UNESCO World Heritage site.

Three of the most important hieroglyphic panels in the Mayan world are found in the Temple of the Inscriptions. The middle room has nine steps leading to the crypt, each of which refers to the nine priests or lords of death and night. This notable funeral crypt connects to a tunnel at the center of the pyramid, which is guarded by five sacrificial youths who accompany the great lord Uaxac ahau, a deified king. The crypt itself is 29.5 feet long and 13 feet wide, and the walls are decorated with the lords of the night. In the center of the crypt is a sarcophagus that is an impressive monolith. Inside is a cavity that contained the dead body of the famous ruler Pakal; it had been covered by a memorial slab. His body was richly dressed, his face covered by a mask of jade mosaic, and he had a diadem with earrings, a hanging necklace, rings, and precious bracelets.

Palenque's landscape is one of the most varied in Mexico. Palenque itself was built in a flat jungle; about forty miles away from the archaeological site are the beautiful Agua Azul waterfalls. These are formed by a tributary of the Tulijá River that feeds a series of waterspouts forming natural pools distinguished by their various shades of blue water. In the center of Palenque is the palace, which is superimposed on a staggered-step base that is 327 feet north to south and 246 feet east to west. The palace is reached by a nearly 1,000-foot-long stairway that leads to a series of galleries grouped around four patios. One of the buildings forming the palace has a rectangular four-tier tower that perhaps served as an astronomical observatory or as a lookout tower in times of war. In the building where the priests lived there are notable works of art such as the reliefs of the Writer and the Speaker.

above
The majestic waterfalls
of Agua Azul.

left
A view of the archaeological
complex.

below
The palace at Palenque.

SAN CRISTÓBAL
A CULTURAL CRUCIBLE

San Cristóbal de las Casas had a dramatic beginning. In 1524, the Spanish arrived in this peaceful valley intent on conquering it; instead they were repulsed by the natives. Four years later the Spanish returned with a larger army but the natives preferred to drown themselves before yielding to the invaders. The victors then founded a city they called Ciudad Real (The Royal City). It was much later that the city was renamed San Cristóbal de las Casas in honor of Fray Bartolomé de las Casas, the great apostle to the indigenous people and the first historian to denounce the horrors of the conquest.

San Cristóbal is located in a completely indigenous area in Chiapas, a region that contains more ethnic groups than any other in Mexico. A favorite destination of some European and American tourists, San Cristóbal often has the feel of being the destination for anthropological pilgrimages. A local joke is that the average family there consists of a father, a mother, three children, and an anthropologist.

Traditional dance and music performances take place here often and once attracted an audience in colorful native dress. But today San Cristóbal is no longer just an indigenous and colonial town; instead, it has become something more international, and it is possible to hear at least a half-dozen languages being spoken in the streets. It is not only San Cristóbal that attracts visitors to the exotic Mexico. Many tourists take excursions to the small neighboring towns such as San Juan Chamula or Zinancantán, in whose small churches Christian rituals co-exist with ancient Indian beliefs. This phenomenon occurs in a large part of Mexico where pre-Hispanic communities and languages have been preserved. Studies have shown that even five hundred years after the Spanish conquest, more than seventy native languages are still in use.

San Cristóbal de las Casas has beautiful examples of colonial architecture, and perhaps the most impressive is the cathedral, constructed in the seventeenth century. At this time the baroque style had been fully embraced in Mexico. Santo Domingo Church is one of the most attractive in San Cristóbal. It has a baroque facade and its nave incorporates a flowery design with niches to hold small figures of saints while the image of a martyr is accompanied by two lions; these images appear to be more like pets than wild beasts.

Gilded retablos can be found in the interior and are distinct from those found in central Mexico. More simple and plain, they are decorated here with enormous floral patterns and portraits of the saints in heaven.

An intimate street in San Cristóbal leading to the arch at El Carmen's tower.

facing page
A night view of San Cristóbal de las Casas Cathedral's elegant facade.

San Cristóbal's town design followed a well-ordered historical model in which the buildings are low-lying and compact. Its important houses have large patios surrounded by colonnaded arcades with fountains in the center. A profound Renaissance influence can be found in the Casa de la Sirena, which dates from the sixteenth century. The most magnificent building from the seventeenth century is the house of Diego Mazariegos, the facade of which combines both indigenous and Spanish influences. Inspired by the typical architecture of Castile, Spain, the large entryway is flanked by two columns, each finished with lions sculpted in the purest indigenous tradition, a style that in Mexico is called *tequitqui,* or vassal style.

During the sixteenth century a number of buildings were built there influenced by two styles that are rare in Mexico—the Gothic and the Renaissance. The Gothic style arrived very late in Spain and was exported to Mexico, but in a rather diluted way; there is no important example of the Gothic in Mexico. In reality, the "Gothic" buildings found in Mexico are the result of a revival during the nineteenth century. The Renaissance style had more success but only lasted a century after its arrival. The style central to the colonial era was the baroque, of which there are many regional variations. A brilliant example of this is the massive cathedral, a sober building that is horizontal in design and exhibits a strong sense of equilibrium complemented by smooth, clear, and well-decorated spaces.

In addition to the neighborhoods where the Spanish lived, San Cristóbal was divided into other sections, each of which has its own personality and some of which are ethnic. The first neighborhoods were named for Spanish allies in the conquest: Mexicanos and Tlaxcala. Later, San Diego, Cuxtitali, and San Antonio were built and are considered the traditional neighborhoods, in existence before recent population growth. Each neighborhood is characterized by purely local traditions, including crafts and foods. La Merced is home to wax makers who create beautiful, artistic candles; in El Cerillo, craftspeople work with wrought iron; in San Ramón they make sweets; and in Mexicanos they work with wood. When there is a neighborhood celebration, marimba music is always played. The marimba is a traditional wooden percussion instrument and its music is reminiscent of that heard in Bali and southeast Asia.

above
Folk dancers perform at the
31st of March Square.

left
A panoramic view of the town with
San Cristóbal de las Casas Cathedral
and its bright yellow facade.

below
An arcaded building
in San Cristóbal.

225

YAXCHILÁN
CITY ON THE RIVER

GETTING TO YAXCHILÁN IS ONE OF THE MOST INTERESTING JOURNEYS IN MEXICO. Visitors must first take a boat trip along the Usumacinta River, which constitutes the border between Guatemala and Mexico. The boat travels through the lush green jungle surrounding this river, which varies from 228 and 327 feet wide. Visitors arrive at Yaxchilán in about forty-five minutes. It is several feet above the river, and to visitors it must seem as if they are entering a paradise as they climb upward and the great Mayan city comes into view.

Yaxchilán was discovered by the Englishman Alfred P. Maudsley in 1888; he gave it the name Menché Tinamit. Soon after, a French explorer—Desiree de Charnay—rediscovered it and gave it an absurd French name, Ville Lorillard. It was not until Teobert Maler explored the city that it was properly renamed Yaxchilán, which means "green stones" in Mayan. Born in Vienna in 1842, Maler came to Mexico as one of the guards of Emperor Maximilian, the ephemeral Austrian emperor of Mexico. Maler stayed in Mexico even after Maximilian was captured and executed by firing squad.

He then established a photography studio in the town of Ticul in the Yucatán. An architecture aficionado, Maler dedicated his life to recovering the world of the Mayans and wrote an impressive number of books and articles published in several languages.

Yaxchilán flourished between the years A.D. 350 and 810, and it is one of the great sites from the classic Mayan period, A.D. 250 to 900. It had grand leaders such as Cráneo-Mahk'kina I, who began to expand the city in the sixth century. Afterward came leaders such as Shield-Jaguar I, who initiated a dynasty that endured until 808, the date of the final inscription discovered on a stele. Yaxchilán's political history can be followed by studying the thirty steles that have been unearthed. A stele is a typical Mayan form used frequently in the classic period. It is a large vertical stone that features a representation of a great personality on its front; on the reverse side are dates and astronomical terms. Other unique objects at Yaxchilán are beautifully designed lintels carved in stone, seventy of which have been found thus far. These lintels are among the masterworks of Mayan sculpture, as are the fewer than twenty altars that have survived. Though few in number, some remains of richly painted murals were also discovered by Maler. These designs provide clues about the murals found at nearby Bonampak.

Building 33, also known as the Temple of Quetzalcóatl, at Yaxchilán.

facing page
A richly detailed lintel found inside Building 20 at Yaxchilán.

Yaxchilán's architecture is typified by Building 20, a temple. Rectangularly shaped, it is sixty feet long, eighteen feet wide, and nearly twenty-three feet high. Its facade has three doors, each of which is adorned with Yaxchilán's outstanding sculpted lintels. In addition, there is a finely decorated frieze and a finished roof with an impressive crest. This temple, simply known as Building 20, is equal in quality with Building 33, which can be seen from the river. Maler gave this building the whimsical name Temple of Quetzalcóatl. The reason? Inside was a sculpture with a large tuft of quetzal feathers, the sacred bird of central Mexico.

The city, which was built on a natural terrace, contains the grand plaza, various other buildings with smaller plazas, as well as the ubiquitous ball court. But this is only the main part of Yaxchilán. Many paths lead to nearby hills where other buildings were constructed. Teobert Maler drew up a plan that both located and numbered not only buildings but also steles and lintels. One of the nearby hills is known as the Acropolis of the South, where a temple and various steles are located. It was here that Maler discovered richly colored murals depicting human figures and plants. Found here is Stele 11, which dates from A.D. 752. It is thirteen feet high and has the image of a leader who is standing wearing a mask of the sun god.

ZINACANTÁN
UNIQUE ETHNIC MIX

ZINACANTÁN IS A TOWN ABOUT SIX MILES FROM SAN CRISTÓBAL DE LAS CASAS, where the indigenous Tzoltziles live. They are one of Mexico's fifty-nine distinct indigenous groups; many of these have remained fairly unassimilated over time, maintaining their own languages, customs, and traditions. In Chiapas State, where Zinacantán is located, ethnic groups have distinctive clothing, traditions, and language. Sixty-two languages are spoken in Mexico. Chiapas is an anthropologist's paradise, as well as a wonderful place for travelers interested in learning about the indigenous people of Mexico.

Because of the curious cycles of history, pre-Hispanic Zinacantán left the Mayan sphere of influence to become members of the Aztec dominion. This happened in 1486 during the reign of the great Aztec emperor Moctezuma I, who ruled for forty years before the arrival of the Spanish. Aztec interest in this place far away from the rest of its empire was due to a desire for goods produced in a region to Zinacantán's south, called Soconusco. But the Aztec presence was not sufficiently lengthy to change the essential Mayan culture of Zinacantán, considered to be the capital of the Tzoltziles, as well as nearby towns San Juan Chamula and San Andres Larrainzar. However, the Aztecs made Zinacantán an important commercial center with a bustling trade in precious objects such as jade, amber, jaguar skins, and, above all, the precious plumes of the quetzal bird, the most highly coveted Aztec luxury.

After the conquest, the Dominicans came to Zinacantán and built the humble, diminutive San Lorenzo Church. It was constructed from adobe bricks and had a straw roof, a material that was used at the beginning of the conquest for many Mexican churches and cathedrals. Over the years these churches were remodeled according to the tastes of the times. This church received help from Fray Bartolomé de las Casas, a great friend of the indigenous peoples. Here traditional Catholic rituals were celebrated, while at other churches of the region, such as San Juan Chamula, indigenous rituals were incorporated. A historical note is important: after the conquest, the victorious Christians agreed that the Catholicism promulgated in Mexico would combine indigenous traditions.

As a result, Zinacantán has a church dedicated to San Sebastian, the Roman martyr. But the natives transformed his story. He became an army official of the king who wanted to marry the king's daughter. Sebastian fled and was persecuted by the king's troops. He was subsequently brought to Zinacantán where he was killed by arrows. According to legend, soon after Sebastian was buried, the church on this site was miraculously built in three days. Also worth a visit is the Ik'alojov crafts museum located in a traditional house nearby.

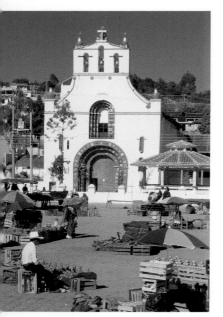

Locals sell their wares during market day in San Juan Chamula. San Lorenzo Church faces the plaza.

facing page
A Tzotzil woman in Zinacantán weaves on a waist loom.

Ik'alojov, the crafts museum in Zinacantán, is in a traditional Indian house. In San Cristóbal, there is another museum, Na Bolom, which is also a nice hotel. San Juan Chamula is a lovely place. This small town about four miles from Zinacantán has a church devoted to San Juan, but it is not dedicated to Catholic worship; instead it celebrates the Chamulas' own rituals—a mix of pre-Hispanic and Christian traditions. Each tradition celebrates its patron saint, and the grand plaza in front of the church is adorned with an array of flowers and candles. While the church can be visited, photographs are forbidden. It is a festive and fascinating place.

Zinacantán's men cultivate flowers and the women weave textiles. The workforce includes young girls, who from six years of age learn the profession they will practice for a lifetime. These woven textiles are made on rope-knot looms, shown in the photograph. In addition, each pueblo in the region around Tzotzil has its own traditional handmade clothing created by the women. In Zinacantán they wear a white top with embroidered necklines and sleeves. The *huipil,* a type of skirt, is black with violet or purple designs. In San Juan Chamula the blouses are blue, while in San Andres they are red. All of the men wear similar clothing, with the exception of respected elders. These revered older men in the community wear clothing specific to their position of authority. On market day in Zinacantán or in San Cristóbal, there is a spectacular display of color mixed with the sound of the many languages spoken in the region.

CAMPECHE
A VIOLENT PAST, A TRANQUIL PRESENT

facing page
The public library behind the fort that surrounds central Campeche.

IN 1517 A SMALL EXPEDITION OF TWO SHIPS LEFT CUBA WITH SCARCELY 110 MEN ON BOARD; among them was Bernal Diaz del Castillo, who would later become the great historian of Mexico's conquest. The ships navigated along the coast of the Gulf of Mexico and came upon a place named Ah Kin Pech. The Spaniards stopped there only for water, continuing on to another village. There they had a fatal encounter with the natives, who killed fifty of the men and wounded the captain; he returned to Cuba where he died. It was more than twenty years before the Spaniards were able to found the Spanish port of Campeche on the site of Ah Kin Pech, which became the principal port of the region and is today the capital of the state of Campeche.

Campeche's history during the colonial era was marked by the constant threat of piracy; as a result, it became a walled fortress. Pirates were attracted to the Gulf of Mexico because of the ships regularly returning to Spain laden with riches. The French were the first pirates to attack Campeche, but without a doubt it was the English, feeling a certain sense of legitimacy for their actions because of the constant wars between England and Spain, who most actively pillaged and destroyed the coastal areas of the empire, especially Campeche. Well-known perpetrators included Englishmen such as Francis Drake (whose actions eventually merited a knighthood), John Hawkins, and William "Peg Leg" Parke, who was greatly feared. The Dutch were also dedicated to piracy; the most notorious among them was Laurent de Graff, known as Lorencillo, who attacked Campeche in 1672.

While the pirates threatened the extensive coastlines of the Spanish empire on both the Atlantic and Pacific coasts, it was the Caribbean and the Gulf of Mexico that were most coveted; this is why the British established the base for their pirate ships in nearby Belize. Fortifications were essential to the defense of Campeche; they are still preserved and give the city its unique character. It was not until the twentieth century that the fortifications were no longer a necessity, solely becoming picturesque remnants of a violent past.

The Plaza de Independencia dates from the founding of the city. This plaza serves many purposes: a market for food and crafts, as well as a gathering place. Important buildings, including the governor's palace, city hall, and a magnificent cathedral, line the perimeter of the plaza. In the past this was where executions took place and where fountains and monuments were built. It was opened as a Plaza Mayor, a grand central plaza, in 1540. In that year, Francisco de Montejo ordered the construction of a small church in honor of the Virgin Mary. The church was in use until it was replaced by the current structure, construction of which was started in the eighteenth century. The construction process went slowly and the new church was not finished until 1916. In the nineteenth century the plaza itself was converted into a garden.

Women wearing traditional dresses embroidered with flowers with the cathedral as a backdrop.

Today the once-tumultuous Campeche is a tranquil town. It is the capital of a state with abundant natural resources—most importantly oil from the Gulf—but its romantic colonial architecture is the most essential aspect of its heritage. Building design was adapted to the hot climate of the port city: walls were thick, open windows were protected by steel bars, homes had high ceilings, corridors had archways, and there were vegetation-filled patios. Campeche has a good museum of archaeology, ethnology and history, as well as a cultural center housed in a mansion dating from the seventeenth century that provides a nice glimpse of what life was like in the past.

Campeche has a slow pace of life. Residents wake up early, accomplishing their work in the morning; all is quiet in the afternoon as people rest during the heat of the day. Refreshed residents return to their activities in the evening. Campeche's cuisine is famous for its mix of Mayan and European influences, as well as for the quality of its seafood. In Mexico, generally the cuisine is better where there were important indigenous civilizations, which led to interesting combinations of ingredients and flavors. Campeche has maintained much of its colonial atmosphere.

E D Z N Á
R U I N S   I N   T H E   J U N G L E

ABOUT FORTY MILES FROM CAMPECHE IN THE STATE OF THE SAME NAME is the Edzná archaeological site. Located in a jungle near the Gulf of Mexico, Edzná remained undiscovered for a long time; consequently, it is less well known and explored than other archaeological sites on the Yucatán Peninsula. However, Edzná is ancient and had a long history, which began around A.D. 600 and was at its zenith around A.D. 900.

These dates are based on the analysis of ceramic remains, so it may actually be older. The history is that a modest community was transformed into a well-governed society able to build enormous monuments and a vast hydraulic water system with thirteen large canals, thirty-one smaller canals, and eighty-four cisterns for excess rain (Edzná is in place that has heavy tropical rainfall). Edzná's government was in the hands of grand leaders who reinforced their power based on their supposed kinship with the gods, a relationship that was depicted in stone and stucco reliefs. At its most successful, Edzná's prosperity was based not only on agriculture but successful commercial routes that crossed through it bringing merchandise from great distances.

In its first phase of development, a style called *petén* was used there. But with the arrival of a new tribe, the Chontales, a different style called *puuc* was employed to renovate Edzná's art and architecture. Petén was simpler, worked with large blocks of stone that were later covered with a thick layer of stucco and then painted in an intense red. Many buildings were decorated with masks and portraits of humans, which were also covered with stucco. The Chontales brought certain refinements and advanced techniques, including capital columns that were previously unknown in Mayan culture but were used in other parts of the world such as Egypt and Crete.

It is very interesting to ponder what might have happened if the Spanish conquest had not occurred. Would indigenous designers have discovered certain basic architectural forms used in the Old World such as the arch, vaulting, or the cupola? Probably not, since the concept of cities and buildings was totally distinct in America. However, we will never know.

A man and horse walk in front of the Uayamón Hacienda.

facing page
Pictured are the Edzná archaeological site central square and the Building of the Five Stories.

Near Edzná is the Hacienda Uayamón, which has had periods of both grandeur and desolation but which has now been restored to its former glory. Built at the end of the sixteenth century, Uayamón was a farming hacienda that was sacked by the pirates Graff and Gramont in 1685. The hacienda had various owners over the years, but in the nineteenth century the Carvajal family transformed it into a major hemp producer. By then it had been converted into a veritable empire with its own railway. But during the revolution it was embroiled in a battle and bombarded. Only recently has it recovered from the damage. Today it is fully restored to its original splendor and has been converted into one of the most luxurious and beautiful hotels in Mexico.

Edzná's most important epoch was between the years A.D. 600 and 900, and during this time Mayan society would grow enormously. It is estimated that the city had around thirty thousand inhabitants; its architecture had great originality, beauty, and grandeur.

Edzná was concealed by jungle foliage until it was accidentally discovered in 1906. It was not until 1927 that restoration work began. The main buildings, separated into two large groups of structures—the Large Acropolis to the east; La Vieja to the west—are spread out over an area of over two and a quarter square miles. There is a great plaza adjacent to the acropolis as well as another neighboring plaza; its most important building is the Edificio de Cinco Pisos, one of the most significant structures of Mayan architecture. Four levels of this building contain various rooms; on the fifth level is a temple crowned by a crest. Other buildings are the Casa de la Luna and the northern and southern temples. There is also a small acropolis where the Templo de las Estrellas is located and where dated calendars were produced from A.D. 672 to 810.

CHICHÉN ITZA

A WONDER OF THE WORLD

CHICHÉN ITZÁ IS A MAYAN CITY THAT EXISTED DURING TWO DIFFERENT PERIODS. In around the year A.D. 435, the first Chichén Itzá was founded by the Itzae, a Mayan tribe. They lived there until the year 700, after which they abandoned the city. The tribe's reason for leaving is uncertain, though possibly it was because of earth tremors. But in 948 they returned and lived there for another two hundred years. By the time the Spanish arrived, the city had been abandoned once again. Both the conquistador Francisco Montejo and Bishop Diego de Landa visited the site; the latter wrote about the Mayans. Subsequently, many travelers have studied Chichén Itzá, including Edward Thompson, who bought the archaeological site so he could sack and pillage it. Later, many of the stolen pieces were returned to Mexico. Its official restoration began in 1923, though there are still hundreds of small structures to study.

The nunnery at Mexico's incomparable Chichén Itzá archaeological site.

facing page
Chichén Itzá's castle, a remarkable structure.

Chichén Itzá stretches about two miles from north to south and one and a quarter miles from east to west. The buildings are divided according to their age. First are those from the classic period such as the Templo de las Monjas (also called Akab D'zib), the Casas de los Venados, and Los Falos. Structures from the second period are Maya-Tolteca in design, because of the influence of central Mexico. The largest and most well-known buildings are El Castillo, Templo de los Guerreros, Juego de Pelota combined with the Mil Columnas, the Muro de los Craneos or Tzompantli, Osario, Plataforma de Venus, and Los Tigres y las Aguilas. There is also an unusual building called El Caracol, which is an astronomical observatory. It is clear that the Mayans were enormously curious about the measurement of time and were excellent astronomers.

El Castillo, a pyramid with multiple tombs, is Chichén Itzá's most spectacular building. It is about 585 square feet and is nearly eighty feet high. It has nine stepped levels with four facades, each one facing one of the four cardinal directions. These facades are decorated with serpents and jaguars and its four stairways each have ninety-one steps that lead to the entrance of the major temple, the most important temple of the site's 365 (a number matching days in the year). Enormous plumed serpent heads guard the principal stairway on the north side. The "new" Chichén Itzá, represented by buildings such as El Castillo, is the sacred space of Kukulcán, the Mayan name for Quetzalcóatl. On the twenty-first day of March and September, the days of the equinox, Kukulcán would visit the city and descend in splendor atop the pyramid appearing with the profile of a serpent.

Chichén Itzá is a rich archaeological site containing notable buildings such as the Templo de los Guerreros, a square pyramid measuring 129 feet on each side. It has four stepped levels that support a building with two salons. The building's columns are carved with priestly figures and the monster of the earth. Masks of Chac and reliefs of Quetzalcóatl ornament the facade; in the vestibule are reliefs of Chac-Mool. The Spanish called this building Las Monjas, and it is a variation connected to other nearby buildings of which the outstanding example is La Casa. Adorning this building are carved steps and decorative patterns that are entirely Mayan. Also notable are Las Monjas's decorative sculptures.

Mexican pyramids such as El Castillo not only have an unusual construction, but in their interiors they contain other pyramids that perhaps were used as tombs. This construction creates a veritable archaeological labyrinth. While it seems practical to construct one pyramid on top of another, it is unclear whether this had a religious purpose.

These new constructions certainly featured stylistic changes. There are additional ancient pyramids in El Castillo's interior, one of which has a red jaguar with a turquoise mosaic as well as a figure of Chac-Mool, a semi-reclining figure poised to present offerings. At Chichén Itzá, the early city clearly belongs to the classic Mayan style; the later city's style is the result of the fusion of the Toltec and Mayan cultures and the significant influence of the new god Quetzalcóatl-Kukulcán. This religious revolution implies an artistic one—the arrival of a new style came with it. Because it has two contrasting styles, Chichén Itzá is somewhat different from other ancient Mayan cities. This is why it is referred to as a "modern" city.

above
A stone sculpted by Mayans.

In 2007 an unusual worldwide competition was held on the Internet. Its purpose was to determine, based on popular opinion, the current "wonders of the world." The initial list created in the ancient world included the Colossus of Rhodes, among other incredible manmade and natural constructions of antiquity. In the 2007 competition, voters tended to choose places in their own countries. The winners were the Taj Mahal, the Christ the Redeemer statue in Río de Janiero, the Roman Coliseum, the Great Wall of China, the Temple of Petra in Jordan, the Great Pyramid of Giza in Egypt, and, last but not least, Chichén Itzá. There were a number of disappointed supporters of the Acropolis, the Eiffel Tower, and the Alhambra in Granada. Though the inclusion of Chichén Itzá was a source of pride among Mexicans, it also concerned many archaeologists who feared that large-scale tourism would hasten deterioration of the site. But that is the price of fame.

below
Chichén Itzá, a World Heritage site and a Wonder of the World, has many incredible buildings including the castle.

right
A group of observatory buildings known as "The Seashell."

IZAMAL
CITY OF MANY CULTURES

IZAMAL IS A MAGICAL TOWN LOCATED IN THE YUCATÁN PENINSULA, only forty minutes away from the better-known Mérida. It was founded by the Mayans in around 300 B.C. and was a living, thriving community at the time of the Spanish conquest. When constructing their own city, the Spanish built over the heart of the Mayan city but it's most important structures remained and were actually conserved. Among these is the great pyramid Kinich-Kakmó; at 114 feet it is the highest pyramid in the Yucatán. In 1560, Fray Diego de Landa wrote about the temple, "it was well known both for its height and beauty and from its top you could see the distant ocean." Itzamatul is another important pyramid and was dedicated to the heroic, mythic deity Zamná.

It seems that Izamal was once the center of a thriving region that was connected by stone-paved roads; these roads were known as *sacbé*. The Spanish Franciscan memoirist Fray Bernardino de Lizana has confirmed that four large avenues radiated from Izamal, each conforming to the four cardinal directions. These were important avenues with a ritual function based on the magical importance of the four directions in the Mayan world.

Izamal was not completely destroyed during the conquest and even up until 1886, when the French traveler Desiré Charnay visited, over twenty original buildings remained in some form. But its overall splendor was covered by the construction of the Spanish, who wanted to build a new Izamal on top of the old. As a result, a unique town was created—a place where it is possible to uncover a Mayan ruin in the backyard of an average home. In this town it is easy to visualize and re-create how one community was literally superimposed upon another.

Izamal is an enchanting town painted entirely in yellow. The most important building here is the Franciscan San Antonio de Padua monastery founded by Fray Diego de Landa in 1533. It has one of the largest ecclesiastical atriums in the world and it is encircled by a magnificent arcade featuring seventy-five arches supported by rough unfinished columns. This atrium reached its highpoint in 1993 when the late Pope John Paul II celebrated an open-air Mass there. It also houses the statue of Our Lady of Izamal, the queen and patroness of the Yucatán and in whose small chapel can be found many valuable relics. This chapel, with its feminine grace, serves as a vesting room for the Virgin.

Izamal is considered the oldest city in the Yucatán peninsula, its archeological site dates from the preclassical era.

The atrium of the Franciscan convent in San Antonio de Padua.

facing page
The stairway up to the entrance of the vibrantly colored Sanctuary at Our Lady of Izamal.

The church of the San Antonio de Padua monastery was designed by a Franciscan architect named Fray Juan Mérida. Its design employed the latest styles brought from Spain, something not found in other parts of Mexico. The entrance to the church was built in the plateresque style. Its plateresque facade has a choral window with clear Arabic influence, and the church itself is covered with a Gothic-inspired vaulted mahogany roof. The architecture of the church itself, along with the ancient retablo, gives the building an archaic flavor, all placed within a wonderful archaeological site that merits exploration.

Fray Juan Diego de Landa is closely connected to the history of Yucatán and of Izamal. He was charged with building Izamal's monastery in 1549 and later was sent to Guatemala where he brought back the statue of the Virgin that is now venerated in Izamal. When he was named provincial of the Franciscans he acted against indigenous people who had returned to their own religion; as a part of this he destroyed valuable codices that documented Mayan history. After he was denounced for abusing his power, he returned to Spain; eventually he was absolved and named Bishop of the Yucatán. As bishop, he began to study the language and culture of the Mayans and, paradoxically, became an expert in both. He wrote the essential text on the Mayan world, *An Account of the Yucatán*.

RUTA CONVENTOS
ROAD OF THE FRANCISCANS

SOME TOURIST DESTINATIONS IN MEXICO are worthy of visits when seen in conjunction with other places; they do not necessarily merit special trips. In these cases, it is the full itinerary that makes the visit worthwhile. The monasteries and friaries of the state of Morelos are examples; individually they would not be of much interest but together they form an interesting Mexican tour or "highway" bordering the Sierra de Tepozteco and ending at the great Itzlaccíhuatl and Popacatépetl volcanoes.

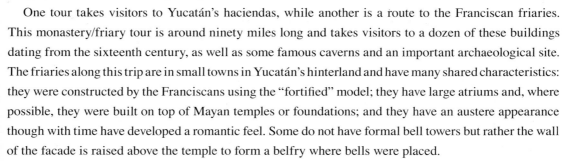

Mama Church along the convent route.

facing page
A magical sunset at Tecoh Church, also along the convent trail.

One tour takes visitors to Yucatán's haciendas, while another is a route to the Franciscan friaries. This monastery/friary tour is around ninety miles long and takes visitors to a dozen of these buildings dating from the sixteenth century, as well as some famous caverns and an important archaeological site. The friaries along this trip are in small towns in Yucatán's hinterland and have many shared characteristics: they were constructed by the Franciscans using the "fortified" model; they have large atriums and, where possible, they were built on top of Mayan temples or foundations; and they have an austere appearance though with time have developed a romantic feel. Some do not have formal bell towers but rather the wall of the facade is raised above the temple to form a belfry where bells were placed.

Acanceh is the closest to Mérida, a city whose center is La Plaza de las Culturas. It contains both Mayan and colonial buildings, such as the church dedicated to the Virgin of the Nativity built in a pure Franciscan style. A little farther on one arrives at Tecoh, where the interior of the sublime church is decorated with numerous paintings; it has two graceful towers. It was built on top of a mound that covers a Mayan pyramid. The custom of the Franciscans to build on top of another sacred structure was also practiced in central Mexico, at the famous church in Cholula, for example. It should be remembered that this was not a practice unique to Mexico; in fact, the Saint Clement Church in Rome is built atop the temple of Mitra.

In Telchaquillo the friars constructed a very austere church that incorporated the talents of local Mayan sculptors, who carved figures that were inlaid in the wall of the facade.

Mayapán is an archaeological site near Telchaquillo and during its apex was one of the great Mayan cities. It flourished between the years A.D. 1200 and 1450 and controlled the northern part of the Yucatán Peninsula.

Some of the towns along this route are famous for other reasons apart from their friaries. Chumayel is the place where the primary tome about Mayan history, *Chilam Balam,* was written. Another is Maní, which was the scene of a terrible auto-da-fé at which Friar Diego de Landa punished heretical natives and then set fire to works of art and invaluable codices. After repenting, Landa was converted into a profound student of Mayan culture. Maní also has exceptional retablos. Other friaries are renowned for their architecture: for example, Mama, with its beautiful campanile, and Teabo with its double belfry. Loltun's caverns are also impressive and tourist-friendly. In addition to the rock formations in these caverns, it's possible to see evidence of human presence from more than 700 years ago.

It is surrounded by a wall that is almost five miles long with six entrances. In its interior there are around thirty-six hundred structures, the majority of which were residences. Its ceremonial center has buildings that are very similar to Chichén Itzá, especially the castle of Kukulcán. While these buildings do not have the refinement of Chichén Itzá, they have a noble simplicity and great architectural force.

A paradox becomes evident along the route of the Yucatán friaries. After the destruction caused by the savage genocidal conquest of Mexico, as well as the force used by the Spanish to evangelize the country, in certain regions the Mayan influence continues to be important. This is especially true in the Yucatán's interior. The majority of the campesinos speak Mayan, which is itself a linguistic miracle. They wear traditional dress, and their lifestyle and values are Mayan. The friaries continue to be a monument to the three hundred years the Franciscans worked to dominate this area spiritually. Tekit has two religious buildings. One chapel is dedicated to Saint Christopher, patron of travelers; the other to Saint Anthony of Padua. After Saint Francis, he is the most popular Franciscan saint, perhaps because the young people turn to him when searching for a good spouse.

RUTA HACIENDAS
A HEMP EMPIRE

DUE TO THE LENGTHY AND BLOODY CONQUEST OF THE YUCATÁN PENINSULA, the ancient Mayan world was replaced by a feudal system. Communal lands were divided among individual owners and many Mayans were forced into slavery. The Spanish called their properties haciendas; these were vast entities (in contrast to ranchos, which were smaller in size and then became the small properties of free farmers). During colonial times the haciendas were either dedicated to ranching or agriculture. But during the nineteenth century, a series of factors changed the way land was used and the Yucatán was converted into the largest hemp-producing region in the world.

Hemp is in the agave *(Agave fourcroydes lemaire)*, or cactus, family, which originates in the eastern Yucatán. Its rigid leaves end with a large needlelike thorn that can be as much as eight feet long. From the time of the Mayans this thorn was the source of fiber that was used to make cords and strong, rough-hewn fabrics. Sixty tons were shipped in 1810; by 1840, over one thousand tons were exported. This made the landowners more ambitious, and they decided to increase hemp production. But this also led to greater exploitation of the campesinos who worked for them, resulting in a series of conflicts called the War of the Castes, a great rebellion of the native population. The landowners prevailed and with the invention first of a fiber gin and later of steam-run machinery, the hemp boom followed.

Hemp production reached eighteen thousand tons in 1879; by the beginning of the twentieth century two hundred thousand tons were shipped. After this, hemp cultivation began in other countries as well as the British colonies in Africa. But with the invention of synthetic fibers as well as other factors, the importance of hemp in the Yucatán began to diminish even though 40 percent of the world supply was produced there. Another factor in the demise of hemp was the Mexican revolution, which resulted in the disbanding of the great haciendas and the division of land among the campesinos. These haciendas, with their magnificent mansions, were history. Many were abandoned; they became overrun with jungle vegetation. The *casta divina* (divine class) of extremely wealthy landowners sought refuge in cities, where they lived with the memories of the splendor that was now gone forever.

Arcaded and beautifully painted Santa Rosa de Lima Hacienda.

facing page
The serene exterior of Temozón Hacienda.

The Hacienda de Santa Rosa de Lima has a rich history. During Mayan times the city of Chunchucmil flourished here and was the center of the coastal salt trade. Chunchucmil's prosperity lasted after the conquest, even after the site was abandoned. Two small towns were built here in the sixteenth century dedicated to agriculture and the salt business. Eventually the agriculture-dedicated haciendas started to focus on livestock instead, and the villages gradually went into decline. It was not until the nineteenth century, when Hacienda de Santa Rosa de Lima converted to hemp production, that it procured its own modern machinery. Its chimney proudly proclaims the date 1901.

In the last several years, with the help of government funding, groups of investors have restored a number of hacienda mansions and converted them into five-star hotels. Another type of Mexican hotel as also appeared: the Yucatán hacienda, where the old mixes with the new.

An estimated 1,170-plus haciendas exist in the Yucatán, the most popular being Xcanatun, Yaxcopoil, San Antonio Cucul, Sotuta del Peón, San Ildefonso Teya, Tecoh, Itzincab, Xcuyum, Kilinché, Holactún, Temozón, Yaxnic, Xcanchacán, Tamanche, Chalmuch, Xmatkuil, and Chacsinkín. It was in Chacsinkín that the first serious efforts to grow hemp were made. Though all of the haciendas were prosperous, it was not until the nineteenth century that growing hemp became a full-time activity. Many elements make Yucatán's haciendas attractive. Their architecture mixes both colonial and nineteenth-century styles. They were the center of small communities, each with a chapel, school, infirmary, and shops. What makes these haciendas truly unique is that they were built in the middle of Yucatán's jungles.

RUTA PUUC
THE CHAAC HIGHWAY

The Mayan nation covered a vast area of southern and southeastern Mexico, as well as territory in Guatemala, Belize, Honduras, and El Salvador. This complex civilization had existed since the fifth millennium before Christ and a great and unique civilization had developed before the conquest. Of course, this culture had contact with the others of Mexico, from the "mother" civilization of the Olmecs to the later cultures such as Teotihuacán. But these groups had little influence on the Mayan culture and did not affect the unique personality of the Mayan civilization. Even though the Mayans were exposed to western culture after the conquest, their society managed to maintain many of its traditions; for example, dozens of variations of the original Mayan language are still spoken today while at the same time the Spanish spoken in this region includes many Mayan words.

Containing more than eleven hundred sites, the vast majority of which are unexplored, the Yucatán Peninsula is both a great Mayan region and one rich in archaeology. Mayan culture in the Yucatán had similar characteristics to those of other regions. The economy was based primarily on a primitive form of growing corn that eventually exhausted the planting fields. At the same time, this need for corn led to trade with the rest of Mexico as well as distant places such as Colombia. This society had two classes: at the top were were priests, political leaders, and businesspeople; below them were the farmers and artisans, as well as slaves destined for sacrifice.

Major intellectual discoveries of the Mayan civilization included numbers and an astonishing knowledge of astronomy, which was focused on the precise measurement of time. Mayan life revolved around a polytheistic religion and its principal gods were those of heaven, Hunab Ku and Itzmaná, and Kinich Ahau, the god of the sun. Ah Puch was the lord of the underworld and Ixchel was the goddess of the moon. Chaac, the god of the rains, had the greatest impact on sculpture and architecture. Unlike those gods worshiped by the great Euro-Asiatic religions, these gods were not omnipotent but required human help through cultic worship and nourishment through human sacrifice.

The Puuc route goes between various Mayan centers in the southern part of the state of Yucatán. *Puuc* signifies the word hill or ridge; along this route are the only mountains found in this otherwise flat region, though none are higher than about 650 feet. In addition to the significant Uxmal, this route has other important cultural centers such as Labná, Kabáh, and Sayil.

The Northern Palace in Sayil, another archaeological site.

facing page
The Arch of Labná at Labná archaeological site.

Kabáh has been cleared and reclaimed and measures about one and a quarter miles from east to west and over half a mile from north to south. This area has dozens of buildings joined in various groupings including a large pyramid and an interesting arch that is found at the end of an avenue and is reminiscent of a Roman triumphal arch. But the most interesting and beautiful structure is Codz Poop, or the Palace of the Masks of Chaac. It is nearly 150 feet long and 19 feet high and has two parallel corridors connected by the extended nose of one of the masks on the facade. Masks of the rain god Chaac completely cover the facade—even its doorways.

Labná is an archaeological site located about seventeen miles from Oxkutzcab. Labná means "old house" in Mayan, and even though its structures are placed irregularly, there are two groups of buildings that are connected by a road, or *sacbé*, that is ten thousand feet long. There are a number of important buildings in Labná, such as a seventy-two-foot-tall temple pyramid with three rooms and a palace connected with several buildings lined up in a row. The most representative building here is known as El Arco, which has two houses on both sides that are richly decorated with latticework panels. El Arco does not have the type of arch typical of European and Asian architecture; instead, a Mayan arch was a simple though elegantly designed opening in a very thick wall.

244

U X M A L
HEART OF THE MAYAN EMPIRE

LOCATED ON THE YUCATAN PENINSULA AT THE HEART OF THE NEW MAYAN EMPIRE, this is one of the most beautiful places in Mexico. Uxmal was built during the sixth century A.D. and flourished between A.D. 600 and 900. Later it was invaded by powerful tribes that came from central Mexico, bringing with them the cult of Quetzalcóatl (Kukulkan in Mayan). A fusion of the two cultures developed, though the aesthetic tradition of the Mayans would always predominate.

However, Uxmal was likely inhabited prior to the Mayans because its principal pyramid, the Soothsayer, is built on top of five other pyramids that had been constructed over the centuries.

Uxmal was built according to the *puuc* style, in which buildings are designed along horizontal lines with flat walls and have richly decorated cornices of rock mosaic. *Puuc* art regularly employed extremely dramatic masks of the rain god Chaac, who is easily recognizable due to his hooked nose that can resemble the trunk of an elephant or a serpent in motion.

Reigning over Uxmal is the Pyramid of the Soothsayer. It is 114 feet high and built on a base fashioned with curved corners, a unique feature among Mexican pyramids; in addition, its walls are covered with specially cut stone. It also has two stairways: one on the west side, the other on the east. The western stairway is the primary one and is oriented so that it directly faces the sunrise of the summer solstice.

The top of the first section of the sixty-five-foot-tall staircase leads to a temple with a rectangular entrance marked by serpents with distended pharynxes representing the god Chaac. It is known as the Temple of the Dwarf, the name referring to a legendary being who was not represented architecturally but was supposed to be the son of a wizard, or the god Itzamná. The temple was supposedly constructed in one night, and this gave the dwarf power. He became the governor of Uxmal and its principal soothsayer or magician.

The Pyramid of the Soothsayer is among the most refined buildings in all of ancient Mexico. More delicate in its design than the pyramids of Teotihuacán or Chichén Itza, it has a unique elegance that dominates the nearby urban landscape, which mirrors its horizontal lines and structures. It is the best example of the fusion between the two great cultures of Mexico, that with its roots in the Mayan culture and that of the northern cult of Quetzalcóatl, the plumed serpent.

Uxmal's Quadrangle of the Nuns.

facing page
A view of the front of the mythical pyramid of the Adivino.

The Quadrangle of the Nuns, in addition to the palaces of Teotihuacán, is one of the most important buildings from the pre-Hispanic world dedicated to worshiping a great religious person. What is most impressive is the purity of the style and the elegance of its long horizontal lines. These form an aesthetic contrast to the smooth texture of the lower walls and the rich, baroque trim of the upper walls, where the work is executed in carved stone. It is important to remember that with indigenous cultures, stone architecture was reserved exclusively for ceremonial sites to worship the deities, while houses were simple and modest.

The Quadrangle of the Nuns was so named because the Spanish thought it was a convent, but the pre-Hispanic cultures did not have religious orders for women. Nonetheless, the name persisted as a way to describe this marvelous example of the *puuc* style of Mayan architecture, which was characterized by flat horizontal walls with delicately designed cornices. Also developed in the *puuc* style was the Mayan arch, which is not technically an arch but instead is a triangular niche or opening in a thick wall; it served as a doorway. Mayan architecture, like that of all ancient Mexico, was very primitive. These early peoples had not discovered the great inventions of the arch and its related forms, the vault and the cupola, that are found in both Europe and Asia.

The Pyramid of the Soothsayer dominates the landscape of Uxmal. Even though it is not particularly tall, at 114 feet, the horizontal layout of the complex makes it the dominant structure of the urban landscape. This pyramid is also unique because of the structures built on it and the stories associated with the mythological soothsayer. Like all ancient Mexican cities, Uxmal is built according to a geometric design that alternates open spaces with massive structures, a pre-Hispanic design concept that is distinctly different from that employed in European and Asian cities. While there were plazas and ceremonial spaces in the Old World, they occupied relatively little space; the city was built principally as a place for citizens to live their daily lives.

above
Steep steps ascend to the
Magician's Pyramid.

below
A close-up view of details at
the Quadrangle of the Nuns.

right
The panorama of Uxmal's
splendid archaeological site.

VALLADOLID
A COLONIAL TOWN WITH MAYAN FLAVOR

THIS CITY IS ON THE HIGHWAY BETWEEN MÉRIDA, THE CAPITAL OF THE STATE OF YUCATÁN, AND CANCÚN, the primary tourist destination in the state. Valladolid has maintained its colonial look and has a tranquil, leisurely atmosphere. It has a significant indigenous population and most of the women wear the typical native white dresses adorned with colorful trim. Many Mayan-influenced crafts can be purchased in Valladolid, and the delicious local cuisine is authentic.

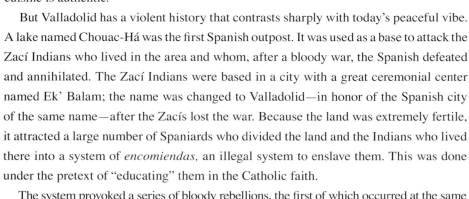

But Valladolid has a violent history that contrasts sharply with today's peaceful vibe. A lake named Chouac-Há was the first Spanish outpost. It was used as a base to attack the Zací Indians who lived in the area and whom, after a bloody war, the Spanish defeated and annihilated. The Zací Indians were based in a city with a great ceremonial center named Ek' Balam; the name was changed to Valladolid—in honor of the Spanish city of the same name—after the Zacís lost the war. Because the land was extremely fertile, it attracted a large number of Spaniards who divided the land and the Indians who lived there into a system of *encomiendas,* an illegal system to enslave them. This was done under the pretext of "educating" them in the Catholic faith.

The system provoked a series of bloody rebellions, the first of which occurred at the same time as the founding of Valladolid in 1546. But the superior military strength of the Europeans prevailed and Valladolid was pacified. Thus began a long colonial period in which the landowners prospered and the Indians endured their slavery. Although Mexico gained its independence at the beginning of the nineteenth century, the social and economic situation changed little.

In July 1847, a native rebellion, today known as the War of the Castes, began. It was a war that was, above all, a genuine indigenous war. Various tribes converged on Valladolid after having conquered the many towns and villages surrounding the city. On January 19, 1848, the natives found themselves on the outskirts of Valladolid and began a struggle for the city; it would last two months. The people took refuge in the main plaza and the church, asking God to save them. Indigenous tribes repeatedly attempted to penetrate the city but, with great difficulty, were repulsed. It took many years for Valladolid to recover and establish the peace and tranquility that exists today. And while many injustices were perpetuated until the Mexican Revolution, lands once lost in the conquest have gradually been returned to their original owners.

Looking down at the remains of Ek' Balam, another archaeological site.

facing page
Sunset at the beautiful San Bernadino Convent.

Because of its unique history, the Mayan community has maintained independence even after being conquered by the Spanish. They still retain many of their cultural traditions and their language. There has not been much intermixing of cultures; as a result, theirs is one of Mexico's purest. Traditional crafts and dress have been preserved, and women can still be seen in their traditional finery of bright colors highlighting white dresses. Mayan women have attracted the attention of innumerable Mexican artists, such as the wonderful sculptor Francisco Zúñiga, who has focused on them in his drawings, painting, and sculpture during his long career.

Valladolid has excellent architecture from the pre-Hispanic to the colonial periods. Ek' Balam was a ceremonial center that had its golden age six hundred to nine hundred years before Christ and was designed in the late classical style. It was eventually abandoned and covered over by an encroaching jungle. It was not rediscovered until 1997 when serious restoration work began. The most significant structure at Ek' Balam is known as the Acropolis; it is 522 feet long and 104 feet high. Important Mayan sculptural works have been discovered in it. The temple was dedicated to the black jaguar, one of the earth gods. San Bernardino Church is a wonderful example of the architecture that the Franciscans brought to the peninsula.

BACALAR
COLORFUL LAGOONS

SPAIN CONSOLIDATED ITS POSITION AS THE PRINCIPAL WORLD POWER IN THE SIXTEENTH CENTURY. At the same time its great enemies, England and France, were trying desperately to steal its riches and diminish its power. King Francis I of France directed his policies toward the seas and lands of America, exhorting the rather small French fleet of privateers to attack the commercial routes of New Spain. Soon after, French pirates such as Jean D'Ango, Jacques Cartier, and Jean Fleury overran the Antilles. They not only became rich but returned to France as heroes, the size of their bounty only increasing the pride of the French. Fleury justified this robbery by referring to the famous treasures violently taken from Moctezuma, the Aztec emperor, by Hernán Cortés.

England also began seizing Spanish ships with little regard for the law. Queen Elizabeth I unconditionally approved of the activities of English pirates, especially of her friend Francis Drake, known as the terror of the Caribbean. For many years, the Spanish tried to stop these attacks through political means but the English Court argued that the Spanish were trying to limit free trade. The English cynically argued that the merchandise was not being robbed but "sequestered"; the goods were a way to repay the expenses incurred by England's military to fight battles in Ireland against supporters of King Philip II of Spain. Other pirates such as John Hawkins and Thomas Cavendish not only benefited from trafficking in slaves, but expanded their activities to Africa and Asia as well. Henry Morgan, who led a band of successful rogues, strengthened his company of pirates and constantly attacked ships and ports.

In these times, privateer was a term used to give legal standing to piracy. A privateer was an armed merchant ship authorized by a government to attack foreign ships during times of war. They were often financed by investors hoping to receive dividends from captured merchandise. In 1621 the Dutch East Indies company was founded. It had more than eight hundred ships and sixty thousand sailors, and it was able to capture more than five hundred enemy ships within a very short time. The celebrated privateer captain Piet Heyn, for example, was able to seize the equivalent of 11 million Dutch florins from a royal Spanish ship in only one attack—half of the original investment in his company. Finally, whether it was legal or not, the Spanish lost an immense amount of riches; however, they were losses similar to those the indigenous peoples of the Americas suffered at Spain's hands.

San Felipe's stalwart fort.

facing page
Seven Colors Lagoon in Bacalar has water comprised of many incredible shades of blue.

For centuries pirates and privateers targeted Bacalar, making it necessary to build San Felipe Fort. Innumerable battles were waged there against the pirates, who were in search of treasure, provisions, weapons, and valuable wood for shipbuilding. Thanks to its superb location and excellent defense systems, the fort also survived attacks during the "caste war" in the Yucatán. During this war, indigenous Mayans revolted against the injustices and abuse committed against them by the Criollos. Today, the fort is a museum. Bacalar is a town with a unique ambience. Its architecture is a mix of tropical colonial buildings and that which uses Mayan construction materials and techniques.

Bacalar's beautiful lagoon is part of a thirty-four-mile-long system of lakes fed by underground currents beneath a surface of smooth white sand. The water's blue hue varies depending on where one looks. It is connected to the Chetumal Bay by the Huay Pix River, supplying the lagoon with an active marine life. This region has junglelike vegetation and is a fascinating place for both eco-tourism and diving. Modern weekend homes have been built on the outskirts of town beside the lagoon. Its romantic atmosphere and surprising natural beauty make Bacalar an ideal place to relax. In the last several years it has become a destination for hundreds of writers, filmmakers, and poets, and it is a popular place for international writer and scriptwriter conferences.

COZUMEL
CORAL PARADISE

Performers take part in the "Dance of the Bottle" at Clock Square.

facing page
Boats are docked at piers on the lovely Mexican Caribbean.

COZUMEL ISLAND IN THE STATE OF QUINTANA ROO IS MUST-SEE DESTINATION FOR LOVERS OF MARINE LIFE. Known worldwide for its excellent diving and snorkeling, Cozumel's rich coral beds and abundant underwater life distinguish it. It has an especially hospitable location in the great Mesoamerican reef system, behind a six-hundred-mile extension of this reef, which allows Cozumel to offer wonderful aquatic adventures. It has a perfect climate, with an average temperature of 80 degrees Fahrenheit, and divers swim in the warm and crystalline Caribbean waters. French oceanographer Jacques Cousteau rated Cozumel as one of the best diving destinations on the planet.

A number of renowned underwater sites at Cozumel are worth exploring. Among these are the coral mounds of Chankanaab; El Cielo, famous for its starfish; and Santa Rosa, known for its underwater caves teeming with fish. Also nearby is the famous wall of San Francisco, with its tunnels filled with gigantic manta rays; Paraiso Bajo y Tormentos, with great facilities for diving; and Yukab, with an abundance of marine life.

Located at the easternmost point of the country, Cozumel is thirty miles long and ten miles wide, and possesses one of the most intimate and beautiful shorelines of the Mexican Caribbean. Thanks to its fine white sands and tranquil turquoise waters, the beaches of Cozumel are a delight.

Certainly it is the island's beauty that inspired the Mayans to build a ceremonial center on Cozumel in honor of the lunar goddess Ixchel. Admired as a creative deity, it was believed her influence extended to the tides, the rains, and the fertility of the harvest. Ixchel was the patroness of maternity, medicine, and divination as well as weaving. The indigenous people of the Yucatán Peninsula visit the Sanctuary of Ixchel to ask for her help in conceiving a child. According to Mayan tradition, Ixchel was grateful for the popular fervor and as a sign of her gratitude adorned the island with thousands of species of birds.

Spaniard Juan de Grijalva discovered the island in 1518. One year later, Hernán Cortés landed here, starting the third Spanish expedition that would finally begin the conquest of Mexico. While there, Cortés encountered Jerónimo Aguilar. Aguilar had survived an earlier Spanish expedition and would later be a diplomat and translator for Cortés.

The island of Cozumel has a unique ambience because of its special cultural mix. It was a Mayan ceremonial site and then, during colonial times, it was not only a Spanish settlement but also a refuge for pirates. During World War II it served as an American military base and today it is an international tourist destination. Foreigners have come to this island for centuries. The majority of the islanders speak Mayan, Spanish, and a conversational level of French and English. The local traditions are a mix, bringing together drinks that originated in the Antilles or festivities from Chiapas, such as the Dance of the Bottle, or recipes adapted from the Yucatán's notable cuisine.

Cozumel was practically unpopulated during the colonial era, but this changed during the indigenous uprising known as the War of the Castes. Hundreds of people fled from the violence on the Yucatán Peninsula and ended up on Cozumel. Today the island combines the charm of a Caribbean pueblo with a rich marine life.

Each year more than two million people visit Cozumel; in fact it receives more cruise visitors than any other port in Mexico. At its piers are everything from small launches for diving and fishing to luxurious transatlantic liners that arrive daily filled with passengers ready to discover the beautiful island. It is a vital place where visitors go to the *malecón,* which has been converted into a huge shopping area for jewelry craftspeople. A typical way to reach the island is by a ten-minute ferry ride from Playa del Carmen. From the air one sees a fertile island outlined by fine beaches and serene turquoise waters. Cozumel has a strong tourist infrastructure, which not only provides gracious hospitality but also preserves the significant natural heritage of the island.

HOLBOX
A PRISTINE ISLAND

ACCORDING TO LEONARDO DA VINCI, "Although human subtlety makes a variety of inventions by different means to the same end, it will never devise an invention more beautiful, more simple, or more direct than does nature, because in her inventions nothing is lacking, and nothing is superfluous." This is particularly applicable to a place like Holbox, where the intervention of humans is at a minimum and that of nature is at a maximum.

The small town of Holbox is in the nature preserve of Yum Balam, which is home to diverse flora and fauna. The island of Holbox is separated from the Mexican coast by a shallow lagoon, Yalahao, a sanctuary for thousands of flamingos, reddish egrets, white ibises, pelicans, and a limitless number of exotic bird species.

Located in the northernmost section of Quintana Roo, Holbox is a great contrast to the state's more famous destinations such as Cancún or Cozumel. This is true primarily because it is little known—there are no young adults on spring break or celebrity jet-setters; instead it caters to ecologically conscious travelers. Waters from the Gulf of Mexico, not the Caribbean, bathe beautiful beaches adorned with pearl-colored conch shells. These waters rush ashore on the smooth white sand. Here there are neither big hotel chains, airports–or modern marinas. On the contrary, Holbox is a peaceful town of fifteen hundred inhabitants with tranquil sandy streets bordered by palms; only bicycles and golf carts pass by. The buildings are simple and houses have Mayan-style thatched roofs. Residents and hotel owners are committed to the environment.

According to legend, Holbox was once a simple indigenous commercial port. Then a Mayan king became fascinated with the island and its surroundings; he decided the island should be reserved for the use of the royal family exclusively. He transformed it into a relaxing place with lovely gardens and sumptuous fountains. In the center he built a pool decorated with jade stones. Only young maidens were allowed to swim in it. With the arrival of the Spanish this majestic place was abandoned. The Spanish then shipped the valuable building material to the coast where it was used to build Mexico's first church, Boca Iglesias, which was both a monastery and the location of the Inquisition in Mexico. Later the island served as a refuge for pirates; toward the end of the nineteenth century it was a modest fishing village. This is why Holbox has been able to maintain intact its richly beautiful natural environment.

A favorite visitor, the whale shark, swims in Holbox's waters.

facing page
Boats anchored at one of Holbox's beaches. A charming fishing village is in the background.

Holbox's best-loved visitors are friendly whale sharks. These sharks are the largest living species of fish and, like whales, only eat plankton and small fish. When moving near the surface, they ingest huge quantities of water in their large mouths, filtering in the smaller fish. They average forty-two feet in length and they can live to be ninety years old. Whale sharks are gentle giants, making it possible to swim next to them. During the summer there are many whale-shark expeditions, a service offered by authorized providers who fully comply with rules and regulations to safeguard this incredible species.

With little more than twenty miles of seashore, the island of Holbox is a lovely oasis with tranquil beaches and exotic fauna. The picturesque town of the same name has become a favorite for people passionate about sports fishing. Many species—tarpon, snooker, snapper, and barracuda, among others—live in the waters. There are also boats that take divers to areas with white turtles, manta rays, and dolphins. For bird lovers, the Yalahao lagoon and the Pájaros and Pasión islands offer great opportunities to watch a range of species. Seafood is the star attraction of the island's cuisine, though curiously, the specialty isn't an indigenous dish but rather a cultural fusion: lobster pizza.

ISLA MUJERES
A RELAXING ESCAPE

Typical colorfully painted homes on Isla Mujeres.

LIKE COZUMEL, ISLA MUJERES WAS A MAYAN CEREMONIAL CENTER IN PRE-COLUMBIAN TIMES, built to honor the goddess Ixchel. In 1517 the Spanish conquistador Francisco Hernández de Córdoba landed on the island. There he discovered a sanctuary dedicated to a deity with statues representing the young maidens of the court—thus his name for the place "Isla Mujeres" (Isle of Women). Later, the Spanish all but abandoned the island and it was transformed into a refuge for both French and English pirates as well as refugees fleeing the battles on the Yucatán Peninsula. By the end of the nineteenth century the island was inhabited by seven hundred people, mostly fishermen. Isla Mujeres was rediscovered in the 1970s, becoming a place to visit because of its natural beauty.

For many tourists, Isla Mujeres is the most relaxing destination in the Mexican Caribbean. Travelers can find refuge from the stresses of the modern world and, most importantly, can completely relax. With its smoothly contoured beaches and beautiful waters, this island embodies the serene atmosphere of a tropical oasis. Here the vegetation, the gracious hospitality, and the warm climate combine to create a genuine sense of serenity. The island is dedicated to restful pleasures. If travelers prefer to be revitalized through more adventurous outdoors experiences, the island offers those as well. Visitors can participate in an endless number of aquatic and sports activities, including fishing, skin diving, snorkeling, sailing, windsurfing, and kayaking. Sport fishing for marlins, golden trevally or golden jack, and flying fish is a very popular tourist activity, with a peak season between April and September. Those who prefer more profound meditative experiences can enjoy those as well.

Fifteen miles north of Isla Mujeres is the nature preserve on Isla Contoy, a 434-acre national park covered with dense foliage that is host to a magnificent bird sanctuary. The island has various lagoons shaded by mangrove trees, where the birds nest and feed on the abundant fish and crustaceans in the area. It is home to more than 150 species of birds, including the frigate, the brown pelican, and the double-crested cormorant. The island also has beaches and sand dunes where hundreds of turtles spawn. Among these can be found the green turtle, the refined Carey turtle hawksbill *(Eretmochelys imbricata)*, the unusual loggerhead, and the immense leatherback turtle, called the *Dermochelys*, that weighs between 550 and 1,545 pounds. Visitors need permits to visit Isle Contoy, but it is well worth it. One can observe the rich flora and fauna accompanied by a resident biologist but also see splendid coral banks—especially Ixlache—which have numerous spiny lobsters, grudges, snails, sardines, and manta rays.

facing page
An aerial view shows the whole of Isla Mujeres, a captivating island.

The town of Isla Mujeres is a tranquil place located at the island's northern end. It still features wood houses painted with bright, joyful colors. Its stores offer a range of jewelry and other products made from conch shells. Four docks in nearby Cancún have frequent ferries that bring passengers back and forth, making the island easily accessible. There is also a landing strip and a marina. Nearby, hundreds of turtles are protected in a refuge that was created in order to both promote adequate reproduction and development before they go out to sea. At the southern end of the island are the Garrafón reefs and inaccessible cliffs.

The beautiful Isla Mujeres is characteristic of the spectacular Mexican Caribbean. Its size fluctuates between nine hundred and twenty-four hundred feet wide, and it is five miles long. Its seven miles of beaches are famous for their smooth white sands, which are ideal for sunbathing or simply resting in a traditional Mayan hammock. Crystal-clear waters are great for innumerable water sports—principally diving and snorkeling in the nearby rich coral reefs and small lagoons. Hospitality on the island is especially gracious. The enchanting small hotels offer their guests a high level of comfort with great attention to detail. In addition to a fabulous cuisine, there are memorable vistas of the Caribbean and unforgettable sunrises and sunsets.

PLAYA DEL CARMEN
A CASUAL PARADISE

IN CONTRAST TO CANCÚN'S DEVELOPMENT, Playa del Carmen maintains an intimate atmosphere combined with a simple, casual style. It existed in pre-Hispanic times when the beaches were the embarkation point for Mayan pilgrims on their way to Cozumel and the sanctuary of the goddess Ixchel. Over time, this small fishing community diversified into the production of palm leaves and, most importantly, the cultivation of the gum tree. In the final decades of the twentieth century, Playa del Carmen rediscovered its natural potential and soon sophisticated residences and lovely hotels were built. Pristine beaches and water, and being a jet-set haven as well as a paradise for relaxation and eating are what this tranquil town is known for today.

Playa del Carmen's unique atmosphere is also created by its natural surroundings. In addition to its beautiful beaches, where thousands of giant turtles spawn, there are also attractive diving areas. Nearby coral reefs are also a delightful place to explore the marine diversity. The underwater cave Dos Ojos, which is connected to the Nohoch Nah Chich caves, is considered the largest underwater cave system in the world. A trip through it offers an opportunity to view illuminated stalagmites and stalactites. Similar to other places in the Mexican Caribbean, there is abundant fishing and an endless variety of water sports. For golf lovers, Playa del Carmen offers a memorable opportunity to play on challenging and beautiful courses expertly integrated with the rich local vegetation.

Sport-fishing boats lined up along a pier.

facing page
Looking down at cheerful Playa del Carmen.

The more one explores this region, the more one discovers that the true temples of Playa del Carmen are not those built to honor saints or pre-Hispanic gods but those dedicated to gastronomy. Food lovers agree that Playa del Carmen is one of the ten major culinary destinations in Mexico. It's no surprise, given that the town is in the Riviera Maya. The Caribbean is teeming with great seafood and the nearby jungle orchards yield a range of exotic fruits and vegetables. Added to this mix is the concentration of delicate flavors and ingredients from the indigenous cuisine of the Yucatán Peninsula. In addition, for years well-known chefs from around the world have adopted Playa del Carmen as their home. As a result, the cuisine is an exquisite fusion of pre-Hispanic and Mestizo dishes, as well as those from across the globe.

Playa del Carmen is dedicated exclusively to enjoyment and rest, and the goal there is to stimulate the senses. After discovering this surprising region there is no other choice but to follow the advice of Oscar Wilde and simply surrender to temptation—in this case to the delectable, seductive, and invigorating temptations of Playa del Carmen.

Playa del Carmen is an ideal place for aquatic activities, especially fishing and diving. You can dive amid the teeming marine life and swim with dolphins. Also offered are whale-watching trips. For those who prefer to go to modern nature recreation areas, great alternatives are the water-themed "eco-parks" Xel-há and Xcaret. From Playa del Carmen it is also possible to organize expeditions to nearby archaeological sites such as Tulúm, Cobá, or Chichén Itza. Bird watchers can view exotic species at the Sian Kan nature reserve.

Playa del Carmen's main boulevard is Fifth Avenue, a lovely paved pedestrian walkway that parallels the coastline. Located along this route are the majority of the town's restaurants, cafés, bars, shops, boutiques, and galleries. Crowded with international visitors, it a very cosmopolitan, festive street with a carnival-like atmosphere. Mimes, musicians, and dancers also contribute to this vibe. It doesn't matter if you visit early or late, because Fifth Avenue is busy all day and night. It is where everything is happening. The dock where the Cozumel-bound ferries arrive is located where Fifth Avenue meets First Street.

TULÚM
WINDOW ON THE CARIBBEAN

TULÚM IS LOCATED SEVENTY-NINE MILES SOUTH OF THE TOURIST CENTER OF CANCÚN on the Mexican Caribbean, and it is in the middle of a national park of nearly sixteen hundred acres. The city has a long history; archaeological evidence indicates it has been inhabited since 400 or 500 B.C., even though its golden age was in the fourteenth and fifteenth centuries. Tulúm was flourishing in the sixteenth century when the Spanish arrived, making it one of the oldest cities in the Americas dating back nearly two thousand years. While other Mayan cities maintained an ephemeral brilliance, Tulúm was able to sustain itself over a long period of time. Perhaps this was because it was located at a strategic point between commercial routes of the region and those from Central America—especially Guatemala—that converged on the Yucatán peninsula. Economic prosperity continued until the Spanish conquest.

At the same time, Tulúm maintained an identity separate from other Mayan cities, akin to the Hanseatic League in Europe, which enabled it to distance itself from the nearby warring Mayan kingdoms. Nevertheless, Tulúm was a natural trading center, which is revealed by the objects from foreign places that have been found there such as jade and obsidian from Guatemala and copper objects traded from the distant highlands of central Mexico.

Tulúm's Temple of the Frescoes.

facing page
Remains of the castle in Tulúm.

Trade was carried out both by land and sea, though pre-Hispanic navigation was primarily coastal using very small boats. In ancient America there were no domesticated animals to transport cargo; traders had to haul goods themselves on foot. People from all Mexican cultures were interested in wide-ranging trade. The distances they had to walk as they carried merchandise across Mexico's varied and often challenging terrain are hard to fathom from today's perspective. But Tulúm's principal activity was fishing, which is understandable given the array of fish that can be found in the Mexican Caribbean, many species of which can be seen in the natural aquatic park Xel-Há located on the coast between Cancún and Tulúm.

Tulúm had a hierarchical society. At the highest level were those in charge of the government and religious rituals, as well as the astronomical scribes. Also among the privileged were the most successful trade and businesspeople, as well as military leaders. Then came the minor functionaries, and after this the artisans and artists. Finally were the more humble workers—the farmers, fishermen, and hunters.

In the Temple of the Frescoes various stages of construction can be seen, though all that is left is a room lavishly decorated with frescoes. As in all pre-Hispanic painting, specific colors were used for each theme; for example, blue represented the sea and the sky; green represented vegetation; yellow, the south; white, the north; red, the east; and black, the west. The use of color in indigenous art was not realistic, but rather was associated with ritual and religious thought. Tulúm was the last of the Mayan strongholds, located beside the sea and resting at the top of a sheer cliff that provided a natural defense from invaders.

Tulúm, which means wall or rampart, is a name only recently given to this Mayan coastal city. In pre-Hispanic times it was called Zamá, which means "the dawn," and was dedicated to the observation and worship of the planet Venus. The ancient Mexicans identified this planet with the god Quetzalcóatl, who the Mayans called Kukulkan. The principal building at Tulúm is known as the castle, but it actually was a temple dedicated to Venus-Kukulc and placed on top of a pyramid. During a 1518 expedition from Cuba led by Juan de Grijalva, the commander wrote that he had discovered "a city as large as Seville" where there was "the largest tower I have ever seen." More than a conquistador, Grijalva was an explorer who traveled along the coasts of the peninsula before returning to Cuba.

Tulúm is intimately bound to the Mexican Caribbean. The Caribbean Sea is characterized by its beautiful blue water with tones of green; in certain parts, the water is incredibly clear. Tulúm's architecture was influenced by the sea, which contrasts with the majority of the Mayan cities that flourished either in jungles or on the flat plains of the Yucatán. The city was abandoned when the Spanish arrived and was rediscovered in the twentieth century. Tulúm's most important temple is of the Descending God, where there is a sculpted figure of a winged god who appears to have come down from the heavens. This could be an image of a solar god, though according to archaeologist Albert Ruz Lhuillier, who discovered the great tomb at Palenque, it is more likely the god of lightning and thunder or of rain. But Venus-Kukulc was the great deity of Tulúm, whose priest-astronomers determined the revolution of Venus and fixed it at 584 days.

above
Beaches at the biosphere reserve in Sian Ka'An.

left
View of the Caribbean from Tulúm.

below
Temple of the Descending God.

265

ADDRESSES

BAJA CALIFORNIA

san felipe

Oficinas de Turismo
Mar de Cortés & Manzanillo 300
phone +52 (686) 577 18 65
sanfelipetur@baja.gob.mx

Hotel San Felipe Marina Resort and SPA
Km. 4.5 Carretera San Felipe – Aeropuerto
phone +52 (526) 577 14 55 / (526) 577 14 55
snmarina@telnor.net
reservaciones@sanfelipemarina.net
www.visitsanfelipebc.com

Restaurant Mariscos Conchita's
Malecon 202
phone +52 (686) 577 02 67

Restaurant de la Hacienda la Langosta Roja
Calzada Chetumal 125
phone +52 (686) 577 04 83

Restaurant The Light House
Guaymas 152
phone +52 (686) 577 25 40

El Nido Restaurant & Bar
Mar de Cortés 348
phone +52 (686) 577 10 28

valle de guadalupe

Hotel La Villa del Valle (Las Brisas del Valle)
Carretera Ensenada–Tecate
phone +45 (646) 183 92 49
info@lavilladelvalle.com
www.lavilladelvalle.com

Hotel Adobe Guadalupe
Parcela A-1 s/n, Col. Rusa de Guadalupe
phone +52 (646) 155 20 94
www.adobeguadalupe.com

Restaurante del Museo Comunitario Ruso
Carretera 3
phone +52 (646) 155 20 30

Restaurante Laja
km. 83, Carretera 3 Tecate-Ensenada
phone +52 (646) 155 25 56

Restaurant La Casa de Campo
Km. 95, Carretera 3 Tecate-Ensenada,
phone +52 (646) 171 75 14

Restaurant El Mesón de Mustafá
Km. 93, Carretera 3 Tecate–Ensenada
phone +52 (646) 155 31 85

L.A. Cetto
Km. 73.5, Carretera 3 Tecate–Ensenada
phone +52 (646) 155 22 64 / (646) 155 22 69
valle@gpocetto.com
www.lacetto.com

Casa de Piedra
Km. 93.5, Carretera 3 Tecate–Ensenada
phone +52 (646) 155 30 97 / (646) 156 52 67
cpiedra@telnor.net
www.vinoscasadepiedra.com

Monte Xanic
Carretera 3, Tecate–Ensenada
phone +52 (646) 174 67 69 / (646) 174 61 55
www.montexanic.com

Bodegas de Santo Tomás
Miramar 666
phone +52 (646) 174 08 36 / (646) 174 08 29
www.santotomas.com.mx

Chateau Camou
Carretera 3, Tecate–Ensenada
phone +52 (646) 177 22 21 / (646) 177 33 03
contacto@chateau-camou.com.mx
www.chateau-camou.com.mx

Casa Pedro Domecq
Km 73.5, Carretera 3 Tecate–Ensenada
phone +52 (646) 155 23 33 / (646) 155 22 49
www.vinosdomecq.com.mx

ensenada

Secretaría de Turismo
Blvd. Lázaro Cárdenas & Calle Las Rocas 1477
Centro
phone +52 (646) 172 30 22 / (646) 172 30 00
fax +52 (646) 172 30 81 / (646) 172 31 18
fpalacios@baja.gob.mx

Información al Turista
phone +52 (646) 178 24 11 / (646) 178 36 75

Hotel Punta Morro
km 106, Carretera Tijuana–Ensenada
phone +52 (646) 178 35 07
reservas@punta-morro.com
www.punta-morro.com

Restaurant El Rey Sol
López Mateos 1000
phone +52 (646) 178 17 33

Restaurant Casa Mar
Blvd. Lázaro Cárdenas 987
phone +52 (646) 174 04 17

Restaurant La Embotelladora Vieja
Miramar & Calle 7A
phone +52 (646) 178 16 60 / (646) 174 08 07

BAJA CALIFORNIA SUR

Oficina de Turismo del Estado de Baja California Sur
Mariano Abasolo s/n, La Paz
phone +52 (612) 124 01 00 / (612) 122 59 39

loreto

Oficina de Información Turística
Edificio Municipal de Loreto
Plaza Cívica
phone +52 (613) 135 04 11
turismoloreto@hotmail.com

Hotel Posada de Las Flores
Francisco. I Madero 78, Centro
phone +52 (55) 5208 22 14
hotel@posadadelasflores.com
jafet@posadadelasflores.com
www.posadadelasflores.com

Hotel The Whales Inn Beach & Golf Resort
Misión de Loreto s/n
phone +52 (613) 133 07 00
reservaciones@whalesinn.com
www.whalesinn.com

Café Olé
Francisco I. Madero 14, Col. Centro
phone +52 (613) 135 04 96

Restaurant El Tío Lupe
Hidalgo & Colegio s/n
phone +52 (613) 135 18 82

Asadero "Super Burro"
Guillermo Pajarito Fernández s/n
Centro

mulegé

Hotel Las Casitas
Madero 50,
Centro
phone +52 (615) 153 00 19
lascasitas1962@hotmail.com
www.bajaquest.com/mulege/casitas.htm

Restaurant Doney Mely´s
Moctezuma s/n, La Paloma
phone +52 (615) 153 00 95

Restaurant Histórico "Las Casitas"
Madero 50.Centro
phone +52 (615) 153 03 19

san ignacio

Casa Lereé
Calle Madero s/n, Centro
phone +52 (615) 154 01 58
janebames@prodigy.net.mx
www.murrietawebdesign.com/test/leree/walk_town_spanish.html

Restaurant Rice & Beans Oasis
Carretera Transpeninsular al este del Pueblo
phone +52 (615) 154 02 83

Restaurant Las Cazuelas
Carretera 1, Km. 74, Hotel La Pinta
phone +52 (615) 154 03 00
Toll free from Mexico 01 800 026 36 05

san josé del cabo

Secretaría Municipal de Turismo
Carretera Transpeninsular
Phone +52 (624) 142 29 60 ext. 150

Hotel Casa Natalia
Blvd. Mijares 4,Centro
phone +52 (624) 146 71 00
fax +52 (624) 142 51 10
nathalie@casanatalia.com
www.casanatalia.com

Hotel Encanto Inn
Morelos 133 esq. C. Comonfort
phone +52 (624) 142 03 88
info@elencantoinn.com
www.elencantoinn.com

Restaurant La Panga Antigua
Zaragoza 20
phone +52 (624) 142 40 41

Restaurant Mi Cocina
Blvd. Mijares 4, Hotel Casa Natalia
phone +52 (624) 142 51 00

Restaurant Da Giorgio
KM. 25, Carretera Transpeninsular
phone +52 (624) 144 51 95 / (624) 144 53 04

Restaurant Damiana
Boulevard Mijares 8
phone +52 (624) 142 04 99

Restaurant Baan Thai
Morelos s/n esquina Álvaro Obregón
phone +52 (624) 142 33 44

cabo san lucas

Oficinas de Turismo
phone +52 (624) 105 16 66

Hotel Casa Bella
Hidalgo 10, Centro
phone +52 (624) 143 64 00
bungson69@prodigy.net.mx
hotelboutiquecb@yahoo.com
www.zonaturistica.com

Hotel The Bungalows Hotel
Blvd. Miguel Angel Herrera s/n
phone +52 (624) 143 50 35
bungalow@prodigy.net.mx
www.zonaturistica.com

Hotel Castillo Blarney Inn
Libertad s/n, Lienzo Charro
phone +52 (624) 143 21 60
www.zonaturistica.com

Hotel Los Milagros
Mariano Matamoros 116, Centro
phone +52 (624) 143 45 66
info@losmilagros.com.mx
ricardo@losmilagros.com.mx
www.losmilagros.com.mx

Restaurant Amarone Ristorante Italiano
Centro Comercial Puerto Paraíso
phone +52 (624) 105 10 34

Restaurant Mariscos Mocambo
Vicario & Calle 20 de Noviembre
phone +52 (624) 143 21 22

santa rosalia

Hotel El Morro
km. 1.5, Carretera Transpeninsular sur
phone +52 (615) 152 04 14

Restaurant El Muelle
Constitución s/n esq. Calle Plaza Centro
phone +52 (615) 152 20 52

Restaurant Miramar
Montoya 6
phone +52 (615) 152 09 32

todos santos

Hotel Hacienda Todos Los Santos
Carretera 19 a Los Cabos
phone +52 (612) 145 05 47 / (612) 145 01 62
haciendadelossantos@prodigy.net.mx
www.mexonline.com/haciendatodoslossantos.htm

Hotel Posada La Poza
Posada La Poza A.P. 10
phone +52 (612) 145 04 00
posadalapoza@yahoo.com
contact@lapoza.com
www.lapoza.com

Hotel The Todos Santos Inn
Legaspi 33
phone +52 (612) 145 00 40
todossantosinn@yahoo.com
www.todossantosinn.com

Restaurant Miguel´s The Best Chiles Rellenos
Degollado esq. Rangel

Caffé Todos Santos
Centenario 33
phone +52 (612) 145 03 00

Restaurant Los Adobes de Todos Santos
Hidalgo s/n
phone +52 (612) 145 02 03

SONORA

Secretaría de Turismo del Estado
Comonfort & Paseo Canal
Col. Centenario, Hermosillo, Son.
phone +52 (662) 217 00 76
Toll free from Mexico 01 800 476 66 72
www.sonoraturismo.gob.mx

álamos

Oficina de Turismo
Juárez 6, Planta baja Hotel Los Portales
phone +52 (647) 428 04 50

Hotel La Puerta Roja Inn
Galeana 46
phone +52 (647) 428 01 42
info@lapuertarojainn.com
www.lapuertarojainn.com

Hotel Hacienda de Los Santos
Molina 8
phone +52 (647) 428 02 22 / (647) 428 00 17
info@haciendadelossantos.com
www.haciendadelossantos.com

Hotel Colonial
Obregón 4
phone +52 (647) 428 13 71
info@alamoshotelcolonial.com
www.alamoshotelcolonial.com

Restaurant Las Palmeras
Cárdenas 9
phone +52 (647) 428 00 65

Restaurant El Africano
Galeana 25
La Colorada
phone +52 (647) 428 12 11

Restaurant Casa de Los Tesoros
Obregón 10, Centro
phone +52 (647) 428 00 10

magdalena de kino

Hotel EL Toro
Niños Heroes & Misión de Dolores
phone +52 (632) 322 03 75
www.zonaturistica.com/sonora/magdalena-de-kino

Restaurant Mariscos Irma
Niños Héroes 313, Centro
phone +52 (632) 318 50 36

Restaurant El Fundador
Del Río 50, Cerro de la Cruz
phone +52 (632) 321 83 11

CHIHUAHUA

Secretaría de Turismo del Estado
Aldama & Guerrero
Centro
phone +52 (614) 429 33 00
Toll free from Mexico 01 800 849 52 00

batopilas

River Side Lodge
phone +52 (635) 456 00 36 / (614) 413 90 20
info@amigos3.com
www.3amigoscanyonexpeditions.com

Restaurant Doña Mica
Plaza de La Constitución

Restaurant El Puente Colgante (The Swinging Bridge)
Plaza de La Constitución
phone +52 (649) 456 90 23

creel

Oficinas de Turismo
Phone +52 (635) 456 05 46
www.3amigoscanyonexpeditions.com

Hotel Villa Mexicana Hotel & Resort
Adolfo López Mateos s/n
phone +52 (635) 456 06 66 / (614) 421 70 88
Toll free from Mexico 01 800 710 64 22
ventas@vmcoppercanyon.com
www.vmcoppercanyon.com

Hotel Divisadero Barrancas
Mirador 4516
Residencial campestre,
Km. 622, Ferrocarril Chihuahua-Pacífico
phone +52 (614) 415 11 99
fax +52 (614) 415 65 75
reservaciones@hoteldivisadero.com
www.hoteldivisadero.com

Cabañas Cañon del Cobre
km 110, Carretera Creel-Guachochi
Cerocahui
phone +52 (635) 456 00 36

Restaurant La Cabaña
López Mateos 36
phone +52 (635) 456 00 68

Restaurant Nuevo Barrancas del Cobre
Francisco Villa 121, Centro
phone +52 (635) 456 00 22

Restaurant Sierra Madre
López Mateos 61, Centro
phone +52 (635) 456 00 71

El Caballo Bayo
López Mateos 25
phone +52 (635) 456 01 36

cerocahui

Restaurant Mision
Address commonly known
Urique
phone +52 (635) 456 52 94 / (668) 818 70 46

Resaturant Paraiso del Oso
Address commonly known
Urique
phone +52 (614) 421 33 72

Wuildeness Lodge
Address commonly known, Urique
phone +52 (635) 456 02 45

divisadero

Restaurant Posada Barrancas Mirador
Address commonly known, Urique
phone +52 (668) 818 70 46

Restaurant Divisadero Barrancas
Address commonly known, Ruta Ch-P km. 622
phone +52 (635) 578 30 60 / (614) 415 11 99

hidalgo del parral

Módulo de Atención Turistica
Riva Palacio 2, Centro
Palacio de Alavarado
phone +52 (627) 522 02 90

Hotel Los Arcos
Dr. Pedro D. Lille 5
El Camino
phone +52 (627) 523 05 97 al 99
Toll free from Mexico 01 800 543 23 39
www.zonaturistica.com/hotel/los-arcos-hidalgo-del-parral/info.php

Hotel American Inn Hotel & Suites
Independencia 412
phone +52 (627) 523 50 10
Toll free from Mexico 01 800 670 88 61
www.americaninnparral.com

Restaurant Bar Calipso
Paseo Gómez Morín 1
phone +52 (627) 522 90 66

Restaurant La Fuente
Collegio & Denon
phone +52 (627) 522 30 88

Restaurant Turista
Plaza Independencia 12
phone +52 (627) 523 72 30 / (627) 522 44 47

nuevas casas grandes

Hotel Las Guacamayas Bed & Breakfast
20 de Noviembre 1101 & Zona Arqueologica
Casas Grandes
phone +52 (636) 692 41 44
maytelujan@msn.com
www.mataortizollas.com

Hotel Hacienda
Juárez 2603, Centro
phone +52 (636) 694 10 46
hotelhacienda@paquinet.commx
www.nuevacasasgrandes.org / hotels.aspx

Restaurant La Hacienda
Benito Juárez 2603, Centro
phone +52 (636) 694 10 48 / (636) 694 17 00

Restaurant El Capulin
Minerva 206
phone +52 (636) 694 01 80

Restaurant Constantino
Benito Juárez & Minerva
Centro
phone +52 (636) 694 10 05

COAHUILA

cuatro ciénegas

Oficinas de Turismo
Juárez s/n
phone +52 (869) 696 05 74

Hotel Misión Marielena
Hidalgo 202
Centro
phone +52 (869) 696 11 51 / (869) 696 11 52
contacto@hotelmisionmarielena.com.mx
www.hotelmisionmarielena.com.mx

Hotel El Nogalito
Km 1, Carretera a Ocampo
phone +52 (869) 696 00 09 / (869) 696 06 22
www.elnogalito.com

Restaurant El Doc
Zaragoza 103, Centro
phone +52 (869) 696 03 69

Restaurant La Casona
Hidalgo 202, Centro
phone +52 (869) 696 00 66 / (869) 696 00 73

parras de la fuente

Promotora Turística de Parras
Km. 3, Carretera Parras-Paila
phone +52 (842) 422 02 59
proturparras@hotmail.com
www.parrascoahuila.com.mx

Hotel Rincón del Montero
Km. 3, Carretera Parras - Paila
phone +52 (842) 422 05 40 / (842) 422 08 21
Toll free from Mexico 01 800 718 40 44
reservaciones@rincondelmontero.com
www.rincondelmontero.com

Restaurantes La Calandria & Los Morillos
Km. 3, Carretera Parras - Paila
dentro del Hotel Rincón del Montero
phone +52 (842) 422 05 40 / (842) 422 08 21

Restaurant Bar La Noria
Ramos Arizpe 301
phone +52 (842) 422 11 13 / (842) 422 25 40

NUEVO LEÓN

Oficinas Generales
Antiguo Palacio Federal
Washington Ote. 648 Piso 1, Centro
Monterrey, N.L.
phone +52 (81) 2020 67 89 / (81) 2020 67 74
Toll free from Mexico 01 800 835 24 38

bustamante

Hotel Ancira
Independencia 108
phone +52 (829) 246 03 10
www.zonaturistica.com

Restaurant Ancira
Independencia 108
phone +52 (829) 246 03 10 / (829) 246 03 40

Restaurant Las Golondrinas
General Miel & Escobedo
phone +52 (829) 246 04 80

villa de garcía

Hotel Los Vientos de García
Escobedo Sur 901, Centro
phone +52 (818) 283 04 62
reservaciones@vientosdegarcia.com
info@vientosdegarcia.com
www.vientosdegarcia.com

Hotel Quinta Real Monterrey
Diego Rivera 500, Valle Oriente
phone +52 (818) 368 10 00 / (818) 368 10 70
Monterrey, N.L.
ventas@quintareal.com
www.quintareal.com

Restaurant Parador Español
Lerdo de Tejada s/n

Restaurant-Bar Los Vientos de García
Escobedo Sur 901, Centro
phone +52 (818) 283 04 62

ZACATECAS

Oficinas de Turismo Zacatecas
Hidalgo 403
phone +52 (492) 924 05 52
Toll free from Mexico 01 800 712 40 78
www.turismozacatecas.gob.mx

Hotel Mesón de Jobito
Jardín Juárez 143
Centro Historico
phone +52 (492) 924 17 22
Toll free from Mexico 01 800 021 00 40
gerenciadeventas@mesondejobito.com
www.mesondejobito.com

Hotel Quinta Real Zacatecas
Ignacio Rayon 434, Centro
phone +52 (492) 922 91 04
Toll free from Mexico 01 800 714 41 57
reserv.zac@quintareal.com
www.quintareal.com

Hotel Santa Rita
Hidalgo 507-A, Centro Histórico
Zacatecas, Zac.
phone +52 (492) 925 41 41
Toll free from Mexico 01 800 560 81 55
contacto@hotelsantarita.com
www.hotelsantarita.com

Hotel Casa Torres
1º de mayo 325
phone +52 (492) 925 32 66
Toll free from Mexico 01 800 581 84 24
reservaciones@hotelcasatorres.com

Hotel la Casona de los Vitrales
Callejón del espejo 104
phone +52 (492) 925 00 96
info@lacasonadelosvitrales.com
www.lacasonadelosvitrales.com

guadalupe

Restaurant Hacienda del Cobre
Blvd. López Portillo s/n
phone +52 (492) 923 13 64

Restaurant Las Costillas de Sancho
Blvd. López Portillo 218
phone +52 (492) 899 11 44 / (492) 899 11 45

jeréz

Oficinas de Turismo
Jeréz de García Salinas
Guanajuato 28
phone +52 (494) 945 68 24

Restaurant Juana Gallo
Calle del Santuario 9
phone +52 (494) 945 51 88

Restaurant La Cofradía
Constitución 19
phone +52 (494) 945 42 86

Restaurant Cenaduría La Paloma
Pino Suárez 27-B
phone +52 (494) 945 34 62

sombrerete

Oficina Municipal de Turismo
Hidalgo s/n, Centro
Phone +52 (433) 935 14 38

Restaurant Gastronómica María Josefina
Hidalgo 181-A, Centro
phone +52 (433) 935 52 28

SAN LUIS POTOSÍ

Secretaría de Turismo
Álvaro Obregón 520, Centro
San Luis Potosí, San Luis Potosí
phone +52 (444) 812 23 57

real de catorce

Dirección de Turismo Municipal
Constitución Núm. 27, Centro
phone +52 (488) 887 50 71

Hotel Ruinas del Real
Libertad esquina Lerdo s/n
phone +52 (488) 882 37 33 / (488) 882 37 33
alexmagno14@yahoo.com
www.zonaturistica.com

Hotel Mesón de La Abundancia
Lanzagorta 11
phone +52 (488) 887 50 44
meson@mesonabundancia.com
www.mesonabundancia.com

Hotel Villas Campestre Alcazaba
Calz. Zaragoza 33 - A
phone +52 (488) 102 07 66
cel. 045 (488) 101 02 44
alcazabatorres@gmail.com
www.realdecatorce.net/alcazaba/index.htm

Restaurant El Cactus Café
Plaza Hidalgo
phone +52 (488) 887 50 56

Restaurant El Candil
Lanzagorta 11,
Hotel Mesón de La Abundancia
phone +52 (488) 887 50 44

Restaurant El Minero
Lanzagorta 6
phone +52 (488) 887 50 64

Restaurant El Tolentino
Terán 7
phone +52 (488) 887 50 92

SINALOA

Coordinación General de Turismo
Insurgentes s/n
Unidad Administrativa
Culiacán, Sinaloa,
phone +52 (667) 717 84 19

cosalá

Oficinas de Turismo
Municipio de Cosalá,
Rosales & Leyva Solano s/n
Centro
phone +52 (696) 965 00 01

Hotel Real del Conde
Rosales 6
Centro Histórico
phone +52 (696) 965 00 06
Toll free from Mexico 01 800 701 68 48
www.cosala.gob.mx/servicios/index.htm

Hotel Ray 4 Hermanos
Arteaga s/n
phone +52 (696) 965 03 03 / (696) 965 00 06
www.cosala.gob.mx/servicios/index.htm

Restaurant El Rincón del Mineral
5 de Mayo 7, Centro
phone +52 (669) 965 02 80

NAYARIT

Oficinas de turismo
Subsecretaría de Turismo
Av. México & Calz. del Ejército Nacional s/n.
Ex Convento de la Cruz, Centro
Tepic, Nayarit.
phone +52 (311) 214 80 71
www.visitanayarit.com

mexcaltitán

Dirección de Turismo de Santiago Ixcuintla
20 de noviembre s/n. Centro
Santiago Ixcuintla, Nayarit
phone +52 (323) 235 05 95

Restaurant El Farallón
Ocampo 132
phone +52 (323) 235 12 00

Restaurant Alberca
Address commonly known
phone +52 (323) 235 60 26

san blas

Hotel Garza Canela
Paredes 106 Sur, San Blas
phone +52 (323) 285 01 12
Toll free from Mexico 01 800 713 23 13
www.garzacanela.com

CENTRAL MEXICO

JALISCO

Secretaría de Turismo
Morelos 102, Plaza Tapatia
Guadalajara, Jalisco
phone +52 (33) 3668 16 00
Toll free from Mexico 01 800 363 22 00
www.jalisco.gob.mx

Hotel De Mendoza
Venustiano Carranza 16, Centro
phone +52 (33) 3942 51 51 / (33) 3613 46 46
Toll free from Mexico 01 800 361 26 00
hotel@demendoza.com.mx
www.demendoza.com.mx

chapala

Oficina de Turismo
Madero 407
phone +52 (376) 765 31 41

Hotel Lake Chapala Inn
Paseo Ramón Corona 23
phone +52 (376) 765 47 86
Toll free from Mexico 01 800 501 94 46
chapalainn@laguna.com.mx
www.mexonline.com/chapalainn.htm

Hotel Villa Montecarlo
Hidalgo 269
phone +52 (376) 765 21 20

Restaurant El Árbol de Café
Hidalgo 236
phone +52 (376) 765 39 08

Restaurant Cazadores
Ramón Corona 18
phone +52 (376) 765 21 62

Restaurant La Ribera de Chapala
Francisco I. Madero 200-A

Restaurant Superior
Madero 415
phone +52 (376) 765 21 80

ajijic

Hotel Mis Amores
Hidalgo 22-B
phone +52 (376) 766 46 40 / (376) 766 46 41
info@misamores.com
www.misamores.com

Hotel Real de Chapala
Paseo del Prado 20
La Floresta
phone +52 (376) 766 00 07 / (376) 766 00 14
reservasrealchapala@yahoo.com.mx
www.realdechapala.com

Hotel La Paloma Bed and Breakfast
Juan Álvarez 56
phone +52 (376) 766 41 40
www.lapalomabb.com

Restaurant La Fonda de Doña Lola
Carretera Poniente 36
phone +52 (376) 766 44 55

Restaurant La Tradicional Posada
Morelos 1
phone +52 (376) 766 07 44

lagos de moreno

Hotel Hacienda Sepúlveda
Km. 4, Carretera Lagos–El Puesto
phone +52 (474) 746 54 01 / (474) 746 54 02
Toll free from Mexico 01 800 503 83 68
info@haciendasepulveda.com.mx
www.haciendasepulveda.com.mx

Hotel Hacienda La Punta
Km. 42, Carretera Aguascalientes–Ojuelos
phone +52 (449) 912 60 48 / (449) 912 60 46
pedro@cadu-inmobiliaria.com
www.haciendalapunta.com.mx

Hotel Hacienda San Rafael
Km. 11 Carretera Lagos de Moreno–S.L.P
phone +52 (474) 742 03 71

Hotel Posada Sierra Vista
Address commonly known
phone +52 (382) 538 07 70 / (382) 538 07 80
Toll free from Mexico 01 800 685 26 86
www.posadasierravista.com

Restaurant Máquina 501
Luis Reina 123
phone +52 (474) 742 04 26

mazamitla

Dirección de Promoción Turística Municipal
Portal 5 de Mayo 4
phone +52 (382) 538 02 30

Hotel Villas Mazamitla
Carretera Guadalajara–Mazamitla s/n
phone +52 (382) 538 12 64

Hotel Rancho Epenche
A 500 mts. de la Ranchería Epenche Grande
phone +52 (33) 3615 57 79
ranchoepenche@hotmail.com
admin@historichaciendainns.com
www.historichaciendainns.com/epencheesp.
html

Restaurant La Troje
Galeana 53
phone +52 (382) 538 00 70

Restaurant Taberna Montecristo
Hidalgo 6

Restaurant Alpina
Reforma 8
phone +52 (382) 538 01 04

puerto vallarta

Oficinas de Turismo
Juárez s/n
Phone +52 (322) 223 25 00 ext. 230

Dirección de Turismo del Edo. de Jalisco
Plaza Marina Local 144 & 146
Marina Vallarta
phone +52 (322) 221 26 76 / (322) 221 26 80

Hotelito Desconocido
Playón de Mismaloya 479-205
phone +52 (322) 222 25 26
hotelito@hotelito.com, hotelito@pvnet.com.mx
www.hotelito.com

Hotel Las Alamandas
Km. 83 Carretera Federal 200
Quemaro, Costalegre
phone +52 (322) 285 55 00 / (322) 285 50 27
infoalamandas@aol.com
www.lasalamandas.com

Hotel Westin Regina Resort
Paseo de la Marina 205
Marina Vallarta
phone +52 (322) 221 11 00 ext. 4202
info@westinpv.com
www.westinpv.com

Hotel El Tamarindo
Km. 7.5, Carretera Melaque–Puerto Vallarta
phone +52 (55) 5257 00 97 / (55) 5257 01 51
info@grupoplan.com
www.grupoplan.com

Hotel Four Seasons Resort
Km. 19, Ramal Carretera Federal 200
Punta Mita, Bahía de Banderas
phone +52 (329) 291 60 00 / (329) 291 60 19
www.fourseasons.com
www.fshr.com/puntamita

Hotel Villa Bella B&B
Calle del Monte Calvario 12
La Cruz de Huanacaxtle
phone +52 (329) 295 51 61
info@villabella-lacruz.com
www.villabella-lacruz.com

Hotel Majahuitas
Playa Majahuitas
phone +52 (322) 293 45 06

Hotel Verana
Address commonly known
phone +52 (310) 360 01 55
Toll free from Mexico 01 (800) 530 71 76
www.verana.com

Café des Artistes Bistro Gourmet
Guadalupe Sánchez 740
phone +52 (322) 222 32 28

Restaurant De Santos
Morelos 771
phone +52 (322) 223 30 52

Restaurant Kaiser Maximilian
Olas Altas 380-B
phone +52 (322) 222 50 58 / (322) 223 07 60

Restaurant 8 Tostadas
Quillas s/n Loc. 28-29
phone +52 (322) 221 31 24

Restaurant El Set
Km. 2.5 Carretera a Barra de Navidad
phone +52 (322) 221 53 42

Restaurant Tacón de Marlín
Blvd. Fco. Medina Ascencio 8106
Villa de las Flores

san sebastian del oeste

**Hotel La Galerita de San Sebastian
Eco-Descanso**
Hacienda la Galera 62, Barrio La Otra Banda
phone +52 (322) 297 30 40 / (322) 297 29 67
lagalerita@hughes.net
lagalerita@direcway.com
www.lagalerita.com.mx

Restaurant Lupita's
Address commonly known

Restaurant El Fortín
Hidalgo 14, Centro
phone +52 (322) 297 28 56

tapalpa

Dirección de Turismo de Tapalpa
Portal Morelos Núm. 1, Centro
phone +52 (343) 432 06 50
www.jalisco.gob.mx

Hostal La Casona de Manzano
Francisco I. Madero 84
phone +52 (343) 432 11 41 / (343) 432 07 67
hostallacasonademanzano@yahoo.com.mx
admin@historichaciendainns.com
www.historichaciendainns.com/casonademan-
zanosp.html

Hotel Tapalpa Country Club
km 5.5, Camino Tapalpa – San Gabriel
phone +52 (343) 432 07 10
reservaciones@tapalpacountry.com
www.tapalpacountry.com

Hotel El Mesón del Ticuz
Priv. de Pedro Loza 1
phone +52 (343) 432 03 51
www.zonaturistica.com

Restaurant El Mesón de los Ángeles
Morelos 71
phone +52 (343) 432 01 95

Restaurant La Troje
16 de septiembre 85 Altos
phone +52 (343) 432 07 83

tequila

Oficina de Turismo de Tequila
José Cuervo 33, Centro
phone +52 (374) 742 00 12
www.tequilajalisco.gob.mx

Hotel Plaza Jardín
José Cuervo 13
phone +52 (374) 742 00 61
www.hotelplazajardin.com

Hotel Casa Dulce María
Abasolo 20
phone +52 (374) 742 32 40

Restaurant Bar Familiar La Posta
Carretera Internacional 604
phone +52 (374) 742 19 59

Restaurant El Callejón
Sixto Gorjón 105
phone +52 (374) 742 10 37

tlaquepaque

Oficinas de Turismo
Centro Comercial Pila Seca Local 2
phone +52 (33) 3635 90 60

Hotel La Villa del Ensueño B&B
Florida 305
phone +52 (33) 3635 87 92
Toll free from Mexico 01 800 777 87 92
vicente@villadelensueno.com
www.villadelensueno.com

Hotel Rosa Morada Cocina & Hotel
Morelos 270
phone +52 (33) 3657 06 27 / (33) 3635 13 91
rosycruz22@hotmail.com

Restaurant El Patio
Independencia 186
phone +52 (33) 3635 11 08

Restaurant Adobe
Independencia 195, Centro
phone +52 (33) 3657 27 92

Restaurant Casa Vieja
Guillermo Prieto 99
phone +52 (33) 3657 62 50

Restaurant Las Divas de Talamantes
Constitución 180-B,
phone +52 (33) 3838 61 53

COLIMA

Secretaría de Turismo
3er. Anillo Periférico
Edificio B Piso 1, Zona Norte.
Colima, Col.
phone +52 (312) 316 20 21

comala

Dirección de Educación, Cultura y Turismo
Miguel Hidalgo
Barrio Alto
Comala, Colima
phone +52 (312) 315 55 47
www.visitacolima.com.mx

Hotel Hacienda de San Antonio
Address commonly known
phone +52 (312) 316 03 00
Toll free from Mexico 01 800 590 38 45
reservations@haciendasanantonio.com
www.haciendadesanantonio.com

Hotel Casa Alvarada B&B
Álvaro Obregón 105
Centro
phone +52 (312) 315 52 29 /
phone 045 312 1116198 / 045 312 1131565
casa_alvarada@hotmail.com
www.casaalvarada.com

Hotel Ceballos
Portal Medellín 12
Toll free from Mexico 01 800 581 97 20
Toll free from USA 1 866 395 08 80
www.hotelceballos.com

Restaurant Campestre Fundador
Prolongación Venustiano Carranza s/n
phone +52 (312) 315 54 26

Hotel América
Morelos 162, Colima
phone +52 (312) 314 44 84

Restaurant Los Naranjos
Barreda 34, Colima
phone +52 (312) 312 00 29

MICHOACÁN

Secretaría de Turismo
Nigromante 79
Palacio Clavijero
Centro Morelia,Michoacán
phone +52 (443) 317 64 26 / (443) 317 64 27
www.michoacan.gob.mx

Oficinas de Información Turística
Tata Vasco 80
Vasco de Quiroga
Morelia, Michoacán
phone +52 (443) 317 80 32 / (443) 317 80 52
Toll free from Mexico 01 800 450 23 00

angangueo

Oficina de Turismo
Plaza Principal s/n
phone +52 (715) 156 00 44

Hotel Plaza Don Gabino
Morelos 147
phone +52 (715) 156 03 22
www.zonaturistica.com

Hotel Albergue Don Bruno
Morelos 92
phone +52 (715) 156 00 26
www.zonaturistica.com

Oficinas de Turismo
Ayala 16
phone +52 (452) 524 71 99
Uruapan, Michoacán

uruapan

Hotel Mansión del Cupatitzio
Calzada de la Rodilla del Diablo 20
phone +52 (452) 523 20 60 / (452) 523 20 90
reservaciones@mansiondelcupatitzio.com
www.mansiondelcupatitzio.com

Hotel Plaza Uruapan
Address commonly known
phone +52 (452) 523 3599 / (452) 523 3488
Toll free from Mexico 01 800 420 02 00
reservaciones@hotelplazaurapan.com.mx
www.hotelplazauruapan.com.mx

Restaurant La Terraza de La Trucha
Calzada de la Rodillla del Diablo 13
phone +52 (452) 524 86 98

Restaurant La Mansion del Cupatitzio
Calzada de la Rodillla del Diablo 20-1
phone +52 (452) 523 20 60

Restaurant Antojitos Yucatecos,
Int. Hotel Cox
Emilio Carranza 31-B, Centro
phone +52 (452) 524 61 52

pátzcuaro

Delegación Regional de Turismo
Buenavista 7, Centro
phone +52 (434) 342 12 14
www.patzcuaro.gob.mx

Hotel Mansión Iturbe
Portal Morelos 59
Plaza Vasco de Quiroga
phone +52 (434) 342 03 68
mansioniturbe@yahoo.com
www.mansioniturbe.com

Hotel La Mansión de Los Sueños
Ibarra 15, Centro
phone +52 (434) 342 57 08
hocasu@ml.com.mx
www.prismas.com.mx

Hotel Posada La Basílica
Arciga 6, Centro
phone +52 (434) 342 11 08
hotelpb@hotmail.com
*www.mexonline.com/michoacan/posadalaba-
silica*

Restaurant El Patio
Plaza Vasco de Quiroga 19
phone +52 (434) 342 04 40

Restaurant Doña Paca
Portal Morelos 59
phone +52 (434) 342 03 68

Restaurant Posada de La Basílica
Arciga 6, Centro
phone +52 (434) 342 11 08

Restaurant Priscilla's
Ibarra 15
phone +52 (434) 342 57 08

Restaurant La Puerta Roja
Ibarra 18
phone +52 (434) 342 58 59

morelia

Hotel Juaninos
Morelos Sur 39
Centro Histórico
phone +52 (443) 312 00 36
reservaciones@hoteljuaninos.com.mx
www.hoteljuaninos.com.mx

Hotel Casa en el Campo
Camelina 830
phone +52 (443) 320 06 20 / ext.103
www.casaenelcampo.com

Hotel La Casa de Las Rosas
Guillermo Prieto 125, Centro Histórico
phone +52 (443) 312 45 45 / (443) 312 38 67
reservaciones@lacasadelasrosas.com
www.lacasadelasrosas.com

Hotel Posada del Artista
Fray Antonio de San Miguel 324, Centro
phone +52 (443) 232 62 46 / (443) 317 94 20
reservaciones@posadadelartista.com
www.posadadelartista.com

Restaurant La Azotea
Morelos sur 39
phone +52 (331) 312 00 36

Restaurant San Miguelito
Camelinas s/n
phone +52 (443) 324 44 11

Restaurant La Casa de las Rosas
Guillermo Prieto 125
phone +52 (331) 312 38 67

tlalpujahua

Módulo de Información Turística
Teléfono: (443) 317 23 71
Toll free from Mexico 01 800 450 23 00

Hotel Estancia Campestre
km 33, Carretera Tlalpujahua
Col. Dos estrellas
phone +52 (711) 125 03 42 / (711) 125 03 43

GUERRERO

taxco

Subsecretaría de Turismo
Av. de los Plateros Núm. 1,
Centro de Convenciones.
phone +52 (762) 622 22 74 / (762) 622 50 73
www.sectur.guerrero.gob.mx

Hotel Posada de La Misión
Cerro de la Misión 32, Centro
phone +52 (762) 622 00 63 / (762) 622 05 33
info@posadamision.com
www.posadamision.com

Hotel De La Borda
Cerro del Pedregal 2
phone +52 (762) 622 02 25 / (762) 622 00 25
info@hotelborda.com
www.hotelborda.com

Restaurant Bar Paco
Plaza Borda 12, Centro
phone +52 (762) 622 00 64

Restaurant Tía Calla
Plaza Borda 1 Bajos, Centro
phone +52 (762) 622 56 02

Restaurant Adobe
Plazuela de San Juan 13 Altos, Centro
phone +52 (762) 622 14 16

Restaurant Del Angel Inn
Celso Muñoz 4 Altos, Centro
phone +52 (762) 622 55 25

GUANAJUATO

dolores hidalgo

Delegación de Turismo
Plaza Principal Núm. 1, bajos Presidencia
phone +52 (418) 182 11 64
www.dolores.gob.mx

Hotel Casa Mia
San Luis Potosí 9 - B
Centro
phone +52 (418) 182 25 60
hotelcasamia@yahoo.com.mx
www.hotelcasamia.com.mx

Hotel Posada Cocomacan
Plaza Principal 4, Centro
phone +52 (418) 182 60 86
www.posadacocomacan.com.mx

Restaurant Carruaje del Caudillo
Plaza Principal 8, Centro
phone +52 (418) 182 04 74

Restaurant-Bar Plaza
Plaza Principal 17-b, Centro
phone +52 (418) 182 02 59

Restaurant El Delfín
Veracruz 2, Centro
phone +52 (418) 182 22 99

guanajuato

Coordinadora de Turismo de Guanajuato
Plaza de la Paz 14, Centro
phone +52 (473) 732 82 75
Toll free from Mexico 01 800 714 10 86
www.guanajuato-travel.com

Hotel Casa Estrella de La Valenciana
Callejón Jalisco 10
phone +52 (473) 732 17 84
msmendezmx@aol.com
www.MexicanInns.com

Hotel Casa de Los Espiritus Alegres
La Ex-Hacienda la Trinidad 1, Marfíl
phone +52 (473) 733 10 13
info@casaspirit.com
www.casaspirit.com

Hotel Quinta Las Acacias
Paseo de la Presa 168
phone +52 (473) 731 15 17
quintalasacacias@prodigy.net.mx
www.quintalasacacias.com

Restaurant La Capellina
Sopena 3
phone +52 (473) 732 72 24

Restaurant Casa Valadéz
Jardín Unión 3
phone +52 (473) 732 11 57 / (473) 732 39 51

Restaurant El Gallo Pitagórico
Constancia 10
phone +52 (473) 732 94 89

Restaurant La Hacienda de Marfíl
Arcos de Guadalupe 3
phone +52 (473) 733 11 48

san miguel de allende

Oficina Regional de Turismo.
Plaza Principal 10, Centro
phone +52 (415) 152 09 00
www.sanmiguelallende.gob.mx

Hotel Casa Linda
Mesones 101, Centro
phone +52 (415) 154 40 07
reservations@hotelcasalinda.com
www.hotelcasalinda.com

Hotel Casa de La Cuesta
Cuesta de San José 32
phone +52 (415) 154 43 24
info@casadelacuesta.com
www.casadelacuesta.com

Hotel Casa Rosada
Cuna de Allende 12
Centro
phone +52 (415) 152 03 82
info@casarosadahotel.com
claudia_tellezcampos@yahoo.com.mx
www.casarosadahotel.com

Hotel Villa Rivera
Cuadrante 3
Centro
phone +52 (415) 152 07 42
hotel@villarivera.com
www.villarivera.com

Hotel Casa de Aves
Rancho Los Fresnos
Montecillo de Nieto
phone +52 (415) 155 96 10
info@casadeaves.com
www.casadeaves.com

Hotel Casa Quetzal
Hospicio 34, Centro
phone +52 (415) 152 21 78
casaquetzalhotel@yahoo.com
cynthiaprice@yahoo.com
www.casaquetzalhotel.com

Hotel Casa Shuck
Garita 3, Centro
phone +52 (415) 152 06 57
casaschuck@gmail.com
casaschuck@yahoo.com
www.casaschuck.com

Hotel Susurro
Recreo 78
phone +52 (415) 152 10 65
rwaters@earthlink.net
www.susurro.com.mx

Hotel La Morada
Correo 10, Centro
phone +52 (415) 152 16 47
info@lamoradahotel.com
www.lamoradahotel.com

Hotel Vista Real
Callejón de Arias 4
phone +52 (415) 152 39 84
hotelvistareal@yahoo.com
laura@vistarealhotel.com
www.vistarealhotel.com

Hotel Doña Urraca
Hidalgo 69
Centro
phone +52 (415) 154 97 70
infosma@donaurraca.com.mx
www.donaurraca.com.mx

Restaurant El Ten Ten Pie
Cuna de Allende 21, Centro
phone +52 (415) 152 71 84

Restaurant La Capilla
Cuna de Allende 10
phone +52 (415) 152 06 98

Restaurant Nirvana
Mesones 101
phone +52 (415) 150 00 67

Restaurant L'Invito
Ancha de San Antonio 20
phone +52 (415) 152 73 33

Restaurant El Pegasso
Corregidora 6, Centro
phone +52 (415) 152 13 51

QUERÉTARO

Secretaría de Turismo
Pasteur Nte. 4,
Querétaro, Querétaro
phone +52 (442) 212 12 41 / (442) 238 50 67
Toll free from Mexico 01 800 715 17 42
www.venaqueretaro.com

bernal

Oficina de Turismo de la Delegación
Hidalgo No. 2, Centro
Bernal, Ezequiel Montes
phone +52 (441) 296 41 26

Hotel Parador Vernal
Lázaro Cárdenas 1
Barrio la Capilla
phone +52 (441) 296 40 58
Toll free from Mexico 01 800 672 58 56
www.paradorvernal.com.mx

Restaurante el Mirador
Lázaro Cárdenas 1
Barrio la Capilla
phone +52 (441) 296 40 58

Restaurant Mesón de la Roca
Hidalgo s/n
phone +52 (441) 296 41 63

Restaurant Piave
Zaragoza 13
phone +52 (441) 296 40 08

Restaurant Portal de Doña Tere
5 de Mayo s/n
phone +52 (441) 296 40 90

sierra gorda

Hotel Misión Hacienda Concá
Km. 32, Carretera 57 Jalpan – Río Verde
phone +52 (487) 877 42 51
Toll free from Mexico 01 800 900 38 00
www.hotelesmision.com

Hotel Inn Misión Jalpan
Fray Junípero s/n
Centro Jalpan de Serra
phone +52 (441) 296 04 45
Toll free from Mexico 01 800 6231004
www.hotelesmision.com

jalpan

Restaurant-Bar "El Trapiche"
Km. 32, Carretera 57 Jalpan – Río Verde
phone +52 (487) 877 42 51
Toll free from Mexico 01 800 900 38 00

Restaurant Rincón Serrano
Fray Junípero s/n
Centro Jalpan de Serra
phone +52 (441) 296 04 45
Toll free from Mexico 01 800 623 10 04

querétaro

Hotel La Casa de La Marquesa
Madero 41, Centro Histórico Qro.
phone +52 (442) 212 00 92
fax +52 (442) 212 00 98
marquesa@abanet.net
www.lacasadelamarquesa.com

Hotel Doña Urraca
5 de mayo 117, Centro
phone +52 (442) 238 54 00
fax +52 (442) 238 54 46
informacion@donaurraca.com.mx
www.donaurraca.com.mx

Restaurant Pasto
Peralta 19-A
phone +52 (442) 214 44 42

Restaurant Mesón de Chucho El Roto
Libertad 60
Phone +52 (442) 212 42 95

Secretaría de Turismo de Hidalgo
Revolución 1300, Periodistas
Pachuca, Hidalgo
phone +52 (771) 107 18 10
Toll free from Mexico 01 800 718 26 00
www.hidalgo.gob.mx

mineral del chico

Oficina de Turismo
Palacio Municipal s/n, Centro
phone +52 (771) 715 09 94

Hotel El Paraiso
Km. 19, Carretera Pachuca – Mineral del Chico
phone +52 (771) 715 56 57 / (55) 3335 16 46
hparaiso@avantel.net
paraiso@mexline.com
www.hotelesecoturisticos.com.mx

Hotel Posada del Amanecer
Morelos 3
phone +52 (771) 715 48 12
Toll free from Mexico 01 800 8226111
hparaiso@avantel.net
paraiso@mexline.com
www.hotelesecoturisticos.com.mx

Restaurant-Bar La Montaña
km. 19, Carretera Pachuca – Mineral del Chico
phone +52 (771) 715 56 57

Restaurant La Peña del Cuervo
Morelos 3
phone +52 (771) 715 48 12
Toll free from Mexico 01 800 822 61 11

huasca de ocampo

Dirección de Turismo de Huasca de Ocampo
Palacio Municipal s/n, Centro
phone +52 (771) 792 02 53
www.hidalgo.gob.mx

Hotel Hacienda San Miguel Regla
Address commonly known
San Miguel Regla
phone +52 (771) 792 01 02
www.sanmiguelregla.com

Restaurante del Lago
Address commonly known
phone +52 (771) 792 01 88

Restaurant El Duende
Av. Principal s/n
phone +52 (771) 792 07 47 / (771) 792 01 01

Restaurant La Casa del Abuelo
Km. 1.5, Carretera Huasca–Tulancingo
phone +52 (771) 792 00 22

real del monte

Dirección de Turismo Municipal
Palacio Municipal
Lic. Ruben Licona Ruiz 1, Centro
phone +52 (771) 797 02 18 / (771) 797 12 18

Hotel Villa Alpina El Chalet
Km. 9.5, Carretera Pachuca – Real del Monte
phone +52 (771) 797 05 55 / (771) 797 00 77
elchalet88@hotmail.com
www.villaalpinaelchalet.com

Hotel Real del Monte
Manuel Timoteo García 5
phone +52 (771) 797 12 02
Toll free from Mexico 01 800 8226111
hparaiso@avantel.net
paraiso@mexline.com
www.hotelesecoturisticos.com.mx

Restaurant El Campo Felíz
El Hiloche 7
Bosque el Hiloche
phone +52 (771) 797 02 75

Restaurant Pastes el Billar
Allende 7, Centro
phone +52 (771) 797 07 95

Restaurante Villa Alpina
Km 9.5, Carretera Pachuca – Real Del Monte
Casas Quemadas
phone +52 (771) 797 00 77

tula de allende

Oficina de Turismo
Plaza del Nacionalismo s/n, Centro
Phone +52 (773) 732 10 82

Hotel Real del Bosque
Cerrada Jacarandas 122, El Mogote
phone +52 (773) 732 53 51
Toll free from Mexico 01 800 500 90 02
info@realdelbosque.com
www.realdelbosque.com

Restaurante Los Negritos
Héroes de Chapultepec 12
Centro
phone +52 (773) 732 37 43 / (773) 732 67 62

Restaurant Tollan Campestre
Km. 31.5, Carretera a Jorobas
phone +52 (773) 732 08 78

pachuca

Casino Español
Blvd. Everardo Márquez 202
phone +52 (771) 718 70 77

Restaurant Alex Steak
Glorieta Revolución 102
phone +52 (771) 713 00 56

ESTADO DE MÉXICO

malinalco

Oficina de Turismo
Palacio Municipal
Phone +52 (714) 147 13 11
www.malinalco.net

Hotel Casa Limón
Río Lerma 103
Barrio Sta. Ma.
phone +52 (714) 147 02 56
leonel@casalimon.com
www.casalimon.com

Hotel Casa Mora
Calle de la Cruz 18
Barrio Sta. Ma.
phone +52 (714) 147 05 72
reserve@casamora.com
alexismora@casamora.net
www.casamora.net

Restaurant Las Palomas
Guerrero 104
phone +52 (714) 147 01 22

Restaurant Los Placeres
Plaza Principal 6-B, Centro
phone +52 (714) 147 08 55

Café La Fe
Guerrero esq. E. Carranza
phone +52 (714) 147 01 77

teotihuacán

Hotel Quinto Sol
Hidalgo 26
Barrio Purificación
phone +52 (594) 956 18 81
quintosol@gshoteles.com.mx
www.hotelquintosol.com.mx

Restaurant La Gruta
Periférico Zona Arqueológica
frente a la Puerta 5
phone +52 (594) 956 01 27

tepotzotlán

Dirección de Turismo de Tepotzotlán
Benito Juárez 1, Centro.
phone +52 (55) 58 76 80 68
www.edomex.gob.mx/portalgem/tepotzotlan

Hotel Posada del Virrey
Insurgentes 13
phone +52 (55) 5876 18 64

Restaurant La Hostería de Tepotzotlán
Plaza Virreynal 1
phone +52 (55) 5876 02 43 / (55) 5876 16 46

valle de bravo

Dirección de Turismo Municipal
Porfirio Díaz esq. Zaragoza
phone +52 (726) 269 62 00

Hotel Rodavento
Km 3.5, Carretera los Saucos – Valle de Bravo
phone +52 (726) 251 41 82
www.rioymontana.com

Hotel Mesón del Viento
5 de mayo 111
Centro Santa María Ahuacatlán
phone +52 (726) 262 00 48
fax +52 (726) 262 51 48
flymexico@prodigy.net.mx
www.mesondelviento.com

Restaurant La Casona
Francisco González Bocanegra 201
phone +52 (726) 262 15 74

Restaurant La Cueva del León
Plaza Independencia 2
phone +52 (726) 262 40 62

D.F.

Secretaría de Turismo
Presidente Masaryk 172
Col. Chapultepec Morales, Distrito Federal
phone +52 (55) 3002 63 00

Dirección General de Servicios Turísticos
Hipódromo Condesa
phone +52 (55) 5212 02 57 Ext. 2403
fax +52 (55) 52 12 02 60 Ext. 2403
e-mail: rodrigorg@mexicocity.gob.mx

polanco

Hotel Casa Vieja
Eugenio Sue 45, Polanco
phone +52 (55) 5282 00 67
sales@casavieja.com
www.casavieja.com

Hotel Habita
Presidente Masaryk 201
Polanco
phone +52 (55) 5280 18 13
reservaciones@hotelhabita.com
www.hotelhabita.com

Restaurant La Valentina
Presidente Mazaryk 393 Loc. 19
phone +52 (55) 5282 28 12

Restaurant L'Olivier
Presidente Masaryk No. 49-C
phone +52 (55) 5545 31 33

la condesa

Hotel Condesa df
Veracruz 102
Condesa
phone +52 (55) 5241 26 00
reservaciones@condesadf.com
www.condesadf.com

coyoacán

Restaurant Los Danzantes
Plaza Jardín Centenario 12
phone +52 (55) 5658 60 54 / (55) 5658 64 51

Restaurant La Dona
Héroes del 47 No. 141
phone +52 (55) 5688 11 18

Restaurant Andre
Miguel Ángel de Quevedo 992
phone +52 (55) 5549 39 00

TLAXCALA

tlaxcala

Oficinas de Turismo
Juárez y Lardizabal
phone +52 (246) 465 09 60 ext. 1519
Toll free from Mexico 01 800 509 65 57
www.tlaxcala.gob.mx

Hotel Posada San Francisco
Plaza de la Constitución 17
phone +52 (246) 462 60 22
reservaciones@posadasanfrancisco.com
www.posadasanfrancisco.com

Restaurant-Café Los Portales
Plaza de la Constitución 8
phone +52 (246) 462 50 02

Restaurant El Tirol
Independencia 7-A
phone +52 (246) 462 37 54

Restaurant La Cacerola
Independencia 9, Centro
phone +52 (246) 466 12 35

MORELOS

cuernavaca

Secretaría de Turismo de Morelos
Morelos Sur 187, Las Palmas
phone +52 (777) 314 39 20
Toll free from Mexico 01 800 987 82 24
www.morelostravel.com

Hotel Casa Colonial
Netzahualcóyotl 37, Centro
phone +52 (777) 312 70 33
hotelcasacolonial@hotmail.com
www.casacolonial.com

Hotel La Casa Azul
Arista 17, Centro
phone +52 (777) 314 36 84
htanikawa@hotelcasaazul.com
lupita57@hotmail.com
www.hotelcasaazul.com.mx

Hotel Hacienda San Gabriel de Las Palmas
Km. 41.8, Carretera Fed.
Cuernavaca–Chilpancingo
Amacuzac
phone +52 (751) 348 01 13 / (751) 348 06 36
gerencia@haciendasangabriel.com
www.haciendasangabriel.com

Hotel Forum
Plutarco Elías Calles 22,
Col. Club de Golf
phone +52 (777) 310 31 96 / (777) 310 31 97
info@hotelforum.com.mx
forbezo@restaurantprovence.com.mx
www.hotelforum.com.mx

Hotel Hacienda Vista Hermosa
Km. 7 Carretera Alpuyeca–Tequesquitengo
phone +52 (734) 345 53 61 / (734) 345 53 82
haciendasyestancias@gmail.com

Restaurant D_' Rivera
Galeana 119
phone +52 (777) 318 32 73

Restaurant Casa Hidalgo
Hidalgo 6, Centro
phone +52 (777) 312 27 49

Restaurant Provence
Plutarco Elias Calles 22
Col. Club de Golf
phone +52 (777) 310 31 96 / (777) 310 31 97

tepoztlán

Regiduría de Turismo
Envila s/n
Centro
phone +52 (739) 395 00 09
www.morelostravel.com/destinos/tepoztlan.html

Hotel Posada del Tepozteco
Paraíso 3
phone +52 (739) 395 00 10
fax +52 (739) 395 03 23
tepozhot@yahoo.com.mx
www.posadadeltepozteco.com

Un Pequeño Hotel Casa Bugambilias
Callejón de Tepopula 007, Valle de Atongo
phone +52 (739) 395 01 58 / (739) 395 44 18
reserva@casabugambilia.com
www.casabugambilia.com

Restaurant Hotel Posada del Tepozteco
Paraíso 3
phone +52 (739) 395 00 10

Restaurant Axitla
Av. Del Tepozteco s/n
phone +52 (739) 395 05 19 / (739) 395 25 55

Restaurant El Ciruelo
Zaragoza 17
phone +52 (739) 395 12 03

tetela del volcán

Restaurant El Rincón del Sabor
Norberto López Avelar 36
Barrio San Bartolo
phone +52 (731) 357 03 31

xochicalco

Hotel Casa Marly
Km 4.5, Carretera a Xochicalco
Alpuyeca
phone +52 (777) 391 52 05
casamarly@hotmail.com
www.casamarly.com

Hotel La Casa de Las Flores
Camino a Perritos s/n, El Rodeo
phone +52 (737) 374 40 84
reservaciones@xochicalco.net
www.xochicalco.net

PUEBLA

Secretaría de Turismo
Calle 5 oriente 3, Centro
Puebla, Puebla.
phone +52 (222) 246 20 44
Toll free from Mexico 01800 326 86 56
www.puebla.gob.mx

cuetzalán

Coordinación de Turismo
Hidalgo 29
Centro
phone +52 (233) 331 00 04 / (233) 331 05 27
Toll free from Mexico 01 800 000 11 22

Hotel La Casa de Piedra
Carlos García 11, Centro
phone +52 (233) 331 00 30 / (233) 331 03 39
www.lacasadepiedra.com

Hotel Villas Cuetzalán
Km. 45, Carretera Zacapoaxtla – Cuetzalan
phone +52 (233) 331 04 23
reservaciones@villascuetzalan.com.mx
www.villas-cuetzalan.com.mx

Hotel Posada Cuetzalán
Zaragoza 12
phone +52 (233) 331 01 54 / (233) 331 02 95
posadacuetzalan@cuetzalanmagico.com
www.posadacuetzalan.com.mx

Restaurant Villa Jaiba
Fracisco y Madero s/n
phone +52 (233) 331 02 89

Restaurant Dandayber
Zaragoza 21
phone +52 (233) 331 01 81

Restaurante Peña Los Jarritos
Adolfo López Mateos 7
phone +52 (233) 331 05 58

Restaurant La Terraza
Hidalgo 33
phone +52 (233) 331 02 62

cholula

Oficinas de Turismo
Calles 12 Ote y Av. 4 Nte
phone +52 (222) 261 23 93

Hotel Estrella de Belem
Calle 2 Oriente 410
phone +52 (222) 261 19 25
fax +52 (222) 261 17 25
belem@estrelladebelem.com.mx
www.estrelladebelem.com.mx

Hotel La Quinta Luna
Calle 3 Sur 702, San Pedro
phone +52 (222) 247 89 15
fax +52 (222) 247 89 16
reservaciones@laquintaluna.com
www.laquintaluna.com

Restaurant La Casona
Calle 3 oriente

Restaurant La Quinta Luna
Calle 3 Sur 702
San Pedro Cholula
phone +52 (222) 247 89 15

PUEBLA

Hotel El Sueño hotel & spa
Calle 9 Oriente 12, Centro
phone +52 (222) 232 64 89 / (222) 232 64 23
recepcion@elsueno-hotel.com
www.elsueno-hotel.com

Hotel Mesón Sacristía de La Compañía
Calle 6 Sur 304
Callejón de los Sapos, Centro
phone +52 (222) 242 35 54
leobardo@mesones-sacristia.com
www.mesones-sacristia.com

Hotel Mesón Sacristía de Capuchinas
Calle 9 Oriente 16, Centro
phone +52 (222) 242 35 54
capuchinas@mesones-sacristia.com
www.mesones-sacristia.com

Restaurant- Bar La Tentación
Calle 9 Oriente 12, Centro Histórico
phone +52 (222) 232 64 89 / (222) 232 64 23

Restaurant Fonda de Santa Clara
Calle 3 Poniente 920
phone +52 (222) 246 19 19

VERACRUZ

veracruz

Oficinas de Turismo
Palacio Municipal
phone +52 (229) 989 88 17
www.veracruzturismo.com.mx

coatepec

Dirección de Turismo Municipal
phone +52 (228) 816 69 01

Hotel Posada Coatepec
Hidalgo 9, Centro
phone +52 (228) 816 05 44
Toll free from Mexico 01800 712 62 56
www.posadacoatepec.com.mx

Hotel Mezón del Alferez
Jiménez del Campillo 47
phone +52 (228) 816 6744 / (228) 816 8471
maferezcoatepec@hotmail.com
www.pradosdelrio.com

Restaurant Arcos de Belem
Miguel Lerdo 9
phone +52 (228) 816 28 73

Restaurant Casa Bonilla
Juárez s/n
phone +52 (228) 816 00 09

papantla

Oficina de Turismo
Azueta 101
phone +52 (784) 842 00 26

Hotel Tajín
José de J. Nuñez y Domínguez 104
phone +52 (784) 842 01 21 / (784) 842 06 44
www.hotel.zonaturistica.com/tajin

monte gordo

Hotel Azúcar
Km 83.5, Carretera Federal Nautla – Poza Rica
phone +52 (232) 321 06 78 / (232) 321 08 04
www.hotelazucar.com

tlacotalpan

Oficina de Turismo
Palacio Municipal

Hotel Posada Doña Lala
Venustiano Carranza 11
phone +52 (288) 884 25 80
www.tlaco.com.mx/hoteldonalala/index.htm
www.zonaturistica.com

Hotel Tlacotalpan
Rodriguez Beltrán 35
phone +52 (288) 884 20 63
hoteltlacotalpan@tlaco.com.mx
www.tlaco.com.mx/hoteltlacotalpan/index.htm

Restaurant Las Brisas del Papaloapan
Blvd. Ribera del Río s/n
phone +52 (288) 884 20 03

Restaurant Doña Lala
Venustiano Carranza No. 11
phone +52 (288) 884 25 80

SOUTHERN MEXICO

OAXACA

Secretaría de Turismo del Estado
Juárez 703, Centro
Oaxaca, Oax.
phone +52 (951) 502 12 00 / (951) 516 01 23
www.aoaxaca.com

oaxaca

Hotel de La Parra
Guerrero 117, Centro
phone +52 (951) 514 19 00 / (951) 516 15 58
Toll free from Mexico 01 800 872 77 27
reservaciones@hoteldelaparra.com
www.hoteldelaparra.com

Hotel Casa Catrina
García Vigil 703, Centro
phone +52 (951) 514 53 22 / (951) 514 54 04
ventas@casacatrina.com.mx
www.casacatrina.com.mx

Hotel Casa Cid de León
Morelos 602, Centro
phone +52 (951) 516 04 14 / (951) 514 18 93
reservaciones@casaciddeleon.com
www.casaciddeleon.com

Hotel La Casona de Tita
García Vigil 805, Centro
phone +52 (951) 516 14 00
www.hotellacasonadetitaoaxaca.com.mx

Hotel Hacienda Los Laureles
Hidalgo 21
San Felipe del Agua
phone +52 (951) 501 53 00 / (951) 501 53 02
bookings@hotelhaciendaloslaureles.com
www.hotelhaciendaloslaureles.com

Hotel Casa Oaxaca
García Virgil 407, Centro
phone +52 (951) 514 41 73 / (951) 516 99 23
reservaciones@casaoaxaca.com.mx
www.casaoaxaca.com.mx

Restaurant Los Danzantes
M. Alcalá 403-3
phone +52 (951) 501 11 84

Restaurant La Teca
Violetas 200-A
phone +52 (951) 515 05 63

Restaurante Temple
García Vigil 409-A
phone +52 (951) 516 86 76

Restaurant Casa Oaxaca
Constitución 104-4
phone +52 (951) 516 88 89

mitla

Hotel Don Cenobio
Juárez 3
phone +52 (951) 568 03 30
mercedes.moreno@hoteldoncenobio.com
informes@hoteldoncenobio.com
www.hoteldoncenobio.com

CHIAPAS

Secretaría de Turismo de Chiapas
Blvd. Belisario Domínguez Núm. 950
Plaza de las Instituciones. Tuxtla Gutiérrez
phone +52 (961) 602 52 98 / (961) 602 51 27
Toll free from Mexico 01 800 208 35 00
www.turismochiapas.gob.mx

comitán de domínguez

Oficinas de Turismo
Calle Central Ote. 6
phone +52 (963) 632 40 47

Hotel Parador Santa María
Km 22, Carretera la Trinitaria
Lagunas de Montebello
phone +52 (963) 632 51 16
paradorsantamaria@prodigy.net.mx
www.paradorsantamaria.com.mx

Hotel Hacienda de Los Angeles
2a. Calle Norte Pte. 6
phone +52 (963) 632 00 74 / (963) 632 00 76
haciendadelosangeles@hotmail.com
www.hotelhaciendalosangeles.com.mx

Restaurant El Portal
Av. Central Sur 15
Centro
phone +52 (963) 632 44 72

Restaurant Matisse
Poniente Nte. 16
phone +52 (963) 632 71 52

chiapa de corzo

Hotel La Ceiba
Domingo Ruiz 300
phone +52 (961) 616 14 97 / (961) 616 03 89
servicios@chiapastours.com.mx
www.chiapastours.com.mx/laceiba/default.htm

palenque

Oficinas de Turismo
Juárez & Abasolo s/n

Hotel Chan-Kah, Resort Village
Km. 3 Carretera Ruinas s/n
phone +52 (916) 345 11 34 / (916) 345 07 62
reservaciones@chan-kah.com.mx
www.chan-kah.com.mx

Hotel Ciudad Real Palenque
Km. 1.5, Carretera Pakal-Na
phone +52 (916) 345 13 15
reserve@ciudadreal.com.mx
www.ciudadreal.com.mx

Restaurant La Selva
Km. 0.5, Carretera Palenque – Ruinas,
phone +52 (916) 345 03 63

Restaurant Maya
Independencia s/n
phone +52 (916) 345 00 42

san cristóbal de las casas

**Delegación de la Secretaría de Turismo
en la Región Altos**
Miguel Hidalgo 1-B, Centro
phone +52 (967) 678 65 70
www.turismochiapas.gob.mx

Dirección de Turismo Municipal
Plaza 31 de Marzo
Bajos del Palacio Municipal
phone +52 (967) 678 06 65

Hotel Parador San Juan de Dios
Calzada Roberta 16, 31 de Marzo
phone +52 (967) 678 11 67 / (967) 678 42 90
sjd@sanjuandios.com

www.sanjuandios.com
Hotel Na Balom
Vicente Guerrero 33
phone +52 (967) 678 14 18
www.nabalom.org

Restaurant El Fogón de Jovel
16 de Septiembre 11
phone +52 (967) 678 11 53

Restaurant Na Bolom
Guerrero 33
phone +52 (967) 678 14 18

Restaurant La Casa del Pan
Dr. Navarro 10
phone +52 (967) 678 58 95

**Restaurant Arco del Carmen
La Casa del Ámbar**
Miguel Hidalgo 14
phone +52 (967) 116 02 00

CAMPECHE

campeche

Secretaría de Turismo
Ruiz Cortines s/n
Plaza Moch-Couoh
Centro
phone +52 (981) 811 92 29 / (981) 811 92 55
Toll free from Mexico 01 800 900 22 67

Modulo de Información
Calle 57 Casa 6
Centro Cultural

Hotel Hacienda Puerta Campeche
Calle 59 No. 71
Puerta de Tierra
phone +52 (981) 816 73 75
reservations1@thehaciendas.com
www.thehaciendas.com

Hotel Hacienda Uayamón
Km 20 Carretera Chiná–Edzná–Uayamón
phone +52 (981) 829 75 26
wolf.kresse@thehaciendas.com
www.thehaciendas.com

Restaurant La Pigua
Miguel Alemán 179-A
phone +52 (981) 811 33 65

Restaurant Tukulná
Calle 10, 333
phone +52 (981) 816 90 88

Restaurant El Langostino
Calle 10-B
phone +52 (981) 815 40 56

Restaurant Casa Vieja
Calle 10, 319-A
phone +52 (981) 811 13 11

Restaurant Marganzo
Calle 8, 267
phone +52 (981) 811 38 98

Restaurant Uayamón
Km. 20 carretera Chiná–Edzná–Uayamón
phone +52 (981) 829 75 26

YUCATÁN

Secretaría de Turismo de Yucatán
Plaza Grande, Calle 61, Mérida, Yucatán.
phone +52 (999) 930 31 03

chichen itza

Hotel Hacienda Chichen
Km 120.5, Carretera Mérida–Puerto Juárez
phone +52 (985) 851 00 45
www.haciendachichen.com

Hotel MAYALAND
Km 120, Carretera Mérida–Cancún
phone +52 (985) 851 01 03
Toll free from Mexico 01 800 719 54 65
www.mayaland.com

Restaurant Las Palapas
Km 120, Carretera Mérida–Cancún
phone +52 (985) 851 01 03
Toll free from Mexico 01 800 719 54 65

Restaurante de Especialidades
Km 120, Carretera Mérida–Cancún
phone +52 (985) 851 01 03
Toll free from Mexico 01 800 719 54 66

maxcanú

Hotel Hacienda Santa Rosa
Address commonly known
reservations1@thehaciendas.com

www.thehaciendas.com
mérida

Hacienda Xcanatún Casa de Piedra
Calle 20 s/n
Comisaría Xcanatun
phone +52 (999) 930 21 40
fax +52 (999) 941 03 19
hacienda@xcanatun.com
www.xcanatun.com

Hotel Hacienda San Pedro Nohpat´
Km. 8, Carretera 180
phone +52 (999) 988 05 42
haciendaholidays@hotmail.com
www.haciendaholidays.com

Restaurant Los Almendros
Paseo Montejo 451
phone +52 (999) 928 54 59

Restaurant Casa del Paseo
Paseo Montejo 465
phone +52 (999) 920 05 28

Restaurant Casa de Piedra
Km. 12, Carretera Mérida–Progreso
phone +52 (999) 941 02 13

Restaurant Villa María
Calle 59, 553
phone +52 (999) 923 33 57

Restaurant La Tratto
Prolongación Montejo 479-A
phone +52 (999) 927 04 34

temozón sur

Hotel Hacienda Temozón
Km. 182, Carretera Mérida–Uxmal
Municipio de Abala
phone +52 (999) 923 80 89
fax +52 (999) 923 79 63
reservations1@thehaciendas.com
www.thehaciendas.com

tixkokob

Hotel Hacienda San José
Km 30 Carretera, Tixkokob–Tekanto
phone +52 (999) 910 46 17 / (999) 923 79 63
reservations1@thehaciendas.com
www.thehaciendas.com

izamal

Dirección de Turismo de Izamal
Calle 30 No. 323
Centro
phone +52 (988) 954 06 92

Hotel Macan ché B&B
Calle 22, No. 305
phone +52 (988) 954 02 87
www.macanche.com

Restaurant Tumben-Lol
Calle 22, No. 302, Centro
phone +52 (988) 954 02 31

Restaurant Kinich-Kakmo
Calle 27, 299-A
Centro
phone +52 (988) 954 04 89

uxmal

Hotel Hacienda Uxmal
Km 78, Carretera Mérida–Campeche
phone +52 (997) 976 20 12
www.mayaland.com

Restaurant Hacienda Uxmal
Km 78, Carretera Mérida–Campeche
phone +52 (phone +52 (997) 976 20 12
Toll free from Mexico 01 800 235 40 79

valladolid

Oficinas de Turismo
Calles 40 y 41
phone +52 (985) 856 18 65

Restaurant Las Campanas
Calle 41 y 42
Centro
phone +52 (985) 856 23 65

Restaurant Hoatería del Marqués
Calle 39, No. 203
phone +52 (985) 856 20 73

QUINTANA ROO

Secretaría de Turismo de Cancún
Km.9, Boulevard Kukulkán
Centro de Convenciones Primer Piso
phone +52 (998) 881 90 00 Ext. 3601

Secretaría de Turismo
Calzada del Centenario 622, Del Bosque
phone +52 (983) 83 5 08 60 Ext. 1808
fax +52 (983) 83 5 08 80
selias@qroo.gob.mx
Chetumal, Quintana Roo

chetumal

Restaurant Nah-Balam
Address commonly known
phone +52 (983) 835 04 00

Restaurant Teranga
San Salvador 441
phone +52 (983) 832 55 40

cozumel

Oficina de Información Turística
Phone +52 (987) 872 75 63

Hotel Casa Mexicana
Rafael E. Melgar 457 Sur
phone +52 (987) 872 90 90
Toll free from Mexico 01 800 227 26 39
reservaciones@casamexicanacozumel.com
www.casamexicanacozumel.com

Restaurant La Cocay
Calle 8 Norte 208
phone +52 (987) 872 44 07

Restaurant Guido's
Rafael E. Melgar 23
phone +52 (987) 872 09 46

Restaurant Pepe's Grill
Rafael E. Melgar s/n
phone +52 (987) 872 02 13

Restaurant Manatí
Calle 8 Nte y Calle 10 Nte
phone +52 (987) 872 51 69

holbox

Hotel Casa Sandra
Igualdad s/n
phone +52 (984) 875 21 71 / (984) 875 24 31
reservations@casasandra.com
www.casasandra.com

Restaurant Evelyn Pizza
Address commonly known

Restaurant El Faro
Juárez y Playa s/n
Address commonly known

Restaurant La Cueva del Pirata
Address commonly known
phone +52 (984) 875 22 17

isla mujeres

Turismo Municipal de Isla Mujeres
Rueda Medina s/n
phone +52 (998) 877 07 67

Hotel La Casa de Los Sueños
Lote 9 A y B, Carretera a Garrafón, Turqueza
phone +52 (998) 877 06 51 / (998) 888 03 69
fax +52 (998) 877 07 08
info@casadelossuenosresort.com
www.casadelossuenosresort.com

Hotel Na Balam
Calle Zazil-Ha 118
Playa Norte
phone +52 (998) 877 02 79 / (998) 877 00 58
nabalam@nabalam.com
www.nabalam.com

Hotel Villa Rolandi
Lotes 15 y 16
Laguna Mar
Carretera Sac–Bajo
phone +52 (998) 877 07 00 / (998) 877 05 00
info@villarolandi.com
www.villarolandi.com

Restaurant Le Bistro Francais
Address commonly known

Restaurant Zazil-Ha
Calle Zazil-Ha 118
Playa Norte
phone +52 (998) 877 02 79 / (998) 877 00 58

playa del carmen

Oficina de Información Turística
phone +52 (984) 873 28 04

Deseo Hotel & Lounge
Quinta Avenida
phone +52 (984) 879 36 20 / (984) 879 36 21
contact@hoteldeseo.com
www.hoteldeseo.com

Hotel Básico
Address commonly known
phone +52 (984) 879 44 48
www.hotelbasico.com

Restaurant Sur
Quinta Avenida s/n
phone +52 (998) 803 32 85

Restaurant Yaxché
Calle 8
phone +52 (984) 873 25 02

Restaurant El Diablito Cha Cha Chá
Calle 12
phone +52 (984) 803 34 16

Restaurant Byblos
Calle 14
phone +52 (984) 803 17 90

tulúm

Hotel Ana y José
Km. 7, Carretera Cancun–Tulúm
Boca Paila
phone +52 (998) 887 54 70 / (998) 892 09 10
fax +52 (998) 887 54 69
reservations@anayjose.com
www.anayjose.com

Hotel Las Ranitas
Km. 9, Carretera Tulúm – Boca Paila
phone +52 (984) 87 785 54
info@lasranitas.com
www.lasranitas.com

Restaurant Mezzanine
Km. 1.5 Tulúm – Boca Paila
phone +52 (984) 804 14 52

Restaurant Diamante K
Km. 1 Tulúm – Boca Paila
phone +52 (984) 876 21 15

Restaurant Ana y José
phone +52 (998) 887 54 70 / (998) 887 54 69

Restaurant Margheritas
Zona Hotelera
phone +52 (984) 100 37 80

SUGGESTED READINGS

ART & ARCHITECTURE

Early, James. *Colonial Architecture of Mexico*. Dallas: Southern Methodist University Press, 2000.

Fernandez, Justino. *A Guide to Mexican Art: From Its Beginnings to the Present*. Chicago: University Of Chicago Press, 1969.

Herrera, Hayden. *Frida Kahlo: The Paintings*. New York: Harper Perennial, 2002.

Kubler, George. *The Art and Architecture of Ancient America*, 3rd ed. New Haven: Yale University Press, 1984.

Paz, Octavio, and Jean Paul Barbier. *Pre-Columbian America: Ritual Arts of the New World*. Milan: Skira, 2000.

Rochfort, Desmond. *Mexican Muralists*. San Francisco: Chronicle Books, 1998.

CULTURE & HISTORY

Cortes, Hernan. *Letters from Mexico*. New Haven: Yale University Press, 2001.

Diaz del Castillo, Bernal. *The Conquest of New Spain*. New York: Penguin Classics, 1963.

Goetz, Delia, and Sylvanus G. Morley. *Popol Vuh*. Oklahoma: University of Oklahoma Press, 1991.

Paz, Octavio. *The Labyrinth of Solitude*. New York: Grove Press, 1994.

Sharer, Robert J. *The Ancient Maya*. Stanford: Stanford University Press, 1994.

Stephens, John Lloyd. *Incidents of Travel in Central America, Chiapas and Yucatan*. Washington, D.C.: Smithsonian, 1993.

LITERATURE

Azuela, Mariano. *The Underdogs*. New York: Modern Library, 2002.

Castellanos, Rosario. *City of Kings*. Pittsburgh: Latin American Literary Review Press, 1993.

Fuentes, Carlos. *The Death of Artemio Cruz*. New York: Farrar, Straus and Giroux, 1991.

Guzman, Martin Luis. *The Eagle and the Serpent*. Gloucester: Peter Smith Publisher, 1969.

Lawrence, D.H. *The Plumed Serpent*. New York: Vintage, 1992.

Lowry, Malcolm. *Under the Volcano*. New York: Harper Perennial, 2007.

Rulfo, Juan. *Pedro Paramo*. New York: Grove Press, 1994.

To Ana Paula and Cristóbal

First published in the United States of America in 2008 by

Rizzoli International Publications, Inc.

300 Park Avenue South

New York, NY 10010

www.rizzoliusa.com

© 2008 Rizzoli International Publications, Inc.

Production: Crigar Monitor, Guadalajara, México

Editor: Cristóbal García

English Translation: Christian Andersen

Editorial Assistant: Juan Carlos Luna

Design: Alejandro Sevilla

Digital Content: Pedro Delgado

Logistics: Marcia Nuñez

Photography: Cristóbal García

2008 2009 2010 2011 2012 / 10 9 8 7 6 5 4 3 2 1

Printed in China

ISBN-13: 978-0-8478-3028-2

Library of Congress Catalog Control Number: 2007937536

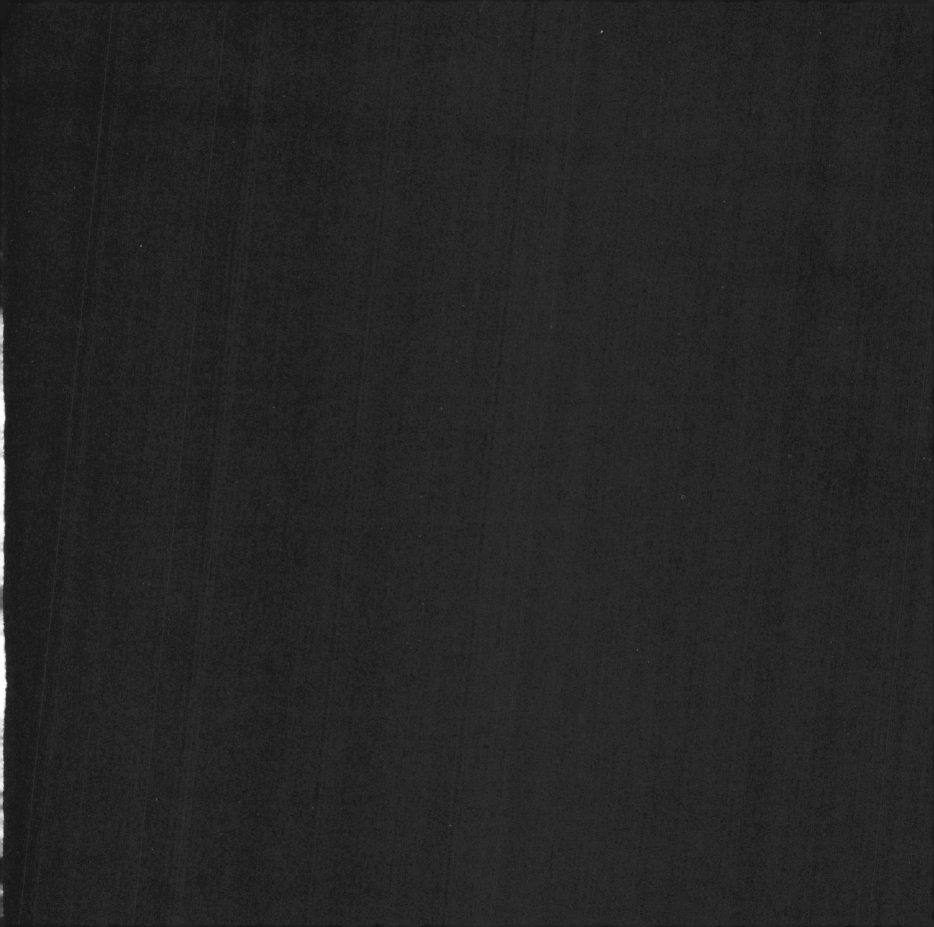